I WILL TEACH YOU TO BE RICH

BY RAMIT SETHI

WORKMAN PUBLISHING

NEW YORK

For my parents, Prab and Neelam Sethi, who taught me that being rich is about more than money

Library of Congress Cataloging-in-Publication Data is available.

ISBN 978-0-7611-4748-0

Cover illustrations by Peter Sucheski

Interior illustrations by Nora Krug

Author photo by Scott Jones

Workman books are available at special discounts when purchased in bulk for premiums and sales promotions as well as for fund-raising or educational use. Special editions or book excerpts also can be created to specification. For details, contact the Special Sales Director at the address below or send an e-mail to specialmarkets@workman.com.

Workman Publishing Company, Inc.
225 Varick Street
New York, NY 10014-4381
workman.com

Printed in the United States of America

First printing February 2009

10 9 8

Acknowledgments

The process of writing this book repeatedly made me wish I were dead. But once I was done, I felt great, my posture improved, my eyesight got clearer, and the world seemed great. I imagine this is what giving birth feels like.

I was fortunate to have a great team of people who helped me turn this book into its final form.

Jeff Kuo is simply the finest researcher I've ever worked with. He was instrumental in helping bring this book together.

I'm grateful to Chris Yeh, who's not only a brilliant marketer but perhaps the most frugal man I have ever met. And to Ben Casnocha, a deep thinker who forced me to dig deeper into everything I wrote.

Noah Kagan and Charlie Hoehn helped me spread the word about this book. Couldn't have done it without them.

Several friends helped immensely by reviewing drafts of this book, including Ben Abadi, Julie Nguyen, Vivek Sankaran, and Jen Tsang.

The folks at Workman were amazing: Margot Herrera, my editor, was incredibly skilled at helping me organize my thoughts into a coherent book. Plus, she's fun: In one of the first chapters, I wrote an over-the-top joke just to see how fast she'd cut it. She just said, "I think we should keep it. It's pretty funny." What more could I ask for? Cassie Murdoch, the perfect complement to Margot, is ultra-organized and constantly thinking two steps ahead.

Many thanks to Peter Workman, who is brilliant and eccentric—exactly as rumored—and to all the people who helped tell the world about this book: Andrea Bussell, Kristin Matthews, David Schiller, Andrea Fleck, and Justin Nisbet. Kudos to Janet Parker, Beth Levy, Barbara Peragine, Doug Wolff, David Matt, and Nora Krug.

Lisa DiMona has now worked with me on two books. You couldn't ask for a better agent.

Seth Godin, who took a chance on a college kid with a cocky attitude and a lot of ambition, got me started in publishing.

BJ Fogg, my mentor and professor, first showed me that you can use psychology for pro-social uses, not just to get people to buy more stuff.

To my family, Prab and Neelam Sethi, Nagina, Ibrahim, Rachi, Haj, and Maneesh—thanks for keeping me motivated for the last two years of writing.

Finally, to my readers. I hope this book helps you on your way to being rich.

Contents

INTRODUCTION

Would You Rather Be Sexy or Rich? 1

Why do people get fat after college? The eerily similar guilt about spending and not working out ■ Counterintuitive but true: We need *less* personal-finance information ■ Common excuses for not managing money ■ Stop debating minutiae and get something done ■ The key messages of *I Will Teach You to Be Rich* ■ "Rich" isn't just about money: What does it mean to you?

CHAPTER 1

Optimize Your Credit Cards 13

How to beat the credit card companies at their own game

Why Indian people love negotiating ■ How credit can help you be rich ■ Picking the best credit card for airline miles, cash back, and rewards ■ Getting a card when you have no income ■ The six commandments of credit cards ■ How to negotiate with your credit card company to get fees waived and receive lower rates ■ Why you should *always* buy electronics, travel, and furniture on your credit card ■ What *not* to do with your cards ■ The burden of student loans ■ When credit cards go bad ■ Five steps to ridding yourself of debt ■ *Week One: Action Steps*

CHAPTER 2

Beat the Banks 49

Open high-interest, low-hassle accounts and negotiate fees like an Indian

Why old people are afraid of online banks—even though they offer the best new accounts you can get ■ How banks rake it in ■ Why you *really* need a separate savings account ■ Opening high-interest, no-fee accounts ■ Five marketing tactics banks use to trick you ■ My personal favorite accounts ■ Negotiate out of fees with your current bank (use my script) ■ *Week Two: Action Steps*

CHAPTER 3

Get Ready to Invest 69
Open your 401(k) and Roth IRA—even with just $50

Why your friends probably haven't invested a cent yet ■ Investing is the single best way to get rich ■ The ladder of personal finance ■ Everything you need to know about your 401(k) ■ The importance of crushing your debt ■ Why everyone should have a Roth IRA ■ *Week Three: Action Steps*

CHAPTER 4

Conscious Spending 91
How to save hundreds per month (and still buy what you love)

Spend less—without making a detailed, irritating budget ■ The difference between cheap and frugal ■ Conscious spending: how my friend spends $21,000 per year going out—guilt-free ■ Using psychology against yourself to save ■ The four buckets: fixed costs, savings, investments, and guilt-free spending money ■ The envelope system for not overspending ■ How to make more money ■ Handling unexpected expenses ■ *Week Four: Action Steps*

CHAPTER 5

Save While Sleeping 125
Making your accounts work together—automatically

The power of defaults: Give yourself fewer choices ■ How to spend only three hours a month managing your money ■ Where does your next $100 go? ■ Setting up a bill-pay and transfer system that works for you ■ Consultants and freelancers: What about irregular income? ■ *Week Five: Action Steps*

CHAPTER 6

The Myth of Financial Expertise 143
Why professional wine tasters and stock pickers are clueless—and how you can beat them

We've been tricked by "expertise"—why financial "experts" can't even match the market ■ You can't time the market ■ How experts hide their poor performance ■ You don't need a financial adviser ■ Pundits worth reading ■ Most mutual fund managers fail to beat the market ■ Why I love index funds

CHAPTER 7

Investing Isn't Only for Rich People **159**

*Spend the afternoon picking a simple portfolio
that will make you rich*

What's your investor profile? ■ The beauty of automatic investing ■ Asset allocation: more important than the "best stock of the year!" ■ Convenience or control? You choose ■ The many flavors of stocks and bonds ■ Creating your own portfolio: How to handpick your investments ■ Investing the easy way: lifecycle funds ■ Feeding your 401(k) and Roth IRA ■ The Swensen model of asset allocation ■ *Week Six: Action Step*s

CHAPTER 8

Easy Maintenance. **199**

*You've done the hard work: Here's how to maintain (and optimize)
your financial infrastructure*

Feed your system—the more you put in, the more you'll get out ■ Ignore the noise ■ The tricky part of managing your own portfolio: rebalancing your investments ■ Don't let fear of taxes guide your investment decisions ■ When to sell ■ For high achievers: a ten-year plan ■ Giving back—an important part of being rich

CHAPTER 9

A Rich Life **219**

*The finances of relationships, weddings, buying a car,
and your first house*

Student loans—Pay them down or invest? ■ Don't let your parents manage your money ■ Role reversal: How to help when it's your parents who are in debt ■ The big conversation: talking about money with your significant other ■ Why we're all hypocrites about our weddings (and how to pay for yours) ■ Negotiating your salary, I *Will Teach You to Be Rich* style ■ The smart person's guide to buying a car ■ The biggest big-ticket item of all: a house ■ The benefits of renting ■ Is real estate *really* a good investment? ■ Planning for future purchases ■ Parting words (cue the violins)

Index. **261**

WOULD YOU RATHER BE SEXY OR RICH?

I've always wondered why so many people get fat after college. I'm not talking about people with medical disorders, but regular people who were slim in college and vowed that they would "never, ever" get fat. Five years later, they look like the Stay Puft Marshmallow Man after a Thanksgiving feast, featuring a blue whale for dessert.

Weight gain doesn't happen overnight. If it did, it would be easy for us to see it coming—and to take steps to avoid it. Ounce by ounce, it creeps up on us as we're driving to work and then sitting behind a computer for eight to ten hours a day. It happens when we move into the real world from a college campus populated by bicyclists, runners, and varsity athletes who once inspired us to keep fit (or guilted us into it). When we did the walk of shame back at school, at least we were getting exercise. But try talking about post-college weight loss with your friends and see if they ever say one of these things:

"Avoid carbs!"
*"Don't eat before you go to bed, because fat doesn't burn
  efficiently when you're sleeping."*
"If you eat mostly protein, you can lose lots of weight quickly."
"Eating grapefruit in the morning speeds up your metabolism."

I always laugh when I hear these things. Maybe they're correct, or
maybe they're not, but that's not really the point.

The point is that we love to debate minutiae.

When it comes to weight loss, 99.99 percent of us need to know only
two things: Eat less and exercise more. Only elite athletes need to do
more. But instead of accepting these simple truths and acting on them,
we discuss trans fats, diet pills, and Atkins versus South Beach.

WHY ARE MONEY AND FOOD SO SIMILAR?

When it comes to food, we . . .	When it comes to personal finance, we . . .
don't track calorie intake	don't track spending
eat more than we know	spend more than we realize—or admit
debate minutiae about calories, diets, and workouts	debate minutiae about interest rates and hot stocks
value anecdotal advice over research	listen to friends, our parents, and TV talking heads instead of reading a few good personal-finance books

Most of us fall into one of two camps in regard to our money: We either
ignore it and feel guilty, or we obsess over financial details by arguing
interest rates and geopolitical risks without taking action. Both options
yield the same results—none. The truth is that the vast majority of
young people don't need a financial adviser to help them get rich. We
need to set up accounts at a reliable no-fee bank and then automate
savings and bill payment. We need to know about a few things to invest
in, and then we need to let our money grow for thirty years. But that's
not sexy, is it? Instead, we watch shows with talking heads who make
endless predictions about the economy and "this year's hottest stock"

without ever being held accountable for their picks (which are wrong more than 50 percent of the time). Sometimes they throw chairs, which drives up ratings but not much else. And we look to these so-called "experts" more than ever in turbulent times like the global crisis of 2008. "It's going up!" "No, down." As long as there is *something* being said, we're drawn to it.

Why? Because we love to debate minutiae.

When we do, we somehow feel satisfied. We might just be spinning our wheels and failing to change anyone's mind, but we feel as if we are really expressing ourselves, and it's a good feeling. We feel like we're getting somewhere. The problem is that this feeling is totally illusory. Focusing on these details is the easiest way to get nothing done. Imagine the last time you and your friend talked about finances or fitness. Did you go for a run afterward? Did you send money to your savings account? Of course not.

People love to argue minor points, partially because they feel it absolves them from actually having to do anything. You know what? Let the fools debate the details. I decided to learn about money by taking small steps to manage my own spending. Just as you don't have to be a certified nutritionist to lose weight or an automotive engineer to drive a car, you don't have to know everything about personal finance to be rich. I'll repeat myself: *You don't have to be an expert to get rich.* You *do* have to know how to cut through all the information and *get started*—which, incidentally, also helps reduce the guilt.

Although I knew that opening an investment account would be a smart financial move, I set up a lot of barriers for myself. "Joey," I said, "you don't know the difference between a Roth IRA and a traditional IRA. There's probably a lot of paperwork involved in getting one of those started anyway, and once it's set up, it's going to be a pain to manage. What if you choose the wrong funds? You already have a savings account; what's wrong with just having that?" Clearly this was the voice of my lazy half trying to talk my body into staying on the couch and not taking action.

—JOEY SCHOBLASKA, 22

Who wins at the end of the day? The self-satisfied people who heatedly debate some obscure details? Or the people who sidestep the entire debate and get started?

Why Is Managing Money So Hard?

People have lots and lots of reasons for not managing their money, some of them valid but most of them poorly veiled excuses for laziness. Yeah, I'm talking to you. Let's look at a few:

INFO GLUT

The idea that—gasp!—there is too much information is a real and valid concern. "But Ramit," you might say, "that flies in the face of all American culture! We need more information so we can make better decisions! People on TV say this all the time, so it must be true! Huzzah!" Sorry, nope. Look at the actual data and you'll see that an abundance of information can lead to decision paralysis, a fancy way of saying that with too much information, we do nothing. Barry Schwartz writes about this in *The Paradox of Choice: Why More Is Less:*

> . . . *As the number of mutual funds in a 401(k) plan offered to employees goes up, the likelihood that they will choose a fund— any fund—goes down. For every 10 funds added to the array of options, the rate of participation drops 2 percent. And for those who do invest, added fund options increase the chances that employees will invest in ultraconservative money-market funds.*

You turn on the TV and see ads about stocks, 401(k)s, Roth IRAs, insurance, 529s, and international investing. Where do you start? Are you already too late? What do you do? Too often, the answer is nothing—and doing nothing is the worst choice you can make, especially in your twenties. As the table on the next page shows, investing early is the best thing you can do.

Look carefully at that chart. Smart Sally actually invests less, but ends up with about $50,000 more. She invests $100/month from age twenty-five to age thirty-five and then never touches that money again. Dumb Dan is too preoccupied to worry about money until he's thirty-five, at which point he starts investing $100/month until he's sixty-five. In other words, Smart Sally invests for ten years and Dumb Dan for thirty years—but Smart Sally has much more money. And that's just with $100/month! The single most important thing you can do to be rich is to start early.

HOW TO MAKE $50,000 MORE THAN YOUR FRIENDS (WITH LESS WORK)

	Smart Sally	Dumb Dan
When beginning to invest, the person is . . .	25 years old	35 years old
Each person invests $100/month for . . .	10 years	30 years
With an 8 percent rate of return, at age 65, their accounts are worth . . .	$200,061. Voilà—the value of starting early	$149,036. Even though he invested for three times as long, he's behind by $80,000

THE MEDIA IS PARTIALLY TO BLAME (I LOVE CASTING BLAME)

Why does just about everything written about personal finance make me want to paint myself with honey and jump into a nest of fire ants? Personal-finance advice has been geared toward old white men and taught by old white men for far too long. I don't understand why newspaper columnists continue to write about tax-optimization strategies and spending less on lattes, hoping that young people will listen. We don't care about that. We care about knowing where our money's going and redirecting it to go where we *want* it to go. We want our money to

WE DON'T WANT TO HAVE TO BECOME FINANCIAL EXPERTS TO GET RICH.

grow automatically, in accounts that don't nickel-and-dime us with fees. And we don't want to have to become financial experts to get rich.

Now, I fully recognize that I'm a big fancy author (that's right, ladies) and am therefore part of the "media." Perhaps it's uncouth to mock my brethren. Still, I can't help myself. Pick up any major magazine and chances are you'll see an article called "10 No-Hassle Tips for Getting Ahead with Your Finances." Amusingly, the same writers who breathlessly encouraged us to buy real estate in 2007 are now advising us on "what to do in the downturn." I'm sick and tired of the same old boring, tired, and frankly horrible financial opinions that are paraded around as "advice." More on this in Chapter 6.

OTHER PEOPLE WE CAN BLAME FOR OUR MONEY PROBLEMS

There are other common excuses for why we don't manage our money. Most of them are complete B.S.:

- "Our education system doesn't teach this," people whine. It's easy for people in their twenties to wish that their colleges had offered some personal-finance training. Guess what? Most colleges *do* offer those classes. You just didn't attend!

- I also often hear the cry that "credit-card companies and banks are out to profit off us." Yes, they are. So stop complaining and learn how to game the companies instead of letting them game you.

- "I'm afraid of losing money," some of my friends say. That's fair, especially after market losses during the global financial crisis, but you need to take a long-term view. Also, you can choose among many different investment options—some aggressive, some conservative— it depends on how much risk you're willing to take. (Because of inflation, you're actually losing money every day your money is sitting in a bank account.) Fear is no excuse to do nothing with your money. When others are scared, there are bargains to be found.

- "What if I don't know where to get an extra $100 per month?" It doesn't have to be $100. And you don't need to earn another penny. I'll show you how to streamline your existing spending to generate that money to invest. Remember, $1 saved per day is $30 saved per month.

Too many of us are paralyzed by the thought that we have to get every single part of our personal finances in order before truly getting started managing our money. Should I use my 401(k) from work or open an IRA? Should I go for mutual funds or individual stocks? Do I need a variable annuity? Here's my answer: Do you need to be the Iron Chef to cook a grilled-cheese sandwich? No, and once you make your first meal, it'll be easier to cook the next most complicated thing. The single most important factor to getting rich is getting started, not being the smartest person in the room.

Put the Excuses Aside

L isten up, crybabies: This isn't your grandma's house and I'm not going to bake you cookies and coddle you. A lot of your financial problems are caused by one person: you. Instead of blaming "the economy" and corporate America for your financial situation, you need to focus on what you can change yourself. Just as the diet industry has overwhelmed us with too many choices, personal finance is a confusing mess of overblown hype, myths, outright deception—and us, feeling guilty about not doing enough or not doing it right. But we can't just blame corporations and the media: With both food and money, we're not taking personal responsibility to step up, learn this stuff, and get started. The result is that many of us end up fat, consumption-minded, and poor. No, seriously: Two-thirds of Americans

> **BECAUSE OF INFLATION, YOU'RE ACTUALLY LOSING MONEY EVERY DAY YOUR MONEY IS SITTING IN A BANK ACCOUNT.**

are overweight or obese, and the average American is nearly $7,000 in debt.

In 2008, when the global financial crisis really erupted in the stock market, the first thing many people did was pull their money out of the market. That's almost always a bad move. They compounded one mistake—not having a diversified portfolio—with a second: buying high and selling low. For all the people who blamed the government, CEOs, and evil banks, had any of them read *one* personal finance book? And yet they expected to get ahead with their money?

Let's put the excuses aside. What if you could consciously decide how to spend your money, rather than say, "I guess that's how much I spent last month"? What if you could build an automatic infrastructure that made all your accounts work together and automated your savings? What if you could invest simply and regularly without fear? Guess what? You can! I'll show you how to take the money you're making and redirect it to the places you want it to go—including substantially growing your money over the long term, no matter what the economy is like.

The Key Messages of
I Will Teach You to Be Rich

I believe in small steps. I want to reduce the number of choices that paralyze us. It's more important to get started than to spend an exhaustive amount of time researching the best fund in the universe. *I Will Teach You to Be Rich* is about taking the first step—understanding the barriers that keep us from managing our money—and then tearing them down and putting our money in the right places so we can achieve our goals. Frankly, your goal probably isn't to become a financial expert. It's to live your life and let money serve you. So instead of saying, "How much money do I need to make?" you'll say, "What do I want to do with my life—and how can I use money to do it?" And instead of being driven by fear, you'll be guided by what history has shown us about investing and growth.

I'll keep it simple: Too many books try to cover everything about money, leaving you holding a book that you "should" read but don't because it's overwhelming. I want you to know enough to get started setting up automated accounts and investing, even with just $50. So here are the essential messages of *I Will Teach You to Be Rich:*

The 85 Percent Solution: Getting started is more important than becoming an expert. Too many of us get overwhelmed thinking we need to manage our money perfectly, which leads us to do nothing at all. That's why the easiest way to manage your money is to take it one step at a time—and not worry about being perfect. I'd rather act and get it 85 percent right than do nothing. Think about it: 85 percent of the way is far better than 0 percent. Once your money system is good enough—or 85 percent of the way there— you can get on with your life and go do the things you really want to do.

It's okay to make mistakes. It's better to make them together now, with a little bit of money, so that when you have more, you'll know what to avoid.

Ordinary actions get ordinary results. Most people are, by definition, ordinary. Yet more than half of a group of college graduates surveyed said they plan to be millionaires by the age of forty, an expectation that is not in line with reality. Look around you: How many of our parents are millionaires? Not many. And if we follow the same ordinary route they did, we'll end up ordinary, too. To be extraordinary, you don't have to be a genius, but you do need to take some different steps than your folks did (like starting to manage your money and investing early).

There's a difference between being sexy and being rich. When I hear people talk about the stocks they bought, sold, or shorted last week, I realize that my investment style sounds pretty boring: "Well, I bought a few good funds five years ago and haven't done anything since, except buy more on an automatic schedule." But investment isn't about being sexy—it's about making money, and when you look at investment literature, buy-and-hold investing wins over the long term, every time. Forget what that money TV station or finance magazine says about the stock-of-the-month. Do some analysis, make your decision, and then reevaluate your investment every six months or so. It's not as sexy as those guys in red coats shouting and waving their hands on TV, but as an individual investor, you'll get far greater returns.

Spend extravagantly on the things you love, and cut costs mercilessly on the things you don't. This book isn't about telling you to stop buying lattes. Instead, it's about being able to actually spend *more* on the things you love by not spending money on all the knucklehead things you don't care about. Look, it's easy to want the best of everything: We want to go out all the time, live in a great apartment, buy new clothes, drive a new car, and travel any time we want. The truth is, you have to prioritize. My friend Jim once called to tell me that he'd gotten a raise at work. On the same day, he moved into a smaller apartment. Why? Because he doesn't care very much about where he lives, but he loves spending money on camping and biking. That's called conscious spending. (Learn how one of my friends consciously spends $21,000 per year going out on page 98.)

I Will Teach You to Be Rich is about sensible banking, saving, spending, and investing. I'll teach you how to set up your accounts to create an automatic financial infrastructure that will run smoothly with minimal intervention. You'll also learn what to avoid, some surprising findings from financial literature (is real estate really a good investment?), and how to avoid common financial mistakes. And you'll start taking action instead of debating minutiae. All this will take you just six weeks— then you'll be on the road to being rich. Doesn't that sound good?

When I was in high school, my parents told me that if I wanted to go to college, I'd need to pay for it with scholarships. So like a good Indian son, I started applying . . . and applying and applying. In the end, I'd applied for about sixty scholarships and had won hundreds of thousands of dollars.

But my best scholarship was the first one—an award for $2,000. The organization wrote a check directly to me. I took it and invested in the stock market—and immediately lost half my money.

Oops. That's when I decided that I really needed to learn about money. I read the personal-finance books, watched the TV shows, and bought the magazines. After a while, I also started sharing what I'd learned. I taught informal classes to friends at Stanford. Then, in 2004, I began writing a blog called "I Will Teach You to Be Rich," where I cover the basics of saving, banking, budgeting, and investing. The rest, as they say, is history.

Why Do You Want to Be Rich?

I've talked to more than a million young people about personal finance over the last four years through my website and speaking engagements. When I do, I always ask two questions:

Why do you want to be rich?

What does being rich mean to you?

Most people never spend even ten minutes thinking through what *rich* means to them. Suckers. Here's a hint: It's different for everyone, and money is just a small part of being rich. For example, my friends all value different things. Dan loves eating out at super gourmet restaurants where a meal might cost $100. Anton loves traveling. And Jen loves buying jeans. If you don't consciously choose what *rich* means, it's easy to end up mindlessly trying to keep up with your friends. I consider myself rich now that I can do these things:

- *Make career decisions because I want to, not because of money*

- *Help my parents with their retirement, so they don't have to work if they don't want to*

- *Spend extravagantly on the things I love and be relentlessly frugal about the things I don't (e.g., spend lots on visiting family in New York, but don't buy the flashiest sports car)*

- *Start a scholarship fund for young entrepreneurs (launched in May 2006!)*

Before you go further, I encourage you to set your goals today. Why do you want to be rich? What do you want to do with your wealth?

What You'll Get Out of This Book

I love to laugh at people when they talk about investing. People think that investing means "buying stocks," so they throw around fancy terms like *hedge funds, derivatives,* and *call options.* Sadly, they actually think you need this level of complexity to get rich because they see people talking about this stuff on TV each day. Guess what? For individual investors like you and me, these options are completely irrelevant.

It sounds sexy, but when individual investors talk about complicated concepts like this, it's like two elementary school tennis players arguing about the string tension of their racquets. Sure, it might matter a little, but they'd be much better tennis players if they just went outside and hit some balls for a few hours each day.

Simple, long-term investing works. This idea gets nothing but yawns and rolling eyes during a conversation. But you need to make a decision: Do you want to sit around impressing others with your sexy vocabulary, or do you want to join me on my gold-lined throne as we're fed grapes and fanned with palm fronds?

SIX
WEEKS OF
ACTION STEPS

I Will Teach You to Be Rich will help you figure out where your money is going and redirect it to where you *want* it to go. Saving for a vacation to China? A wedding? Just want to make your money grow? Here's the six-week program that will let you tackle it.

IN WEEK 1, you'll set up your credit cards and learn how to improve your credit history (and why that's so important).

IN WEEK 2, you'll set up the right bank accounts, including negotiating to get no-fee, high-interest accounts.

IN WEEK 3, you'll open a 401(k) and an investment account (even if you have just $50 to start).

IN WEEK 4, you'll figure out how much you're spending. And then you'll figure out how to make your money go where you want it to go.

IN WEEK 5, you'll automate your new infrastructure to make your accounts play together nicely.

IN WEEK 6, you'll learn why investing isn't the same as picking stocks—and how you can get the most out of the market with very little work.

Plus, there's plenty more. You'll learn to choose a low-cost automatic portfolio that beats typical Wall Street portfolios, and how to maintain your investments by setting up a system that enables you to remain as hands-off as possible while your money accumulates automatically. There are even answers to many specific money questions, including how to buy a car, pay for a wedding, and negotiate your salary.

After reading this book, you'll be better prepared to manage your finances than 99 percent of other people in their twenties and early thirties. You'll know what accounts to open up, ways not to pay your bank extra fees, how to invest, how to think about money, and how to see through a lot of the hype that you see on TV and in magazines every day.

There aren't any secrets to getting rich—it just takes small steps and some discipline, and you can do it with just a little bit of work. Now let's get started.

CHAPTER 1

OPTIMIZE YOUR CREDIT CARDS

How to beat the credit card companies at their own game

You'll never see an Indian driving a two-door coupe. Seriously, think about it. If you have a neighborhood Indian—let's call him Raj—he's probably driving a four-door car, usually a Honda Accord or Toyota Camry. However, Indian people aren't just fanatical about driving practical four-door cars. We're absolutely nuts about hammering down the price to the last penny. Take my dad, for example. He'll bargain for *five straight days* just to buy one car. Dear God, it's not pretty. I've been along for the ride on these weeklong negotiating sessions with him before. Once, as he was literally about to sign the papers, he stopped, asked them to throw in free floor mats (a $50 value), and *walked away when they refused*. This, after he'd spent five days bargaining them down. As he dragged me from the dealership, I just stared straight ahead, shell-shocked.

As you can imagine, by the time I went to buy my own car, I had been steeped in a rich tradition of negotiating. I knew how to make unreasonable demands with a straight face and never take no for an answer. I took a more modern approach, however: Instead of spending a week going from dealership to dealership, I simply invited seventeen dealers in northern California to bid against one another for my business while I sat at home, watched *The Real World,* and calmly reviewed the e-mails and faxes as they came in. (For more about buying a car, see page 244.) In the end, I found a great deal in Palo Alto and walked in ready to sign the papers. Everything was going smoothly until the dealer went to check my credit. He came back smiling. "You know, you have the best credit of anyone I've ever seen at your age," he said.

"Thanks," I replied, actually wanting to say, "AWWW, YEAH, I KNEW IT." That is because I am a weird twentysomething Indian who chooses a four-door Accord for his dream car and prides himself on his credit score.

Then the dealer said, "Hmm."

"Hmm?" I asked.

"Well," he said, "it looks like you have great credit, but not enough credit sources." The bottom line, he told me, was that they couldn't offer me the low-interest option we had talked about. Instead of 1.9 percent interest, it would be 4.9 percent. That didn't sound like much, but I pulled out a notepad and did a quick calculation. The difference would be more than $2,200 over the life of my car loan. Because I was getting such a great deal on the car, I convinced myself that the higher interest rate was okay, and I signed the papers for the loan. But I was still pissed. Why should I have to pay an extra two grand when I had great credit?

How Credit Can Help You Be Rich

People love to pick sexy investments and use fancy words like *distressed securities* and *EBITDA* when they focus on getting rich. But they often ignore something that is so simple, so basic, that it just doesn't seem important: their credit. Ironically, credit is one of the most vital factors in getting rich, but because it's hard to wrap our minds around it, we often overlook it entirely. It's time to wake up and pay attention to it (and not just because of the credit crisis), because establishing good credit is the first step in building an infrastructure for getting rich. Think about it: Our largest purchases are almost always made on credit, and people with good credit save tens of thousands of dollars on these purchases. Credit has a far greater impact on your finances than saving a few dollars a day on a cup of coffee.

What you saw in 2008 was the unraveling of credit, including personal spending that relied on phantom credit from credit cards and home equity. Those days of easy credit are gone (at least for a while until Americans forget history and do it all over again). So understanding your credit is more important than ever.

There are two main components to credit (also known as your credit history): the credit report and the credit score. These boring terms can actually save you tens of thousands of dollars over your lifetime, so listen up. This is what will enable you to justify heading to Vegas and staying at the Hugh Hefner suite at the Palms.

CREDIT SCORE VS. CREDIT REPORT

What your credit score is based on:	What your credit report includes:
35% payment history (How reliable you are. Late payments hurt you.)	■ Basic identification information
30% amounts owed (How much you owe and how much credit you have available, or your credit utilization rate.)	■ A list of all your credit accounts
15% length of history (How long you've had credit.)	■ Your credit history, or whom you've paid, how consistently, and any late payments
10% new credit (Older accounts are better because they show you're reliable.)	■ Amount of loans
10% types of credit (For example, credit cards, student loans. Varied is better.)	■ Credit inquiries, or who else has requested your credit (like other lenders)
Get your credit score at www.myfico.com for about $15.	Get your free credit report once a year at www.annualcreditreport.com.

Your **credit report** gives potential lenders—the people who are considering lending you money for a car or home—basic information about you, your accounts, and your payment history. In general, it tracks all credit-related activities, although recent activities are given higher weight.

Your **credit score** (often called your FICO score because it was created by the Fair Isaac Corporation) is a single, easy-to-read number between 300 and 850 that represents your credit risk to lenders. It's like Cliff's Notes for the credit industry. The lenders take this number (higher is better) and, with a few other pieces of information, such as your salary and age, decide if they'll lend you money for credit like a credit card, mortgage, or car loan. They'll charge you more or less for the loan, depending on the score, which signifies how risky you are.

It's ridiculously easy to check your credit score and credit report—and you should do it right now. Once a year, by law, you're allowed to obtain your credit report for free at www.annualcreditreport.com. It includes basic information about all your accounts and payment history. Be careful to type that URL correctly, not the one that first comes to mind when you think "free credit report."

To get your credit *score,* on the other hand, you'll have to pay. I recommend getting the basic credit report, which will run you about $15. You'll get the option to pick any of the three major reporting agencies. Just pick any one—it doesn't really matter.

Why are your credit report and credit score important? Because a good credit score can save you hundreds of thousands of dollars in interest charges. How? Well, if you have good credit, it makes you less risky to lenders, meaning they can offer you a better interest rate on loans. "But Ramit," you might say naively, "I don't care about this. I don't need to borrow money." Maybe you don't today. But in three or four years, you might need to start thinking about a wedding or a house. What about cars? Vacations? Those ridiculous baby cribs that cost $7,000? And it goes on and on.

So please don't scoff or dismiss what you just read. One of the key differences between rich people and everyone else is that rich people plan before they need to plan.

If you doubt that a loan's interest rate really makes that much of a difference, check out the following table. Assuming you borrowed $200,000 for a 30-year mortgage, look at the differences in what you'd pay based on your credit score.

HOW CREDIT SCORES AFFECT WHAT YOU PAY

On a $200,000 30-year mortgage, if your FICO score is . . .	. . . your APR* (interest rate) will be . . .	. . . with interest, you'll pay a total of . . .
760–850 (best range)	4.384%	$359,867
700–759	4.606%	$369,364
680–699	4.783%	$377,021
660–679	4.997%	$386,381
640–659	5.427%	$405,515
620–639 (worst range)	5.973%	$430,427

*APR calculated in January 2009.

As you can see, a high credit score can save you hundreds of thousands of dollars over your lifetime—and that's just on a mortgage. While other people spend many hours cutting coupons, growing food in their gardens to save on grocery bills, or being frugal with lattes, they're failing to see the bigger picture. It's fine to be frugal, but you should focus on spending time on the things that matter, the *big wins*. So, let's dig into tactics for improving your credit, which is quantifiably worth much more than any advice about frugality.

Building Credit with Credit Cards

Credit comes in many forms (car loans, mortgages, and so on), but we're going to start with credit cards because almost all of us have one, and most important, they're the fastest and most concrete way to optimize your credit. Most people are making at least one or two major mistakes with their credit cards. The good news is that it's incredibly easy to fix this by learning a little bit about how credit cards work.

GUESS HOW MUCH AN iPOD COSTS IF YOU FINANCE IT WITH A CREDIT CARD?

One of the biggest problems with credit cards is the hidden cost of using them. It may be incredibly convenient to swipe your card at every retailer, but if you don't pay your bill the same month, you'll end up owing way more than you realize. Take, for instance, an iPod. It looks like it costs $250, but if you buy it using a credit card with the average 14% APR and a 4% minimum payment, and then only pay the minimum each month, you'll be out almost 20 percent more in total.

Let's say you buy this . . .	Paying minimum payments, it will take this long to pay it off . . .	You'll pay this much in interest . . .
$250 iPod	2 years 6 months	$47
$1,500 computer	7 years 9 months	$562
$10,000 furniture	13 years 3 months	$4,062

If you paid only the minimum monthly balance on your $10,000 purchase, it would take you more than 13 years and cost you more than $4,000 in interest alone. Remember, this doesn't even factor in your "opportunity cost": Instead of paying off a $10,000 sofa for 13 years, if you'd invested the same amount and earned 8%, it would've turned into about $27,000! Try calculating how much your own purchases really cost at www.bankrate .com/brm/calc/minpayment.asp

From one perspective, credit cards are like a delightful gift from heaven. If you pay your bill on time, they're actually a free short-term loan. They help you keep track of your spending much more easily than cash, and they let you download your transaction history for free. Most offer free warranty extensions on your purchases and free rental car insurance. But unfortunately, there's more to them than that.

Credit cards are also convenient enemies. Almost everyone has a bad story about late fees, unauthorized charges, or overspending. Not surprisingly, many pundits (and parents) have a knee-jerk reaction to credit cards: "Using credit cards is the worst financial decision you can make," they shout. "Cut them all up!" What an easy battle cry for people who want simple solutions and don't realize the benefits of multiple sources of credit.

The truth about credit cards lies somewhere between these two extremes. As long as you manage them well, they're worth having. But if you don't completely pay off your bill at the end of the month, you'll owe an enormous amount of interest on the remainder, usually about 14 percent. This is what's known as the annual percentage rate, or APR. Credit card companies also tack on a whopping fee every time you miss a payment—usually around $35. And don't forget the fees for making a payment even just a day or two late. It's also easy to overuse credit cards and find yourself in debt, as most American credit card users have done.

Most of us don't think about these fees. We just charge away and then make our monthly payments, right? Unfortunately, although they're not obvious, credit card charges are some of the largest unnecessary fees you'll ever pay—much more than the costs of eating out once a week or buying that nice outfit you've been eyeing.

This isn't meant to scare you away from using credit cards. In fact, I encourage you to use credit cards *responsibly.* If you can avoid the unreasonable fees and tricks, credit cards offer exceptional benefits (more on this later). To get the most out of using credit, you need to optimize your credit card(s) and use them as a spearhead to improve your overall credit. This is all the more important in the wake of the credit crisis; if you don't have good credit, it may be difficult to get an affordable home loan—even if you have a high income. By the end of this chapter, you'll know how to squeeze the credit card companies for everything they're worth—without paying unnecessary fees or late charges—and you'll know how to use your cards to boost your all-important credit score. Let's do it.

Getting a New Card

Whether you've never had a credit card before or you're thinking about getting an additional card, there are a few things to think about.

Avoid those credit card offers you receive in the mail. Let's cut to the chase: If you hate those credit card offers in the mail as much as I do, visit www.optoutprescreen.com to get off their lists. The average American receives twenty credit card offers every year, and four out of every thousand people accept them. The numbers are markedly different for students. Out of every thousand students who are mailed offers, 150 accept them, an astonishingly high number. Students—and young people in general—are especially susceptible to these offers because they don't know any better. Let's get real. Taking a credit card offer you get in the mail is like marrying the first person who touches your arm—99 percent of the time it's the easy decision, not the right one. Most people know better and go out and find what's best for them; they don't just settle for the horrible offers that fall in their lap. For something as important as your credit, make the effort and pick a good card.

Avoid cash-back cards, which don't actually pay you much cash. People get really mad at me when I say this, but cash-back cards are worthless. "Get 1 percent back on all your spending!" Wow, if I spend $2,000 per

Getting a Credit Card When You Have No Income

A while ago, one of my friends called me and asked if she could borrow my credit card to buy something online. "How come? Don't you have a credit card?" I asked. Given all the benefits of having a card (assuming you use it wisely), you can imagine how angry I was when I learned that she didn't have a card of her own. In my mind, this was the equivalent of one of Dr. Koop's friends being morbidly obese because of eating only butter.

Anyway, I told her to get a credit card and start building her credit. Her response: "I can't get approved for a credit card because I have no income."

Okay, fair enough. Getting your first credit card can be tricky, especially if you're young. But there's an easy solution: Get a secured credit card. These are cards that require you to put down a few hundred bucks in a savings account, and then the bank uses that as collateral to issue you credit. After a few months, assuming you've behaved responsibly, you can graduate to a regular ("unsecured") credit card. To get one, call your bank and ask about it.

month on my credit card, I'll get back $20. "But Ramit," you might say, "twenty dollars is better than nothing." Sure, but what if you could save more by getting a free $500 flight? It wouldn't be as obvious as receiving money each month, but in the long term, you'd save more with a travel rewards card.

Compare cards online. The best way to find a card that is right for you is by researching different offers online (try www.bankrate.com). In most cases, the simplest credit cards are offered by your bank, so this is often a good place to look. They'll connect with your bank account and you can choose from a variety of options, including credit limit, rewards, and more. On the plus side, they're easy to get without much research. The downside is that the rewards are usually fairly mediocre.

Rewards are important. You're going to be using this card a fair amount, so make sure the rewards it offers are something you'll actually want. I travel a lot, so I got an airline card that gives me free companion tickets, free flights, and points for every dollar I spend and every mile I fly. I get multiple free flights per year, and each one saves me about $350. But if you hardly ever travel, this card wouldn't make sense for you. Bottom line: If you're getting a rewards card, find one that gives you something you value.

Don't go card crazy. Now that you're in the market, you might be tempted by any number of card offers. But don't overdo it. There's no magic number of cards you should have. But each additional card you get means added complexity for your personal-finance system. Two or three is a good rule of thumb. (The average American has four credit cards.) Your credit score is based on overall sources of credit. Remember, there are other sources of credit besides credit cards. These include installment loans (such as auto loans), personal lines of credit, home equity lines of credit, and service credit (such as utilities). "Take it slow," Craig Watts of Fair Isaac Corporation says, cautioning against prescribing a specific number of credit sources. "It depends on how long you've been managing credit. The less information in your credit report, the higher the prominence of each new report. For example, if you're in college and you only have one credit card in your name, when you open another account, the weight of that action is more than it would be ten years down the line. If you limit yourself to opening one card a year, you'll be doing yourself a favor."

The Six Commandments of Credit Cards

Now it's time to take full advantage of your cards as a means to improving your credit. Optimizing your credit is a multi-step process. One of the most important factors is getting out of debt, which we'll tackle at the end of the chapter. But first, we'll set up automatic credit card payments so you never miss a payment again. Then, we'll see how to cut fees, get better rewards, and take everything you can from the credit card companies. (Hey, it's business, and they're in it to get your money, too.)

1. Pay off your credit card regularly.

Yeah, we've all heard it, but what you may not know is that your debt payment history represents 35 percent of your credit score—the largest chunk. In fact, the single most important thing you can do to improve your

Awful Consequences

If you miss even one payment on your credit card, here are four terrible, horrible, no good, very bad results you may face:

1. Your credit score can drop more than 100 points, which would add $240/month to an average thirty-year fixed-mortgage loan.

2. Your APR can go up to 30 percent.

3. You'll be charged a late fee, usually around $35.

4. Your late payment can trigger rate increases on your other credit cards as well, even if you've never been late on them. (I find this fact amazing.)

Don't get too freaked out: You can recover from the hit to your credit score, usually within a few months. In fact, if you're just a few days late with your payment, you may incur a fee, but it generally won't be reported to the credit bureaus. Turn the page to find out what to do if you miss a payment.

credit is to pay your bills on time. Whether you're paying the full amount of your credit card bill or risking my wrath by paying just part of it, *pay it on time*. Lenders like prompt payers, so don't give your credit card company the opportunity to raise your rates and lower your credit score by being a few days late with your payment. This is a great example of focusing on what will get you rich, not on what's sexy. Think about your friends who catalog every single website to get the best deals on travel or clothes. They might be thrilled after saving $10—and they can brag to everyone about all the special deals they get—but you'll quietly save thousands by understanding the invisible importance of credit, paying your bills on time, and having a better credit score.

"Paying your bills on time is absolutely critical," says FICO's Craig Watts. "It's by far the most important thing you can do to improve your credit rating." If you miss a credit card payment, you might as well just get a shovel and repeatedly beat yourself in the face. The credit card companies are going to get you—and the worst part is, you earned it.

Most people pay their credit card bills online now, but if you haven't set up automatic payment yet, log on to your credit card's website to set it up now. Note: Don't worry if you don't always have enough money in your checking account to pay off the full amount you owe on your credit card. You'll get an e-mail from your card company each month before the payment goes through so that you can adjust your payment as needed.

I just totally forgot the due date for my credit card. So not only did they charge me a late fee, but they charged me interest on that month's and the previous months' purchases. I called up the customer service line of my credit card and told them that I had been a good customer in the past, and asked if they could do anything for me with the fees. The representative removed the late fee and refunded $20 of the interest charge back to my account. They returned a total of $59 to me with one phone call.

—ERIC HENRY, 25

---

2. Get all fees waived on your card.

This is a great, easy way to optimize your credit cards because your credit card company will do all the work for you. Call them using the phone

What to Do If You Miss a Payment

Nobody's perfect. Despite my warnings, I understand that accidents happen and you might miss a payment at some point. When this happens, I use my Indian heritage to beat the companies by negotiating with them, and you can, too:

YOU: Hi, I noticed I missed a payment, and I wanted to confirm that this won't affect my credit score.

CREDIT CARD REP: *Let me check on that. No, the late fee will be applied, but it won't affect your credit score.*

(Note: If you pay within a few days of your missed bill, it usually won't be reported to the credit agencies. Call them to be sure.)

YOU: Thank you! I'm really happy to hear that. Now, about that fee ... I understand I was late, but I'd like to have it waived.

CREDIT CARD REP: *Why?*

YOU: It was a mistake and it won't happen again, so I'd like to have the fee removed.

(Note: Always end your sentence with strength. Don't say, "Can you remove this?" Say, "I'd like to have this removed.") At this point, you have a better-than-50-percent chance of getting the fee credited to your account. But just in case you get an especially tough rep, here's what to say.

CREDIT CARD REP: *I'm very sorry, but we can't refund that fee. I can try to get you our latest blah blah marketing pitch blah blah....*

YOU: I'm sorry, but I've been a customer for four years and I'd hate for this one fee to drive me away from your service. What can you do to remove the late fee?

CREDIT CARD REP: *Hmm ... Let me check on that.... Yes, I was able to remove the fee this time. It's been credited to your account.*

You don't believe me that it can be so simple? It is. Anyone can do it.

number on the back of the card and ask if you're paying any fees, including annual fees or service charges. It should go a little something like this:

YOU: Hi, I'd like to confirm that I'm not paying any fees on my credit card.

CREDIT CARD REP: *Well, it looks like you have an annual fee of $50. That's actually one of our better rates.*

YOU: I'd rather pay no fees. Which card can you switch me to that doesn't charge fees? I'd like to make sure my credit score isn't affected by closing this account, too. Can you confirm?

Yes, I really talk like that.

The vast majority of people don't need to pay any annual fees on their credit cards, and because free credit cards are so competitive now, you rarely need to pay for the privilege of using your card. The only exception is if you spend enough to justify the extra rewards a fee-charging account offers. (If you do pay an annual fee, use the break-even calculator on my website to see if it's worth it.)

Most people should switch from a for-fee card to a free card, so ask your credit card company what they'll do for you. If they waive your fees, great! If not, switch to a no-fee credit card. I suggest you do this at the same credit card company to simplify your life—and so you don't have to close one account and open another, which will affect your credit score. If you decide to close the account and get a new credit card, look for one with no fees and good rewards (read more about those on page 29).

3. Negotiate a lower APR.

Your APR, or annual percentage rate, is the interest rate your credit card company charges you. The average APR is 14 percent, which makes it extremely expensive if you carry a balance on your card. Put another way, since you can make an average of about 8 percent in the stock market, your credit card is getting a great deal by lending you money. If you could get a 14 percent return, you'd be thrilled—you want to avoid the black hole of credit card interest payments so *you* can earn money, not give it to the credit card companies.

So, call your credit card company and ask them to lower your APR. If they ask why, tell them you've been paying the full amount of your bill on time for the last few months, and you know there are a number of credit cards offering better rates than you're currently getting. In my experience, this works about half the time. It's important to note that your APR doesn't technically matter if you're paying your bills in full every month—you could have a 2 percent APR or 80 percent APR and it would be irrelevant, since you don't pay interest if you pay your total bill each month. But this is a quick and easy way to pick the low-hanging fruit with one phone call.

4. Keep your cards for a long time and keep them active.

Lenders like to see a long history of credit, which means that the longer you hold an account, the more valuable it is for your credit score. Don't get suckered by introductory offers and low APRs. If you're happy with your card, keep it. And if you're getting a new credit card, don't close the account on your old one. That can negatively affect your credit score. As long as there are no fees, keep it open and use it occasionally, because some credit card companies will cancel your account after a certain period of inactivity. To avoid having your account shut down, set up an automatic payment on any card that is not your primary card. For example, I set it up so that one of my credit cards pays a $12.95 monthly subscription through my checking account each month, which requires zero intervention on my part. But my credit report reflects that I've had the card for more than five years, which improves my credit score. Play it safe: If you have a credit card, keep it active using an automatic payment at least once every three months.

5. Get more credit. (Warning! Do this only if you have no debt.)

This one is counterintuitive, and to explain it, I had to reach into personal-finance lessons of yore. Many people don't realize this, but in the classic '80s Salt 'N Pepa song "Push It," when they say that the dance isn't for everybody—"*Only the sexy people*"—they are actually detailing a sound personal-finance strategy:

Bbefore I explain, I want to first acknowledge that yes, I did just quote Salt 'N Pepa in an actual, published book. Anyway, when Salt 'N Pepa talk about "only the sexy people," what they really mean is "this tip is only for the financially responsible people." I'm serious about this warning: This tip is only for people who have no credit card debt and pay their bills in full each month. It's not for anyone else.

It involves getting more credit to improve something called your *credit utilization rate*, which is simply how much you owe divided by your available credit. This makes up 30 percent of your credit score. For example, if you owe $4,000 and have $4,000 in total available credit, your ratio is 100 percent (4,000 ÷ 4,000 × 100), which is bad. If, however, you owe only $1,000 but

Always Track Your Calls to Financial Companies

Unfortunately for you, credit card companies are very good at using B.S. late fees to increase their revenues. Unfortunately for them, I'm giving you lots of tactics for getting these fees reversed. One of the best ways to improve your chances of getting fees waived is by keeping track of every time you call your financial institutions, including credit card companies, banks, and investment companies. This is especially true of credit card companies, whom you should treat just slightly better than you would an armed militia coming after your younger sister. It's tempting, when calling, to be really nasty, but because I was raised right, I don't scream or threaten violence. Instead, when I call to dispute anything, I open a spreadsheet that details the last time I called them, whom I spoke with, and what was resolved. If only all criminals were as diligent as I am.

The Pocket Tracker for Tracking Credit Card Calls

Call Date	Time	Name of Rep	Rep's ID#	Comments

Download this spreadsheet from www.iwillteachyoutoberich.com.

Whenever you make a call regarding a dispute on your credit card, you wouldn't believe how powerful it is to refer back to the last time you called—citing the rep's name, date of conversation, and your call notes. Most credit card reps you talk to will simply give in because they know you came to play in the big leagues.

When you use this to confront a credit card company or bank with data from your last calls, you'll be more prepared than 99 percent of other people—and chances are, you'll get what you want.

The Cards I Use

I have two credit cards. My primary credit card is a Citibank Premier Pass Elite. Citibank offers no-fee and for-fee versions of this card (the no-fee card offers half the rewards). I ran the calculations and decided to pay the $75 annual fee because I spend enough to justify the cost. With this card, I earn one point for every dollar I spend and one point for every mile I fly, plus free companion fares for domestic flights over $379. You can check this card out, along with the free version, at www.citicards.com.

I also have a United Airlines student card that I got many years ago. I use this card only to maintain my credit history, so I've set up an automatic charge of $12.95/month for a music subscription site (see page 26 for why this is important). You can learn more details about this card at www.united.com.

have $4,000 in available credit, your credit utilization rate is a much better 25 percent ($1,000 ÷ $4,000 × 100). Lower is preferred because lenders don't want you regularly spending all the money you have available through credit—it's too likely that you'll default and not pay them anything.

To improve your credit utilization rate, you have two choices: Stop carrying so much debt on your credit cards (even if you pay it off each month) or increase your total available credit. Because we've already established that if you're doing this, you're debt-free, all that remains for you to do is to increase your available credit.

Here's how: Call up your card company and ask for a credit increase.

YOU: Hi, I'd like to request a credit increase. I currently have five thousand dollars available and I'd like ten thousand.

CREDIT CARD REP: *Why are you requesting a credit increase?*

YOU: I've been paying my bill in full for the last eighteen months and I have some upcoming purchases. I'd like a credit limit of ten thousand dollars. Can you approve my request?

REP: *Sure. I've put in a request for this increase. It should be activated in about seven days.*

I request a credit-limit increase every six to twelve months.
Remember, 30 percent of your credit score is represented by your
credit utilization rate. To improve it, the first thing you should do is
pay off your debt. If you've already paid off your debt, *only then* should
you try to increase your available credit. Sorry to repeat myself, but
this is important!

---

*When my husband and I were in college, we got a free T-shirt or
something and got credit cards with reasonable limits ($500)
Sure, I had no income, but that didn't seem important at the time.
Wouldn't you know it, I was responsible enough to have my limit
raised to $2,000 after a very short period of time! Except that
I wasn't actually responsible, and I paid thousands of dollars in
interest and late fees and wrecked my credit rating for several
years. It took many years for us to clear up this debt. I can't name
one purchase that was truly necessary either.*

—**MICHELE MILLER, 38**

---

6. Use your rewards!

Before I get into rewards programs, let me say this: Just like with car
insurance, you can get great deals on your credit when you're a responsible
customer. In fact, there are lots of tips for people who have *very good*
credit. If you fall in this category, you should call your credit cards and
lenders once per year to ask them what advantages you're eligible for.
Often, they can waive fees, extend credit, and give you private promotions
that others don't have access to. Call them up and use this line:

"Hi there. I just checked my credit and noticed that I have a 750 credit
score, which is pretty good. I've been a customer of yours for the last four
years, so I'm wondering what special promotions and offers you have
for me . . . I'm thinking of fee waivers and special offers that you use for
customer retention."

Credit cards also offer rewards programs that give you cash back,
airline tickets, and other benefits, but most people don't take advantage
of all the free stuff they can get. For example, when I had to fly to a
wedding in an obscure town in Wisconsin, I redeemed my credit card's
travel reward to save more than $600 on the flight. That's an easy one,
but there's better: Did you know that credit cards automatically give you

Disputing a Charge: How to Mobilize Your Credit Card's Army for You

Once, when I canceled my Sprint cell phone service, they told me my account had a $160 charge. For what? I asked. Wait for it. . . . "An early cancellation fee."

Yeah, right. I knew I didn't have a contract, and I had negotiated out of an early cancellation fee a long time before that. (Cell phone companies make a lot of money from trying these shady moves, hoping customers will get frustrated, give up, and just pay.) Unfortunately for them, ever since Sprint had started trying to rip me off three years before, I had kept records of every phone conversation I'd had with them. The customer-service rep was very polite, but insisted she couldn't do anything to erase the charge.

Really? I've heard this tune before, so I pulled out the notes I had taken the previous year and politely read them aloud to her.

As soon as I read them, I experienced a miraculous change in her ability to waive the fee. Within two minutes, my account was cleared and I was off the phone. Amazing!!!!! Thank you, madam!!!

Wouldn't it be great if that were the end of the story? Although they told me they wouldn't charge me, they did it anyway. By this point, I was so fed up that I called in the big guns.

Many people don't know that credit cards offer excellent consumer protection. This is one reason I encourage everyone to make major purchases on their credit card (and not use cash or a debit card).

I called my credit card company and told them I wanted to dispute a charge. They said, "Sure; what's your address and what's the amount?" When I told them about my experience with Sprint, they instantly gave me a temporary credit for the amount and told me to mail in a form with my complaint, which I did.

Two weeks later, the complaint was totally resolved in my favor.

What happens in disputes like this is that the credit card company fights the merchant for you. This works with all credit cards. Keep this in mind for future purchases that go wrong.

amazing consumer protection? Here are a few examples you might not know about:

- Automatic warranty doubling: Most cards extend the warranty on your purchases. So if you buy an iPod and it breaks after Apple's warranty expires, your credit card will still cover it up to an additional year. This is true for nearly every credit card for nearly every purchase, automatically.

- Car rental insurance: If you rent a car, don't let them bully you into getting the extra collision insurance. It's completely worthless! You already have coverage through your car insurance, plus your credit card will usually back you up to $50,000.

- Trip-cancellation insurance: If you book tickets for a vacation and then get sick and can't travel, your airline will charge you hefty fees to re-book your ticket. Just call your credit card and ask for the trip-cancellation insurance to kick in, and they'll cover those change fees—usually up to $1,000 per year.

- Concierge services: When I couldn't find LA Philharmonic tickets last year, I called my credit card and asked the concierge to try to find some. He called me back in two days with tickets. They charged me (a lot, actually), but he was able to get them when nobody else could.

Most important, your credit card makes it easy for you to track your spending. For these reasons I put almost all my purchases on a credit card—especially the large ones. Call your credit card company and ask them to send you a full list of all their rewards. Then use them!

My digital camera broke about eighteen months after I bought it. The manufacturer's warranty expired after twelve months, but I knew that American Express extended warranties on electronics for an extra year. I called American Express and explained the problem. They just asked how much I had paid for the camera, and one week later I had a check for the full purchase price in my mailbox.

—RAVI GOGIA, 26

Mistakes to Avoid

Avoid closing your accounts (usually). Although closing an account doesn't technically harm your credit score, it means you then have less available credit—with the same amount of debt. (For example, having $2,000 in debt and $8,000 in available credit is better than having the same debt with only $4,000 in credit. This is your credit utilization rate from page 28.)

The bottom line is that it's usually a bad idea to close your credit card accounts unless you *know* yourself and you know you're going to spend any credit you have available. (Hey, it happens. At least you're being honest with yourself.)

People with zero debt get a free pass. If you have no debt, close as many accounts as you want. It won't affect your credit utilization score.

Manage debt to avoid damaging your credit score. "If you close an account but pay off enough debt to keep your credit utilization score the same," says Craig Watts of FICO, "your score won't be affected." For example, if you carry $1,000 debt on two credit cards with $2,500 credit limits each, your credit utilization rate is 20 percent ($1,000 debt ÷ $5,000 total credit available). If you close one of the cards, suddenly your credit utilization rate jumps to 40 percent ($1,000 ÷ $2,500). But if you paid off $500 in debt, your utilization rate would be 20 percent ($500 ÷ $2,500) and your score would not change.

Think ahead before closing accounts. If you're applying for a major loan—for a car, home, or education—don't close any accounts within six months of filing the loan application. You want as much credit as possible when you apply.

However, if you know that an open account will entice you to spend, and you want to close your credit card to prevent that, you should do it. You may take a slight hit on your credit score, but over time, it will recover—and that's better than overspending.

Don't play the zero percent transfer game. Some people have started playing the 0 percent transfer game to profit off of credit cards by making balance transfers or taking cash advances. They take the introductory zero percent APR that you get when you open many credit cards (which usually only lasts for six months). Then they borrow money from the card at this

Oh No!
My Credit Score Just Dropped

Some of my Type-A readers worry too much about their credit scores. If your credit score suddenly drops, first you should figure out why by getting a copy of your credit report and score (see page 15). Then what's important is how you deal with it going forward. Your credit score can start recovering immediately as more positive information is reported, like paying your bills on time. So work to manage your credit wisely and consistently. As FICO's Craig Watts notes, "The natural movement of these scores is to slowly grow. How do you think people end up with scores in the mid-800s? It's through years and years of consistently boring credit management."

low rate and stick it in a high-interest savings account, which allows them to profit off the interest. Some actually invest the money in short-term CDs or even stocks. At the end, they plan to return the money and keep the interest. I find these 0 percent credit card games so moronic. Sure, you can make a few bucks a year, or maybe even a few hundred, but the waste of time, risk of mismanaging the process, and possibility of screwing up your credit score just aren't worth it. Most important, this is a distraction that gets you only short-term results. You're much better off building a personal-finance infrastructure that focuses on long-term growth, not on getting a few bucks here or there. Dave Ramsey, a popular personal-finance author and radio host, specializes in helping people get out of debt. He says, "I have met with thousands of millionaires in my years as a financial counselor, and I have never met one who said he made it all with Discover Card bonus points. They all lived on less than they made and spent only when they had cash." Focus on the big wins if you want bigger results.

Avoid getting sucked in by "Apply Now and Save 10 Percent in Just Five Minutes!" offers. Stay away from the cards issued by every single retail store. These cards might as well have "You Are a Dumbass" written on them in thirty-six-point type. I can't count the number of times I've seen someone standing in front of me at The Gap or Bloomingdale's who gets suckered into these cards. "If you sign up today, you'll get 10 percent off

Rate Chasers: Wasting Time Earning $25/Month

One of my blog readers, a guy named Mike, wrote in to tell me about his rate chasing. In this case, it was savings accounts, not credit cards, but they're very similar: It's just moving money around from one account to another to eke out a few additional percentage points.

Mike admitted, "I'm one of those rate-chasers, so [with $40k in emergency savings], I've consistently been earning anywhere between 0.65 and 0.85 percent higher than my operating money market account. . . . That's an extra $300/year in interest, which is definitely worth changing banks every four to six months for me."

MY RESPONSE: "Mike, if you were smart enough to sock away $40k in an emergency fund (which is really impressive, by the way), I bet you're smart enough to spend your time doing something better than earning $300/year—something that will let you earn much more sustainably. You're only earning $0.82/day doing that! How about spending the same time optimizing your asset allocation? (see page 170) That step alone is probably worth thousands per year. Or starting a side business? Or even spending those few hours with your family? I don't know what you value, but in my eyes, any of those things would produce more value than $300/year . . . especially for someone who's so far ahead of everyone else, like you are. This is just my two cents . . . about 1/40th of what you earned today (sorry, couldn't resist)."

Focus on the big wins to get the big results. They may not be as obvious or sexy as jumping from account to account and getting a few extra bucks, but the big wins will make you rich over the long term.

your purchase!" the clerks say. They forget to mention that these cards, with an average APR of 21 percent and low credit limits, are issued to people with little regard for how credit-worthy they are. And, predictably, they contain some of the most onerous terms of any cards, including tremendous rate increases if your payment is late even once. And for what? Twenty dollars off a single purchase? Ask yourself if it's worth it. Here, I'll just tell you: It's not. Stay away from retail cards.

Don't make the mistake of paying for your friends with your credit card and keeping the cash—and then spending it all. Finally, please don't do the same dumb thing I keep doing. The last few times I've gone out to dinner, the bill has come, everyone has plopped down cash, and I've realized I can just pay on my credit card and earn some miles. Here's where things go horribly wrong. Don't wake up the next day and say, "Wow! I have $100 extra cash in my wallet!" NO!!! Put it in the bank!! I forget to do this all the time and end up regretting it. Last time, I checked my statement and had shared-meal charges of $50, $64, $25, and so on. Then, my mouth agape, I opened my wallet and saw . . . one $1 bill. Great.

Debt, Debt, Debt

S tatistically speaking, being in debt is normal. And yet, think about it: Is it really normal to owe more than you have? Maybe for certain things, like a house or education, but what about for random purchases on a credit card?

Some people differentiate debts by calling them "good debt" and "bad debt," depending on if the debt appreciates (education) or depreciates (car) over time. Others despise debt altogether. Whatever the case, most of us have a lot of it. And it doesn't feel good.

I want to talk about student loans and credit card debt, the two largest types of debt facing most twentysomethings and thirtysomethings. They get in the way of your getting rich, so I want to help you knock these barriers down with a simple plan.

THE BURDEN OF STUDENT LOANS

I'm not going to lie to you: Getting rid of student loan debt is hard. The average student graduates with about $20,000 in student loan debt, but lots of my friends have more than $100,000 in loans to pay off. Unfortunately, it's not like you can just wave a magic wand and make it disappear. In fact, even if you declare bankruptcy, you'll still have to pay your student loans. However, even if you have huge student debt, I want you to pay attention to how much money you're putting toward the monthly payments. Because the loan amounts are so large, even an extra $100/month can save you years of payments.

Let's look at an example. "Tony," a friend of mine who graduated from Stanford, has $20,000 in student loan debt. If he pays off the loan over ten years, his monthly payment will be about $230/month, meaning he'll pay just over $7,600 in interest. But if he pays just $100 more/month, he'll have to pay only $4,571 in interest—and he'll pay off his loan in 6.3 years.

Most of us accept our student debt as is. We get a bill each month, we pay it, and we shrug, frustrated about the burden of our loans but not really sure if we can do anything. Guess what: *You can change your student loan payments.*

First, to inspire you to take action on paying off your student debt, play with the financial calculators at www.dinkytown.net. You'll be able to see how paying different amounts changes the total amount you'll owe.

Second, I want to encourage you to put at least $50 more each month toward any debt you have. Not only is it a psychological victory to know that you're consciously working to pay off your debt, but you'll also be able to focus on investing sooner. Make sure this is automatic, drawing right out of your checking account, so you don't even see the money. (I describe automatic payments in Chapter 5.)

Finally, if you find that, no matter how you run the numbers, you're not going to be able to pay your loan off in any reasonable amount of time, it's time to call your lender. Look at the phone number on that monthly bill you keep ignoring. Call them up and ask them for their advice. I can't emphasize this enough: *Call them.* Your lenders have heard it all, from "I can't pay this month" to "I have five different loans and want to consolidate them." You'll want to ask them the following:

- *What would happen if I paid $100 more per month? (Substitute in the right amount for you.)*

- *What would happen if I changed the time line of the loan from five years to fifteen years?*

- *If you're looking for a job, you might ask, What if I'm looking for a job and can't afford to pay for the next three months?*

Your lender has answers to all these questions—and chances are they can help you find a better way to structure your payment. Typically, they'll help you by changing the monthly payment or the time line. Just think: With that one call you could save thousands of dollars.

WHEN CREDIT CARDS GO BAD

Just like with gaining weight, most people don't get into serious credit card debt overnight. Instead, things go wrong little by little until they realize they've got a serious problem. If you've ended up in credit card debt, it can seem overwhelming. When you watch Dr. Phil, you wonder why those people can't figure out how to solve their problems when the answers are so clear: "Yes, you should leave him! He hasn't had a job for the last eight years! And he looks like a rat. Are you blind?" But when we have our own problems, the answers don't seem so simple. What should you do? How do you manage your day-to-day finances? And why do things keep getting worse? The good news is that credit card debt is almost always manageable if you have a plan and take disciplined steps to reduce it. Yes, it's hard, but you *can* get out of debt.

Now, almost nothing makes people feel guiltier than having credit card debt. Seventy-five percent of Americans claim they don't make major purchases on their credit card unless they can pay it off immediately. Yet from looking at actual spending behaviors, 70 percent of Americans carry a balance and fewer than half are willing to reveal their credit card debt to a friend. Those numbers are an indication that American consumers are ashamed of their debt levels, says Greg McBride, a senior financial analyst from www.bankrate.com, which commissioned the study. Referring to a recent study on consumer behavior, he told me, "They [are] more willing to give their name, age, and even details of their sex life than provid[e] the amount of their credit card debt." Really? Their sex lives? I would like to talk to these people . . . alone.

When I was engaged, I asked my credit union to raise my Visa limit of $500 to $1,500. This was a horrible mistake. My wedding dress budget of $500 suddenly became $1,200 when I "fell in love" with a dress in a boutique. I've paid only the minimum balance on my Visa each month, since emergency expenses seem to be keeping our budget stretched paper-thin, so I'm throwing away $30 or more per month in interest for a credit card balance from just one day in my life. My husband and I will most likely be paying for the wedding for years to come.

—CLAIRE STUBBLEFIELD, 24

This shame means that those in debt often don't educate themselves on how to stop the madness. Instead, they fall victim to the credit card companies' nefarious practices, which prey on the uninformed—and the undisciplined. These companies have become very good at extracting more money from us, and we've become very bad at knowing enough to say no.

For instance, the number one mistake people make with their credit cards is carrying a balance, or not paying it off every month. Astonishingly, of the 115 million Americans who carry a monthly credit card balance, half of them pay only their minimum monthly payments. Sure, it's tempting to think that you can buy something and pay it off little by little, but because of credit cards' insanely high interest rates, that's a critical mistake.

Let's say it again: The key to using credit cards effectively is to pay off your credit card in full every month. I know I said that prosaically, in the same way someone would ask you to pass the salt, but it is REALLY IMPORTANT. Ask your friend with $12,000 in credit card debt how it happened. Chances are he'll shrug and tell you he decided to "just pay the minimum" every month.

I'm not going to belabor the point, but you would be *shocked* by how many people I talk to who charge purchases without knowing how much they'll actually end up paying once interest is figured in. Paying the minimum amount on your credit card is the grown-up equivalent of a little boy letting the school bully take his lunch money on the first day of school, then coming back with his pockets jingling every single day afterward. Not only are you going to get your ass kicked, but it's going to happen again and again. But by learning how the system works, you can figure out how to avoid the card companies' traps and get out of debt more quickly.

PAY YOUR DEBT OFF AGGRESSIVELY

If you've found yourself in credit card debt—whether it's a lot or a little— you have a triple whammy working against you:

- First, you're paying tons of high interest on the balance you're carrying.

- Second, your credit score suffers—30 percent of your credit score is based on how much debt you have—putting you into a downward spiral of trying to get credit to get a house, car, or apartment, and having to pay even more because of your poor credit.

- Third, and potentially most damaging, debt can affect you emotionally. It can overwhelm you, leading you to avoid opening your bills, causing more late payments and more debt, in a downward spiral of doom.

It's time to make sacrifices to pay off your debt quickly. Otherwise, you're costing yourself more and more every day. Don't put it off, because there's not going to be a magic day when you win a million dollars or "have enough time" to figure out your finances. You said that three years ago! Managing your money has to be a priority if you ever want to be in a better situation than you are today.

Think about it: The average interest rate on credit cards is a hefty 14 percent, which means you're likely paying a tremendous amount of interest on any balance you're carrying. To see how this plays out, let's assume someone has $5,000 in debt on a card with 14 percent APR. If Dumb Dan pays the monthly minimum payment, it will take him more than eight years to pay off this debt—assuming he doesn't rack up more debt, which you know he will. Over the entire process, he'll pay more than $1,900 *in interest alone*. Smart Sally, by contrast, decides to pay $400 each month, which is double the minimum payment. It takes her just over five years to pay off the full debt, and she cuts the amount of interest by more than *half*. Plus, since it's automatically withdrawn from her checking

DUMB DAN VS. SMART SALLY: PAYING OFF $5,000 CREDIT CARD DEBT AT 14% APR

Dumb Dan pays the minimum monthly payment		
His monthly payment is . . .	Paying minimum payments, it will take this long to pay off . . .	Total amount of interest he pays is . . .
$200	2 years, 8 months	$1,313.96
Smart Sally pays twice the minimum monthly payment		
Her monthly payment is . . .	Paying twice the minimum payments, it will take this long to pay off . . .	Total amount of interest she pays is . . .
$400	14 months	$436.46

account each month, she doesn't even notice the extra money she's paying.

That's just from paying $200 extra each month. Don't have $200 extra? How about $50? Or even $20? Any increase over the minimum helps.

If you set up automatic payments (which I discuss on page 131) and work your debt down, you won't pay fees anymore. You won't pay finance charges. You'll be free to grow your money by looking ahead. In the credit card companies' eyes you'll be a "deadbeat," a curious nickname they actually use for customers who pay on time every month and therefore produce virtually no revenue. You'll be worthless in their eyes, which is perfect in mine. But to beat them, you have to prioritize paying off whatever you already owe.

The day I paid off my last credit card bill was surreal. I had spent four years in college racking up debt that I was certain I'd pay off so easily once I started working. I Spring Break-ed in Las Vegas, Mexico, and Miami. I bought Manolo Blahnik shoes. I went out several nights a week. I had no idea then that I'd spend five post-college years paying that debt off—five years in which I could not vacation, could not buy fancy shoes, and could not go out very much at all. So on the day when I sent my final payment to my credit card company, I decided that that payment would be my last. I promised myself that I would never go back into debt again.

—JULIE NGUYEN, 25

Five Steps to Ridding Yourself of Credit Card Debt

Now that you see the benefits of climbing out of debt as quickly as possible, let's look at some concrete steps you can take to get started. *I Will Teach You to Be Rich* is a six-week program, but obviously paying off your loans will take longer than that. Even if you're carrying debt, you should still read the rest of the book now, because there are important lessons on automating your finances and getting conscious about your spending. Just keep in mind that you won't be able to invest as aggressively as I recommend until you pay off your debt. Yeah, it sucks, but that's a reasonable cost to pay for incurring your debt. Now, here's what to do.

1. Figure out how much debt you have.

You wouldn't believe how many people don't do this and continue blindly paying off any bills that come in with no strategic plan. This is exactly what the credit card companies want, because you're essentially just dumping money into their mouths. You can't make a plan to pay off your debt until you know exactly how much you owe. It might be painful to learn the truth, but you have to bite the bullet. Then you'll see that it's not hard to end this bad habit. In fact, you can get the credit card companies to help you: Look at the back of your credit cards for their numbers, call them, and let them tell you the answers to fill in this spreadsheet.

HOW MUCH DO YOU OWE?

Name of credit card	Total amount of debt	APR	Monthly minimum payment

Download this spreadsheet from www.iwillteachyoutoberich.com.

Congratulations! The first step is the hardest. Now you have a definitive list of exactly how much you owe.

2. Decide what to pay off first.

Not all debts are created equal. Different cards charge you different interest rates, which can affect what you decide to pay off first. There are two schools of thought on how to go about this. In the standard method, you pay the minimums on all cards, but pay more money to the card with the *highest APR*, because it's costing you the most. In the Dave Ramsey Snowball method, you pay the minimums on all cards, but pay more

PRIORITIZING YOUR DEBT

	Snowball method: lowest balance first	Standard method: highest APR first
How it works	Pay the minimum on all cards, but pay more on the card with the lowest balance. Once you pay off the first card, repeat with the next-lowest balance.	Pay the minimum on all cards, but pay more on the card with the highest interest. Once you pay off the first card, repeat with the next-highest-APR card.
Why it works	This is all about psychology and small wins. Once you pay off the first card, you're more motivated to pay off the next one.	Mathematically, you want to pay off the credit card that's costing you the most first.

money to the card with the *lowest balance* first—the one that will allow you to pay it off first.

This is a source of fierce debate in credit card circles. Technically, the Snowball method isn't necessarily the most efficient approach, because the card with the lowest balance doesn't necessarily have the highest APR. But on a psychological level, it's enormously rewarding to see one credit card paid off, which in turn can motivate you to pay off others more quickly. Bottom line: Don't spend more than five minutes deciding. Just pick one method and do it. The goal is not to optimize your payoff method, but to get started paying off your debt.

3. Negotiate down the APR.

I'm a huge fan of taking 50/50 odds if the upside is big and it takes only five minutes of my time. Accordingly, try negotiating down your APR. It works surprisingly often and if it doesn't, so what? Just call your card companies and follow this script:

YOU: Hi, I'm going to be paying off my credit card debt more aggressively beginning next week and I'd like a lower APR.

CREDIT CARD REP: *Uh, why?*

YOU: I've decided to be more aggressive about paying off my debt, and that's why I'd like a lower APR. Other cards are offering me rates at half what you're offering. Can you lower my rate by 50 percent or only 40 percent?

CREDIT CARD REP: *Hmm . . . After reviewing your account, I'm afraid we can't offer you a lower APR. We can offer you a credit limit increase, however.*

YOU: No, that won't work for me. Like I mentioned, other credit cards are offering me zero percent introductory rates for twelve months, as well as APRs of half what you're offering. I've been a customer for X years, and I'd prefer not to switch my balance over to a low-interest card. Can you match the other credit card rates, or can you go lower?

CREDIT CARD REP: *I see . . . Hmm, let me pull something up here. Fortunately, the system is suddenly letting me offer you a reduced APR. That is effective immediately.*

It doesn't work every time, but when it does, you can save a significant amount of money with a five-minute conversation. Make the call, and if you're successful, don't forget to recalculate the figures in your debt spreadsheet.

I fell behind in my payments to my Sears Gold MasterCard. I racked up $3,400 in debt, so I called and told them I was having difficulties paying my bill. They offered me 0 percent financing on my balance for twelve months to help me get back on track.

—CHRIS MANCINI, 25

---

4. Decide where the money to pay off your credit cards will come from.

One common barrier to paying off debt is wondering where the money should come from. Balance transfers? Should you use your 401(k) money or your savings account? How much should you be paying off every month? These questions can be daunting, but don't let them stop you.

- **BALANCE TRANSFERS.** Many people begin by considering a balance transfer to a card with a lower APR. I'm not a fan of these. Yes, it can help for a few months and save you some money, particularly on large balances. But this is just a Band-Aid for a larger problem (usually your spending behavior, when it comes to credit card debt), so changing the interest rate isn't going to address that. Plus, balance transfers are a confusing process fraught with tricks by credit card companies to trap you into paying more, and the people

(continued on page 46)

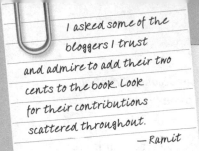

ADVICE FROM THE BLOGOSPHERE

SO, YOU'VE DECIDED TO GET OUT OF CREDIT CARD DEBT

Here's How to Do It Right

By Flexo of www.consumerismcommentary.com

It's fine to use credit cards as tools for convenient spending and to rack up "bonus points," as long as you're aware of the possibility *you are subtly spending more due to the ease of use. I would even understand it if you use* a credit card in an emergency situation when no other options are available. But when you use that same card to buy products or experiences you cannot afford, it's time to admit your behavior is damaging and get a grip on your situation.

You're reading this book because you want to improve your money situation—perhaps even get rich—and the only way to tread that path is to get out of credit card debt. Here's how.

FIRST, YOU NEED THE CASH FLOW. To eradicate debt, you need to have enough income every month to meet your regular obligations like groceries, utilities, your mortgage, and the minimum payments on your credit cards, plus enough to throw toward putting that debt away for good. If you do not have enough income to cover more than your minimum payments, you have to clear that hurdle by earning more money, negotiating with your credit card issuers to lower your minimum payments, or working with a legitimate, nonprofit debt consolidation organization that negotiates with creditors on your behalf, not one that provides you with a loan. (Try the National Foundation for Credit Counseling at www.nfcc .org and read about nonprofit debt consolidation on HowStuffWorks at http:// money.howstuffworks.com/personal-finance/debt-management/non-profit-debt-consolidation.htm.)

NEXT, PRIORITIZE YOUR CREDIT CARDS. The best way to do this is to list your debts from highest interest rate to lowest. If you do a little research, you *may find some people—vocal professionals with motivational seminars and radio talk shows—who disagree with this premise. They want you to list your credit cards with the lowest balances as the most important, the ones to fully pay off first. They claim that the emotional "quick win" of paying off the first card as quickly as possible will motivate you to continue paying off debt. (This sounds more like a "quick win" for the credit card industry because they will get more of your money from interest.) You're already motivated—and it could well be your emotions that got you into this mess of debt in the first place. Leave your emotions at the door and get out of debt the quickest, cheapest, and most efficient way possible.*

PAY THE MINIMUM ON EVERYTHING EXCEPT THE TOP CARD.
Once your credit cards are ranked properly, pay the minimum amount due listed on the statement for every card except the one at the top of the list. Dedicate all the extra funds you have to paying it off. Do this every month until that first credit card balance disappears. Then move to the second card on the list.

STOP USING YOUR CARDS. *When you're paying off debt, you don't want to be adding more at the same time. Eliminating debt is more than just paying off your balances, it's also about resisting consumerist temptations. Don't cancel your cards, but stop using them. Some people have found resisting the temptation to spend to be easier when the credit cards are out of sight. One creative method is to literally "freeze your credit": Freeze your plastic into a block of ice as described at www.calculatorweb.com/calculators/creditcardcalc.shtml.*

Repeat this monthly payment process until the credit card debt is gone. This method will get you there quickly as long as you stick to it diligently. Don't believe me? Check out the "snowball calculator" at www.whatsthecost.com/snowball .aspx?country=us.

Additional resources that might help you eliminate credit card debt:

- *How much will that $350 jacket really cost on a credit card? Find out by entering the price paid for a product as the "current account balance." www.calculatorweb.com/calculators/creditcardcalc.shtml.*

- *Use the "social" financial management application Mint to analyze your credit cards and provide you with suggestions for lowering your interest rates. www.mint.com.*

- *Eliminating your credit card debt should have a positive effect on your credit score. Get your current score for free from CreditKarma and simulate scenarios to see how your future score might change with improved money habits. www.creditkarma.com.*

Flexo blogs about personal finance, the economy, and current financial events at www.consumerismcommentary.com.

I've known who do this end up spending more time researching the best balance transfers than actually paying their debt off. As we just discussed, a better option is to call and negotiate the APR down on your current accounts.

- **TAKING MONEY FROM A 401(K) OR HOME EQUITY LINE OF CREDIT (HELOC).** I don't recommend either of these options. You're trying to reduce complexity, not increase it, even if it costs slightly more. Using your 401(k) money double-taxes the money you contributed to your retirement account. Again, there's the behavioral problem: People with credit card debt often find it difficult to reduce spending and end up getting back into debt after tapping their 401(k) or HELOC. Tough to hear, but true. If you use your HELOC money to pay off credit cards, you'll risk losing your home if you run up more debt.

- **REDUCING SPENDING AND PRIORITIZING DEBT.** Not sexy, but it works. The most sustainable way to pay off credit card debt is also the least sexy. Unlike balance transfers or HELOC borrowing, which you can brag to your friends about, it's not very exciting to tell people you decided to spend less on other things so you could pay off your debt. But it works.

Let me ask you a question. Right now, for every $100 you earn, how much of it goes to debt? Two dollars? Maybe $5? What if you paid $10 toward your debt? You'd be surprised that many people don't even have to cut much spending to pay off debt quickly. They just have to stop spending on random items, get conscious about making debt a priority, and set up aggressive automatic transfers to pay off their credit card debt. I don't want to make this sound easy, because paying off your credit card debt is extremely difficult. But millions of others have done it.

As you read the rest of this book, think of yourself as being on a little treasure hunt to figure out where to get the money to pay off your credit card debt. Pay special attention to these discussions:

- "The Next $100" Principle on page 128.

- Figuring out how much you can afford to put toward your debt using the Conscious Spending Plan on page 103.

- The "Save $1,000 in 30 Days" Challenge on page 115.

- Setting up automatic payments on page 23.

You'll notice that I haven't offered you a simple secret or cute sound bite about how to pay off your debt with no work. That's because there isn't one. If there were, I would be the first to tell you. But truthfully, paying off debt just takes hard work and a plan. It may seem like pure agony for the first few weeks, but imagine the relief you'll feel when you see your debt growing smaller and smaller with each passing month. And sometime after that, you'll be debt-free! Then you can focus all your energy on getting ahead, investing, and living your life. It may not happen overnight, but if you pay off your credit card debt as aggressively as possible, you'll soon be on the road to getting rich and staying rich.

5. Get started.

Within the coming week, you should start paying more money toward your debt. If you find yourself taking more time than that to get started, you're overthinking it. Remember the philosophy behind the 85 Percent Solution: The goal is not to research every last corner to decide where the money will come from, it's action. Figure out how much debt you have, decide how you want to pay it down, negotiate your rates, and get started. You can always fine-tune your plan and amount later.

My biggest mistake was not thinking about the future, and using credit cards to live beyond my means. I got myself into debt in my mid-twenties by spending, spending, spending—and on stupid things like clothes, eating out, DVDs, etc. Once I allowed myself to carry a balance that first time, it got easier to let it build up. I learned my lesson, and am now living within my means on a strict budget that will allow me to be debt-free in two years. Being in debt means giving up choices, means staying at a job you hate because it pays good money, means not being able to build a decent savings account. On a happier note, all of my debt is now on cards with APRs between 0 and 4.99 percent. I have a small but growing savings account, a 401(k), and a plan to achieve financial freedom.

—MELISSA BROWN, 28

WEEK ONE

1 **Get your credit report and credit score (one hour).** Check them to make sure there are no errors and to get familiar with your credit. You can access your report and score at www.my fico.com. If you don't want to pay the $15 fee at www.myfico.com, at least get your free credit report from www.annualcreditreport.com.

2 **Set up your credit card (two hours).** If you already have one, call and make sure it's a no-fee card. If you want to get a new credit card, check out www.bankrate.com.

3 **Make sure you're handling your credit cards effectively (three hours).** Set up an automatic payment so your credit card bill is paid off in full every month. (Even if you're in debt, set up an automatic payment for the largest amount you can afford.) Get your fees waived. Apply for more credit if you're debt-free. Make sure you're getting the most out of your cards.

4 **If you have debt, start paying it off (one week to plan, then start paying more).** Not tomorrow, not next week, today: Give yourself one week to figure out how much you owe, call the lender to negotiate down the APR or restructure your payments (in the case of student loans), and set up your automatic payment with more money than you're paying now. Getting out of debt quickly will be the best financial decision you ever make.

That's it! You've mastered improving your credit by using your credit card. You've waived your card fees, negotiated your rates down, and even set up automatic payments. And if you have debt, you've taken the first steps toward paying it all off. Congratulations! In the next chapter, we're going to optimize your bank accounts. You'll earn more interest, pay no fees, and upgrade to better accounts than the worthless checking and savings accounts we grew up with. Once you've tackled your credit card and bank accounts, you'll be ready to start investing—and growing your money significantly.

CHAPTER 2

BEAT THE BANKS

*Open high-interest, low-hassle accounts and
negotiate fees like an Indian*

Last week, you got your credit cards organized, and now in Week 2 we're going to get your bank accounts set up right. Since they're the backbone of your personal-finance infrastructure, we're going to spend a little time picking the right ones, optimizing them, and making sure you're not paying unnecessary fees. The good news is that this can be done in just a few hours over the next week, and once you do it, your accounts will basically run themselves. The bad news is that the bank account you have—probably from your neighborhood Big Bank—is most likely a big fat rip-off with fees and minimums that you don't need to be paying. See, banks love young people because we're new to banking, and they think we don't know any better about things like monthly fees and overdraft protection. With this chapter, that's going to change. I'll show you how to pick the best bank and the best accounts so you can earn the maximum amount of interest.

How Banks Rake It In

Fundamentally, banks earn money by lending the money you deposit to other people. For example, if you deposit $1,000, a Big Bank will pay you 0.5 percent to hold on to that money, and then they'll turn around and lend it out at 7 percent for a home loan. Assuming that everyone repays the full amount they're loaned, the bank makes a fourteen-times return on their money for simple arbitrage. (To be fair, banks don't get 100 percent of their principal plus interest back, so they do incur some risk and should be compensated accordingly. But fourteen times is a lot of money.) To me, this is a lot like a lazy Godzilla outsourcing a city's destruction to the Stay Puft Marshmallow Man while he sits around and eats a big old pizza, then takes a nap.

FEES, FEES, FEES. Banks also make money from fees—a lot of money. In 2006, banks made more than $10 billion from overdraft fees alone. For example, if you're using a debit card and accidentally buy something for more money than you have in your checking account, you'd expect your bank to decline the charge, right? Nope. They'll let the transaction go through, and then they'll helpfully charge you around $30 for an overdraft fee. Even worse, banks can charge you multiple overdraft fees in one day, leading to horror stories of more than $100 in fees levied in a single day. But there are some positives! Bank of America is nice enough to charge you only $20 for the first overdraft (but $35 for each subsequent overdraft). What a great deal! Check out Bank of America's ridiculous "fees and processes" site, which offers FULL-SCREEN VIDEO and thousands of words but, crucially, does not actually tell you the amount they charge.

NO MORE OVERDRAFTS. One overdraft fee at your crappy neighborhood bank wipes out your interest for the entire year and makes you hate your bank even more than you already do, if that's even possible. More than half the people I've spoken to during my personal-finance talks have had at least one overdraft. One night back in college, I was out for dinner and my friend "Elizabeth" started asking me questions about overdrafts. They got increasingly complex, which weirded me out because I wondered how she knew so much about them. (I thought I was the only nerd who read up on overdraft fees for fun.) Then I asked her a simple question: "How many overdrafts have you had?" She suddenly got quiet, which forced me to interrogate her like Mike Wallace. I ended up learning that she'd incurred more than $400 in overdraft fees over four years of college by simply not paying attention to how much money she had in her account. I screamed at her so much. The sad thing is that she could have negotiated her way out of the first few and then set up a system so that it never happened again. For more on negotiating bank fees, see page 65.

Remember, your bank's fees are often more important than the interest rate it offers: If you have $1,000 and another bank has a 1 percent higher interest rate, that's a difference of $10 per year. *Just one overdraft fee equals three times that amount. Costs matter.*

I'm going to admit my bias up front: I'm a big fan of online banks like ING Direct and Emigrant Direct because they offer simple banking with great rewards and almost no downsides. Most important, they don't try to nickel-and-dime you with fee after fee. These online banks have realized that by eliminating overhead, they can offer dramatically higher interest rates and better customer service than the traditional Big Banks. Online banks have no branches and no tellers and spend very little on marketing, which allows them to accept lower profit margins than conventional banks. That savings is passed on to you as lower fees and higher interest rates. I also love the fact that online banks cut off problem customers. ING Direct, for instance, has found that once customers' balances rise above $600,000, they tend to start demanding a higher level of service than ING Direct is built for. They want to keep costs low for everyone else, so if these high-value account holders require too much service, ING Direct gently suggests that they move to another bank. Man, it takes some balls to tell your highest rollers to take a walk! This is the opposite of brick-and-mortar banks, who love to up-sell products to their high-balance customers.

The result is that online high-interest savings accounts offer interest rates about six to ten times higher than you'd get at your neighborhood bank. That's right: For the first time in history you can actually make a decent return by simply parking your money in an online savings account.

Plus, up to $100,000 held in a savings account is insured by the Federal Deposit Insurance Corporation (FDIC), which is basically the government. (That amount was temporarily raised to $250,000 until 2010, but may change.) Even in the mother of all crises, politicians will move heaven and earth to protect ordinary Americans' savings. It would be political suicide not to.

Here's the funny thing: Try to get your parents to open one of these high-interest accounts, and they'll stop and stare at you like you just backhanded Grandma at the family picnic. Online banks are scary for older people, especially after a few name-brand banks failed during the credit crisis. (A number of people I know actually withdrew their money and kept it—just in case—in their houses. I didn't know whether to scream at them or rob them.) Fortunately, you and I are comfortable doing business online, so we can take advantage of the higher interest rates.

The Nuts and Bolts

Now that I've got my bank rants out of the way, let's go over a few account basics. You may think you know all this stuff (and a lot of it you probably do), but bear with me.

CHECKING ACCOUNTS

As you know, checking accounts let you deposit money and withdraw money using debit cards, checks, and online transfers. I think of my checking account like an e-mail inbox: All my money goes in my checking account, and then I regularly filter it out to appropriate accounts, like savings and investing, using automatic transfers. I pay most of my bills through my credit card, but occasionally there are bills that I can't pay with my card—like rent or my car payment—that I pay directly from my checking account using automatic transfers. (In Chapter 5, I'll show you how to make these transfers and bill paying work automatically.) Traditionally, banks paid no interest on checking accounts, but this is changing. Most online banks now offer checking accounts with interest, blurring the line between checking and savings accounts. Checking accounts are the number one place where unnecessary fees are levied, which we're going to fix.

HOW MUCH YOU EARN AT ONLINE BANKS VS. BIG BANKS

If you saved . . .	Online high-interest banks: At 3% interest, you'd earn . . .	Big useless banks: At 0.5% interest, you'd earn . . .
$1,000	$30 per year	$5 per year
$5,000	$150 per year	$25 per year
$10,000	$300 per year	$50 per year
$25,000	$750 per year	$125 per year
$50,000	$1,500 per year	$250 per year

SAVINGS ACCOUNTS

Think of savings accounts as places for short-term (one month) to midterm savings (five years). You want to use your savings account to save up for things like a vacation, Christmas gifts, or even longer-term items like a wedding or down payment on a house. The key difference between checking accounts and savings account is this: Savings accounts pay interest (although, as we saw, the lines are being blurred with new interest-bearing checking accounts). Typically, Big Banks paid about 0.5 percent interest on savings accounts, meaning that if you put $1,000 in a savings account, you'd earn $0.41 in monthly interest, or $5 per year. I find more than $5 in pennies on my way to the bathroom each morning, so I'm not very impressed by that kind of return. Interestingly, if your money were sitting in one of these Big Banks (like Wells Fargo or Bank of America), you'd actually be losing money every day because inflation is about 3 percent. That's right: You may be earning 0.5 percent interest on your savings account, but you're losing 2.5 percent every year in terms of real purchasing power.

The most important practical difference between checking accounts and savings accounts is that you withdraw money regularly from your checking account—but you rarely withdraw from your savings account (or at least that's the way it should be). Checking accounts are built for frequent withdrawals: They have debit cards and ATMs for your convenience. But your savings account is really a "goals" account, where every dollar is assigned to a specific item you're saving up for.

Most people keep their savings account and checking account at the same bank, although this is increasingly changing as electronic transfers become the industry standard. In fact, with electronic transfers and online banks, options have gotten considerably better for consumers. Online banks pay a higher interest rate for savings accounts—about 2.5 to 5 percent, which would produce $25 to $50 interest per year on that $1,000, compared with $5 per year on the Big Bank savings account. And as with any savings account, your money just keeps growing and compounding, meaning it is working for you by just sitting there.

There is one downside to having an online savings account: It can take a few business days to access your money. Typically, if you want to withdraw your money, you'll log in to your online savings account, initiate a free transfer to your checking account, and then wait three to five days for it to happen. If you need your money immediately, this could cause a problem—but then again, you shouldn't be withdrawing very frequently from your savings account, so most likely this won't be a big issue.

To see how much you'd make from an online bank versus a Big (Bad) Bank, plug in your own numbers using the online spreadsheet at my website, iwillteachyoutoberich.com.

WHY YOU NEED BOTH A SAVINGS ACCOUNT AND A CHECKING ACCOUNT

Having your money in two separate accounts makes money management easy. One basic way of looking at it is that your savings account is where you deposit money, whereas your checking account is where you withdraw money. Yet there's something profoundly different about having two accounts: If your friends want to go out on Friday night, you're not going to say, "Hold on, guys, I need three business days to transfer money to my checking account." If you don't have the money available in your discretionary (checking) account because you've spent your "going out" money, you're staying in that night. Having a separate savings account forces you to keep your long-term goals in mind instead of just blowing them off to have a few rounds of drinks.

Right now, you might be saying to yourself, "Why should I bother with a savings account? I only have $300." I hear this all the time. It's true, the interest you'll be earning on that kind of money isn't really that much.

How My Bank Accounts Work

It's not easy being me. Just as the paparazzi follow Paris Hilton and Lindsay Lohan, wanting to know what they're wearing and which clubs they're going to, people are always dying to know about my personal-finance infrastructure.

MY ACCOUNTS. All of my money goes through my interest-bearing Schwab online checking account. Deposits happen through direct deposit and by mailing checks in preaddressed, prestamped Schwab envelopes. I have a brick-and-mortar Wells Fargo checking account because it was required to open my savings account and I haven't gotten around to closing it. But in general, once you've opened the online account, you can close your brick-and-mortar account any time.

MY SYSTEM. My finances work on a monthly cycle, and my system automatically disburses money where it needs to go. I've set up accounts to draw from my checking account. For example, my ING Direct savings account automatically withdraws a certain amount every month from my checking account, as does my investment account (more about these in Chapter 3). For consumer protection, I pay my bills using my credit card. The credit card is automatically paid in full every month by my online checking account. For cash expenses, I use the Schwab ATM card to withdraw money at any ATM nationwide. All ATM charges are fully reimbursed at the end of the month. Generally, I use my ING Direct account as a receiver, not a sender: I rarely transfer money out of there unless I need to cover a temporary shortage in my checking account or want to spend savings money on something important, like a vacation or birthday gift.

And that's how I do it.

But it's not just about your immediate earnings—being young is about developing the right habits. We're cutting our teeth with small amounts of money, but as our savings accounts increase from $5,000 and $10,000 to $100,000 to $1 million, the habits really start to matter. Start small now so that when you *do* have a lot of money, you'll know what to do with it.

FINDING THE PERFECT ACCOUNT SETUP

I wish I could suggest the one best checking and savings account for everyone, but each person is different. (Don't worry, I'm not going to cop out and hold back my bank recommendations. I'll give you my favorite accounts in a few pages.) Before you go about finding the specific banks and accounts you want to use, take a minute to consider the bigger picture of how you want to organize your accounts. I'll take you through simple and advanced setups for your checking and savings accounts, but pick the one that works well with your personality. You have to know yourself: Do you value simplicity? Or are you the kind of person who wants to spend your time building a complicated system for a slightly larger payout? For most people, the second option—"basic option + small optimization"—is perfect.

Most basic option (good for lazy people). This is the bare minimum. All you need is a checking account and a savings account at any local bank. Even if you already have these accounts, it's worth talking to your bank to be sure you're not paying fees.

Basic option + small optimization (recommended for most people). This option means opening accounts at two separate institutions: a no-fee checking account at your local bank and a high-yield online savings account. With the checking account, you'll have immediate access to your money and the ability to transfer cash to your high-interest online savings account for free. If you already have this, great! Just call to make sure you're not paying unnecessary fees. (*Note:* Most online banks require you to have a brick-and-mortar bank, so don't close your old account before checking with your online bank.)

Advanced setup + full optimization (perfect for people who read things like lifehacker.com and The 4-Hour Workweek*).* This setup consists of several checking accounts and savings accounts at different banks, usually to eke out the most interest and services that various banks have to offer. For example, I have a basic checking account at a brick-and-mortar bank, an interest-bearing checking account at an online bank, and a savings account at yet another online bank. Although you can set up automatic online transfers, having multiple banks means multiple websites, multiple customer-service numbers, and multiple passwords. Some people find this overly complicated—if you're one of them, stick to one of the more basic setups, unless it's very important to you to fully optimize your bank accounts.

SO MANY CHOICES, SO LITTLE TIME

Depending on what accounts you already have and what setup you've opted to go with, getting this part of your financial infrastructure squared away may be as easy as making small changes to accounts you've had for a while. Or you may need to open new accounts, which can be pretty overwhelming. Imagine walking into a strip club in Vegas where you can see everyone lined up and take your pick. I am really hesitant to go further into this analogy because my mom is going to read this book, but suffice it to say that both strippers and banks want your money. Also, there are a lot of choices. That's all, Mom!!!

As usual with financial decisions, we have too many options, leading most of us to make less-than-ideal choices—like opening a bank account in college and then staying with that bank forever. There are some good accounts out there, but of course banks don't always make these deals easy to find.

Why Use a Credit Union Over a Bank?

I'm a big fan of credit unions. Credit unions are like local banks, but they're not-for-profit and are owned by their customers (or, in credit union parlance, "members"). As a result, credit unions usually provide better loan rates and more personalized service than other brick-and-mortar banks. Most are wide open to the public for you to establish a checking account, savings account, or loan, although some require membership in associations like teachers' unions. When you're looking for a car loan or home loan, you'll of course compare rates online, but be sure to also check out your local credit union at www.creditunion.coop/cu_locator. (Full disclosure: I've spoken at a number of their national conferences to help them understand how to reach young people, which I loved doing because I hope they succeed in reaching out to other twentysomethings.)

Most traditional banks offer different checking and savings accounts to serve customers with different needs and amounts of money. They start at student accounts, which are bare-bones accounts with no fees, no minimums, and few value-added services. These are usually perfect for young people. Next, they offer accounts that have nominal monthly fees—around $3 to $5. They also offer ways for you to get these fees waived, like using direct deposit (where your paycheck is automatically sent to your bank every month) or maintaining a minimum balance. If your employer offers direct deposit, these accounts might be a good choice. Finally, banks offer higher-end accounts with higher minimums—often $5,000 or $10,000—and more services like commission-free brokerage trades (which you should avoid, since banks charge exorbitant fees for investments), "bonus" interest rates, and discounts on home loans. These accounts are worthless. Avoid them. If you have that much money lying around, I'll show you how to put it to work in Chapter 7 and earn more than any bank could give you.

You should research the options at a few different banks. I suggest calling (or even going in) and asking them if they can help you find a no-fee, no-minimum account. Ideally they'll be able to offer you a few options. Remember, even if the accounts have fees or minimums, ask about ways (like direct deposit) to get them waived. Here are some phone numbers to get you started:

Bank of America: ....(800) 432-1000

Chase: ....(877) 682-4273

Citibank: ....(800) 374-9700

Washington Mutual: ....(800) 788-7000

Wells Fargo: ....(800) 869-3557

Emigrant Direct Online Savings Account: ...(800) 836-1997

HSBC Direct: ....(888) 404-4050

ING Direct Orange Savings: ....(800) 464-3473

Beyond just the type of accounts offered, there's more to consider when choosing your bank(s). I look for three things: trust, convenience, and features.

Five Shiny Marketing Tactics Banks Use to Trick You

1. Teaser rates ("6 percent for the first two months!"). Your first two months don't matter. You want to pick a good bank that you can stick with for years—one that offers overall great service, not a promo rate that will earn you only $25 (or, more likely, $3). Banks that offer teaser rates are, by definition, to be avoided.

2. Requiring minimum balances to get "free" services like checking and bill paying.

3. Up-sells to expensive accounts ("Expedited customer service! Wow!"). Most of these "value-added accounts" are designed to charge you for worthless services.

4. Holding out by telling you that the no-fee, no-minimum accounts aren't available anymore. They are. Banks will resist giving you a no-fee, no-minimum account at first, but if you're firm, they'll give you the account you want. If they don't, threaten to go to another bank. If they still don't, walk out and find one that will. There are many, many choices and it's a buyer's market.

5. Bundling a credit card with your bank account. If you didn't walk in specifically wanting the bank credit card, don't get it.

Trust. For years, I've had a Wells Fargo account because their ATMs are convenient, but I don't trust Big Banks anymore. I'm not the only one. At the moment, Big Banks are looking around wildly, wondering why young people like me are moving to high-interest accounts online. Perhaps it's because Big Banks pay a meager 0.5 percent interest, and they try to nickel-and-dime us for every small service. Perhaps it's because they secretly insert fees, like the filthy double charges for using another ATM, then count on our inaction to make money off us. There are still some good banks out there, though. The best way to find one is to ask friends if they have a bank they love. You should also browse the major bank websites. Within about five minutes, you should be able to tell which banks are trustworthy and which are not by seeing how straightforward they are with their accounts and fees. Your bank shouldn't nickel-and-dime you through minimums and fees. It should have a website with clear descriptions of different services, an easy setup process, and 24/7 customer service available by phone. Another thing: Ask them if they send you promotional material every damn week. I don't want more junk mail! Stop sending crap! A couple of years ago, I switched my car insurance because they would not stop sending me mail three times a week. Go to hell, 21st Century Insurance.

Convenience. If your bank isn't convenient, it doesn't matter how much interest you're earning—you're not going to use it. Since a bank is the first line of defense in managing your money, it needs to be easy to put money in, get money out, and transfer money around. This means its website has to work, and you need to be able to get help when you need it—whether by e-mail or phone.

Don't Be a Rate Chaser

Do me a favor: If your bank account offers 3 percent and another bank starts offering 3.1 percent, don't change accounts. Half the time, those rates are simply introductory teaser rates that will drop after six months. I'd rather take a slightly lower interest rate if it's at a bank I can trust to give me great service over the long term. But there are a lot of dorks who spend every waking hour online digging up the best interest rate and switching to it immediately. "OMG!!!!" they say. "Emigrant Direct increased its rate from 2.25 percent to 2.75 percent!! Now it's 0.02 percent higher than ING Direct! I must switch accounts right away!! Onward!!!" If you do this, you are a moron. Do you really want to spend each month figuring out which bank is offering a slightly better rate? That's a colossal waste of time for most of us, since a 0.5 percent difference equals just a few dollars per month more in interest. Plus, interest rates change over time, so rate chasing doesn't even make sense. I plan on sticking with my bank for the next few *decades,* and I'm sure you have better things to do with your time. So focus on the big problems, not on rate jumping.

My bank's website is TERRIBLE. It's horrible—most of it isn't in plain English, and they seem to think that everyone should speak like a stock trader. Even worse, it obfuscates how much you actually have versus how much you owe, and doesn't give you streamlined access to moving things around. For example, on a recent charge I made, I can see it online but I can't pay it. I will have to call them and authorize them to pay it. How messed up is that?

—ELEANOR P., 25,

Features. The bank's interest rate should be competitive. If it's an online bank, it should offer value-added services like prepaid envelopes for depositing money and convenient customer service. Transferring money around should be easy and free because you'll be doing a lot of it, and you should have free bill paying. It's nice if the bank lets you categorize your spending and get images of canceled checks, but these aren't necessary.

The Best Accounts

As we've seen, there's a lot that goes into finding the right accounts. Here are a few specific options that I've found work well for many people:

CHECKING ACCOUNTS

Your local bank or credit union's checking account with no fees and no minimums. Yes, I hate Big Banks, but their checking accounts are usually the most convenient ones available. As we just discussed, you can get no-fee and no-minimum accounts with student accounts, direct deposit, or negotiation. Bill paying and new checks are generally free with some concession, such as a minimum amount in the account or direct deposit. These accounts pay little or no interest, but because you won't be storing much money here, that's no big deal. Using the criteria I laid out on the last few pages, you should be able to find a local bank or credit union that you'll be happy with.

Schwab Bank Investor Checking with Schwab One Brokerage Account
(www.schwab.com/public/schwab/home/account_types/brokerage/
schwab_one_with_ic.html, or just Google it): If you've decided an online
checking account is right for you, Schwab offers a stunningly good
account with 3 to 5 percent interest on money in your checking account,
no fees, no minimums, no-fee overdraft protection, free bill pay, free
checks, an ATM card, automatic transfers, and unlimited reimbursement
of *any* ATM usage. Deposit money by transfer, direct deposit, or mailing
in checks. When I saw this account, I wanted to marry it. Although you
need to open a Schwab brokerage account to get all fees waived, you
don't have to use it if you have another discount brokerage account.
(See Chapter 3 for more on brokerage accounts.) Overall, it's a fantastic
checking account.

ING Direct Electric Orange (http://home.ingdirect.com/products/
products.asp): This online checking account has many benefits: It can be
tightly integrated with ING Direct savings accounts, and it provides an ATM
card, free ATM access at 32,000 Allpoint ATMs (but surcharges for usage at
other ATMs), automatic overdraft protection, easy bill pay, and a simple
interface. Billed as a "paperless" account, there are no personal checks
to use—you issue checks electronically through your account or transfer
money outbound. You can deposit money by transfer, direct deposit, or
mailing in checks. The only reason I don't absolutely love this account
is the fact that only some ATM withdrawals are free, which means you'll
have to look up which ATMs you can withdraw from (or face fees).

SAVINGS ACCOUNTS

I would not encourage anyone to use a standard Big Bank savings
account. Online savings accounts let you earn dramatically more interest
with lower hassle. And because you'll primarily be sending money there,
not withdrawing it, what does it matter if it takes three days to get your
money?

ING Direct Orange Savings (http://home.ingdirect.com/products/
products.asp): I use ING Direct for my online savings account. This
excellent bank lets you keep virtual sub-accounts (which means you can
specify savings goals like a car, wedding, and so on) and set up automatic
transfers to other accounts ("Transfer $100 on the 1st of every month
from my checking account and send $20 to my investment account on the

5th of every month"). You can use this in conjunction with an ING Direct checking account, and there are no fees, no minimums, and no tricky up-sells or annoying promotions. It's not always the highest interest rate, but it's always close.

Emigrant Direct (https://emigrantdirect.com): Another great bank that a bunch of my friends use. Their account generally has the highest or second-highest interest rates available.

HSBC Direct (www.hsbcdirect.com): Also highly recommended. Like Emigrant Direct, HSBC generally has the highest or second-highest interest rates available.

Now you've got all the information you need to open a new checking or savings account. It shouldn't take more than three hours of research and two hours to open each account and fund it. Get it done!

Optimizing Your Bank Accounts

Whether they're accounts you just opened or already had, you need to optimize your checking and savings accounts. This means you shouldn't be paying fees or minimums. The key to optimizing an account is talking to an actual customer-service rep, either in person or on the phone. Yes, nerds, you have to get out of your chair and either go over to the bank or pick up the telephone. For some reason, half my friends are afraid of talking to people on the phone and it ends up costing them lots of money. I have a friend who recently lost his bank password and, for security reasons, had to call the bank to prove who he was. He turned into a Stockholm Syndrome victim in front of my eyes, muttering, "It's not that important. I'll just wait until I go into the bank" over and over. He didn't get his password for four months! What the hell is wrong with people? You may not like to talk on the phone, but most of the special deals I'll show you how to get require talking to someone in person or on the phone. So suck it up.

AVOIDING MONTHLY FEES
Maybe I'm too demanding, but if I'm lending a bank my money to re-lend out, I don't believe I should have to pay them additional fees. Think about

Alert to Students

If you're a student, there's no reason you shouldn't have an account with no fees and no minimums. If you decide to stick with a Big Bank account, make sure you're in a student account with no annual fees. Here's how the conversation will probably go:

YOU: Hi, I'm a student and I'd like to get a savings account and a checking account with no annual fees. I'd like free checking and no minimum balance, please.

BANKER: *I'm really sorry, but we don't offer those anymore.*

YOU: Really? That's interesting because [Bank of America/Wells Fargo/Washington Mutual/other competitor] is offering me that exact deal right now. Could you check again and tell me which comparable accounts you offer?

(Eighty percent of the time, you'll get a great account at this point. If not, ask for a supervisor.)

SUPERVISOR: *Hi, how can I help you?*

YOU: (Repeat argument from the beginning. If the supervisor doesn't give you an option, add this:) Look, I've been a customer for X years and I want to find a way to make this work. Plus, I know that your customer-acquisition cost is more than two hundred dollars. What can you do to help me stay a customer?

SUPERVISOR: *What an astounding coincidence. My computer is suddenly allowing me to offer the exact account you asked for!*

YOU: Why, thank you, kind sir. (Sip Darjeeling tea.)

You're in a customer group that's very profitable for banks: ING Direct and the American Bankers Association put the cost of acquiring a new customer between $100 and $3,500—including all of their advertising, personnel, and technology costs. They don't want to lose you over something as small as a $5 monthly fee. Use this knowledge as leverage whenever you contact any financial company.

it: If your Big Bank charges you a $5 monthly fee, that basically wipes out any interest you earn. This is why I'm fanatical about my savings and checking accounts having no fees of any kind, including monthly fees, overdraft fees, or setup fees. If you already have an account at a bank you like, but they're charging a monthly fee, try to get them to waive it. They will often do this if you set up direct deposit, which lets your employer deposit your paycheck directly into your account every month.

Banks will also try to trick you by demanding "minimums," which refer to minimum amounts you must have in your account to avoid fees or to get "free" services like bill pay. These are B.S. Imagine if a bank required you to keep $1,000 sitting in its low-interest account. You could be earning twenty times that much by investing it.

If you can't do direct deposit because your job doesn't offer it or if you can't get the bank to waive a "minimum," I strongly recommend that you switch to an online high-interest account, which has no fees and no minimums.

Note: Certain charges are okay for services like money orders and reordering checks. Please don't run into your bank screaming, "BUT RAMIT TOLD ME NO FEES!!!!" when you're trying to order more checks. That would be cool, though.

ALMOST ALL BANK FEES ARE NEGOTIABLE

The most painful and expensive fees are usually overdraft fees—which is the fee your bank charges you if you don't have enough money in your checking account to cover a purchase. Of course, the best way to avoid overdraft fees is to not let them happen in the first place. Set up automatic transfers and keep a cash cushion in your account (I keep about $1,000 in my checking at all times). But mistakes do happen. Most banks understand that people are occasionally forgetful and they'll waive a first-time fee if you ask. After the first time, it gets harder but can still be done if you have a good excuse. Remember: They want to keep you as their customer. A well-executed phone call can often make a difference. But when calling, keep in mind that you should have a clear goal (to get your fee erased) and should not make it easy for companies to say no to you.

Here's how I negotiated my way out of a $20 overdraft fee and a $27.10 finance charge from Wells Fargo.

I had transferred money from my savings account to my checking account to cover a temporary shortage, and the transfer arrived one day late. I saw the overdraft fee, sighed, and called the bank to get it waived.

RAMIT: Hi, I just saw this bank charge for overdrafting and I'd like to have it waived.

BANK REP: *I see that fee . . . hmm . . . Let me just see here. Unfortunately, sir, we're not able to waive that fee. It was [some B.S. excuse about how it's not waiveable].*

Bad Things to Say Here:

"Are you sure?"
Don't make it easy for the rep to say no to your request.

"Is there anything else I can do?"
Again, imagine if you were a customer-service rep and someone said this. It would make your life easier to just say no. As a customer, don't make it easy for companies to say no.

"Well, this Indian blogger dude told me I could."
Nobody cares. But it would be cool if a thousand customers called their banks and said this.

"Okay."
Don't give up here. Despite what you learned in sex ed, "no" does not mean "no" when it comes from a bank.

Try this instead:

RAMIT: Well, I see the fee here and I'd really like to get it waived. What else can you do to help me? (Repeat your complaint and ask them how to constructively fix it.)

At this point, about 85 percent of people will get their fees refunded. I have hundreds of comments from people on my blog who have taken this advice and saved thousands of dollars in fees. But in case the rep is obstinate, here's what you can do.

BANK REP: *I'm sorry, sir, we can't refund that fee.*

RAMIT: I understand it's difficult, but take a look at my history. I've been a customer for more than three years, and I'd like to keep the relationship going. Now, I'd like to get this waived—it was a mistake and it won't happen again. What can you do to help?

BANK REP: *Hmm, one second, please. I see that you're a really good customer. . . . I'm going to check with my supervisor. Can you hold for a second?*

(Being a long-term customer increases your value to them, which is one reason you want to pick a bank you can stick with for the long term. And the fact that you didn't back down at the first "no" makes you different from 99 percent of other customers.)

BANK REP: *Sir, I was able to check with my supervisor and waive the fee. Is there anything else I can help you with today?*

That's all I had to do! This doesn't just work for overdraft fees—it can also work for certain processing fees, late fees, and even ATM fees. I learned this lesson the hard way. I lived in New York for a summer when I was doing an internship. I decided not to open a bank account while I was there because it would take time and I was lazy. So I just used those ATMs left and right and ate the $3 charges ($1.50 from my bank, $1.50 from the ATM) each time. Now I feel dumb because I just talked to a friend who recently moved to New York for a few months. She didn't want to open a bank account for such a short time either, but instead of just shrugging and saying "Oh, well," she actually called her bank. She just asked them if they would waive the ATM fees while she was there. "No problem," they said. She saved more than $250 just by making a phone call! Remember, with a customer-acquisition cost of more than $200, banks want to keep you as their customer. So use this information to your advantage, and next time you see any fees levied on your account, make the call.

While many bank fees are ridiculous, I find that they are quite willing to wipe them for a good customer. I had a bounced-check fee wiped because I stupidly wrote a check out of the wrong account. I simply walked into the bank and asked, and they did it right there on the spot. I didn't have to do any convincing or anything. Plus, I'd been a customer for about five years.

—ADAM FERGUSON, 22

ACTION STEPS

WEEK TWO

1 **Open a checking account or assess the one you already have (one hour).** Find an account that works for you, call the bank (or go in), and open the account. If you've already got one, make *absolutely sure* it is a no-fee, no-minimum account. How? Review your last bank statement or, if you don't have that, call your bank and say, "I'd like to confirm that my bank account has no fees and no minimums whatsoever. Can you confirm that?" If you discover you've been paying fees, use the negotiating tactic on page 64 to get your account switched to a no-fee, no-minimum account. Be aggressive in threatening to leave if they don't switch you. If you decide to switch, check out www.bankswitcher.com.

---

2 **Open an online high-interest savings account (three hours).** You'll earn more in interest and pay less in fees. Plus, it's psychologically powerful to have your savings account separate from your checking: You're much less likely to dip into your savings if it's not immediately reachable through your normal banking. Spend a couple of hours comparing the banks I recommended on page 61. To see a more comprehensive list, got to www.bankrate.com. My favorite savings account: ING Direct.

2a **Optional: Open an online checking account (two hours).** This isn't absolutely necessary—but if you're ready to be more advanced and earn a higher interest rate, go ahead and do it. Remember, the main benefits of an online checking account are a high interest rate and fewer tricky fees. My favorite checking account: Schwab Investor Checking.

---

3 **Fund your online savings account (one hour).** Leave one and a half months of living expenses in your checking account, or as close to it as you can manage. (This prevents overdrafts as you're getting used to transferring money between accounts. Remember, most transfers take three to five business days.) Transfer the rest to your savings account— even if it's only $20.

Congratulations! Now that you've got the backbone of your personal financial infrastructure up and running, we're going to open your investment account.

CHAPTER 3

GET READY TO INVEST

Open your 401(k) and Roth IRA—even with just $50

There's something special about Indian parents. To understand what I mean, ask any Indian kid you know what happened when he excitedly brought home his straight-A report card. His parents probably gleamed with pride, gave him a huge hug, and then immediately frowned. "Vijay, this is very good! But why did you get this A minus? What happened?" they said. As you can imagine, this approach tends to promote a slightly warped view of the world for Indian children. I can't wait to do this to my future kids someday.

Perhaps the fact that I grew up with this worldview explains why, when people finally start thinking about their finances, I congratulate them for approximately six seconds before I secretly judge them because I know they're not doing enough. In the last chapter we talked about saving, and I'm happy you've opened up a high-interest savings account. I really am. But it's not enough! Saving a little money here and there is not enough, despite what you read in the myriad books and blogs filled with tips and tales of frugality. "Buy 200 cases of orange juice," these fantastic articles say, "and you can save 6 percent! Amazing!"

Get a life. The sad fact is, if you do only the bare minimum—for example, if you get frugal and save $100 a month in an online savings account—the results will not be especially impressive. Even if you're earning a competitive 3 percent or higher from a high-interest online savings account, it will take you a long, long time to get a substantial return. You need a way to put that money to work for you so it earns more than even the highest-yielding savings account, and investing is the first and best way to do it. "Compounding," Albert Einstein said, "is mankind's greatest invention because it allows for the reliable, systematic accumulation of wealth."

Rather than earning 0.5 percent interest like most people do in their savings account, or even six times that amount with a high-interest savings account (like the one you now have, right?), you can earn around 8 percent per year over the long term by investing: Over the twentieth century, the average annual stock-market return was 11 percent, minus 3 percent for inflation, giving us 8 percent. To put that in perspective, if you invested $1,000 at age twenty-five and didn't touch it until age sixty-five, it would be worth about $3,000 in your 3 percent high-interest savings account, but if you put it in an investment account that earned 8 percent, you'd have more than $21,000.

Investing may seem intimidating, especially considering the volatility of the markets during the global financial crisis. But it's actually quite painless. I'll walk you through it, and by the end of this chapter, you'll have opened an investment account. You don't actually have to worry about choosing where to invest yet—that comes in Chapter 7. For now, we'll set up the right accounts so that when you're ready, you can simply set up automatic transfers to funnel cash there each month.

There must be something about turning 40 that causes you to evaluate where you've been and where you are going. My husband was offered a new position with better pay, but even with a $15,000 increase in salary our debt load has been so high we have continued to struggle. The turning point was when we received a fairly sizable inheritance and used it to pay down our debt, but even that wasn't enough to pay it off.

—**ANN BERG, 40**

Why Your Friends Probably Haven't Invested a Cent Yet

Before we go any further, let's take a minute to understand why young people are not investing. Then you can secretly scorn them once you've opened your own investment accounts.

Ask any of your friends how much they've invested and they'll say things like, "Huh?" or "I don't earn enough to invest." Most of them will say, "I don't know how to pick stocks," which is ironic because INVESTING ISN'T ABOUT PICKING STOCKS. Although it's true that some of them might participate in a 401(k)—a type of retirement account—that's probably the extent of their investments. And yet these are the most important investing years of our lives!

Another reason young people don't invest is that they're scared. You can hear the media scream "Global financial crisis!" only so many times before you decide to opt out altogether. And yet, a drop in the stock market is a *good* thing for young people. It means investments are essentially on sale, so we can buy stocks for less now and then let our

Three Startling Stats About Young People and 401(k)s

Remember, a 401(k) is just a type of investment account—one that offers huge benefits that I'll cover on page 78. Here's what's stunning: Of employees age twenty-five and under,

- Less than one-third participate in a 401(k);

- Less than 4 percent max out their contributions;

- And, astonishingly, only 16 percent contribute enough to get the full company match. The company match is literally free money, so 84 percent of young employees are losing thousands of dollars per year because they haven't spent a few hours to learn how this stuff works.

OLDER PEOPLE REGRET NOT INVESTING

I'm not a crotchety old man yet, but when I see these numbers, it's tempting to run around with a cane and a vodka tonic in hand, screaming at young people. Not only do we fail to invest our money, but we don't even know why it's important!

Age of employee	Percentage who participate in a 401(k)	Percentage of pay they Contribute	Median balance of their 401(k)	My comment
18–25	31.3%	5.6%	$1,280	Too busy watching *The Hills*.
26–41	63.1%	7.2%	$14,730	These people have realized that perhaps saving money is important.
42 and up	72.0%	8.3%	$44,330	These older folks are wishing they could go back in time and beat themselves for not saving more, like Biff in *Back to the Future II*.

Source: Hewitt and Associates (http://articles.moneycentral.msn.com/CollegeAndFamily/MoneyInYour20s/YoungAdultsAllButIgnore401ksIRAs.aspx)

money grow for decades. When people say "buy low, sell high," this is what they're talking about.

Remember, knowing how to invest isn't obvious. And that's the problem. When it comes to money, it's actually very easy to end up like most other people: You just . . . do nothing. After years of talking to young people about money, I have come to a couple of conclusions: First, I pretty much hate everyone. Second, I believe there are three categories of people: the As, the Bs, and the Cs. The As are already managing their money and want to optimize what they're doing. The Bs, the largest group of people, are not doing anything but could be persuaded to change that if you figure out what motivates them. The Cs are an unwashed mass of people who are a lost cause. Theoretically, they *could* be motivated,

I have a friend who loves cycling and movies. He never liked to "dress up," preferring dirty jeans and T-shirts, and didn't want a boring office job. I don't think he's ever received more than $9 an hour in his life. He has spent all of his money on lighter bike parts and VHS movies. When DVDs came out, he started rebuying the same movies on DVD because they were "better quality." Meanwhile, he filed for bankruptcy to get out from under credit card debt and now lives in a trailer behind his parents' house, with his sister paying most of his bills.

—**RONALD WAGNER, 25**

but it's impossibly hard to get through their knuckleheaded reasons and excuses for putting money management so far down their list of priorities.

Sadly, although some people are limited by circumstances, most people will never get rich simply because they have poor attitudes and behaviors about money. In fact, most people in their twenties are Bs: not great, but not bad. There's a lot of time left for them to set aggressive investment goals, but if they don't take any action, they end up inevitably drifting toward being a C. Don't let this happen to you!

Why do so many of us have such poor attitudes toward money? You could make a convincing case for a lack of education, too much information, confusing messages from the media, or simply a lack of interest. Whatever the reason, we *know* young people aren't investing enough.

Financial institutions have noticed an interesting phenomenon: When people enter their forties, they suddenly realize that they should have been saving money all along. As a result, the number one financial concern Americans have is not having enough money for retirement. "Even a majority of Americans in upper-income households say they are 'very' or 'moderately' worried about their retirement income," says Lydia Saad of the Gallup News Service. To bring this close to home, ask your parents what they worry about most. I'll bet you their answer is, simply, "money." Yet we're not paying much more attention to our finances than our parents did.

Although it's easy to "plan" on winning the lottery to get rich, the real way to do it is actually much simpler: Of America's millionaires, 80 percent are first-generation affluent, meaning their parents weren't rich. They collected their significant wealth through controlling their spending,

A FIFTH OF YOUNG PEOPLE THINK THEY'LL GET RICH THROUGH THE LOTTERY

Percentage of young people . . .	. . . Who believe they'll get rich . . .	My comment
21%	By winning the lottery	I hate you.
11%	Through an inheritance	I hate you.
3%	Via an insurance settlement	How about the insurance of doing some actual work to learn about your money?

regular investing, and in some cases, entrepreneurship. Not as sexy as winning the lottery, but much more realistic.

On average, millionaires invest 20 percent of their household income each year. Their wealth isn't measured by the amount they make each year, but by how much they've saved and invested over time. In other words, a project manager could earn $50,000 per year and be richer than a doctor earning $250,000 per year—*if* the project manager has a higher net worth by saving and investing more over time.

American culture doesn't help us think about investing our money. We see shows like *My Super Sweet 16* that show us the *results* of being rich, not *how to get there*. Not surprisingly, as such TV shows have become more popular, our attitudes have changed. According to a Roper Center study in 1975, a lot of Americans thought "the good life" meant a happy marriage, one or more children, an interesting job, and a home. By 1999, the responses were more materialistic: "a lot of money," a second car," "a second TV," "a vacation home," "a swimming pool," and "really nice clothes."

Despite this preoccupation with material goods and a dizzying array of information sources—including 24/7 financial-news channels and dozens of personal-finance magazines—most of us don't seem to be concerned with managing our financial situation. Even high-income earners don't handle their money well: 34 percent of those who earned $250,000 or more said the need to pay everyday bills was the top reason why they weren't saving more. One in ten said they weren't making enough to make ends meet, according to an HSBC Bank report in 2007.

Even though lots of young people have naive and often delusional ideas about money, you don't need to be one of them. I'm going to help you confront reality and take a few simple steps to get rich. Ten years from now—hell, maybe even three months from now—you'll see an investment account full of money that is automatically added to each month. You'll be earning while you sleep. And instead of waiting for a magical lottery win, you'll consciously use your investment account to get rich.

INVESTING IS THE SINGLE MOST EFFECTIVE WAY TO GET RICH

By opening an investment account, you give yourself access to the biggest moneymaking vehicle in the history of the world: the stock market. Setting up an account is an excellent first step toward actually investing, and you don't have to be rich to open one. Many account providers will waive minimums (the amount required to open an account) if you set up an automatic monthly transfer (more on this in Chapter 5).

INVEST NOW...
YOU'RE NOT GETTING ANY YOUNGER

What if you had started investing $10 per week five years ago, receiving an average 8 percent return? Guess how much you'd have? It turns out that by now, you'd have thousands of dollars—all from investing a little more than $1 per day. Think about that $10 a week—where did it go, anyway? If you're like most people, it probably slipped through your fingers on random things like cab rides and lunches. Despite wild rides in the stock market, with a long term perspective, the best thing you can do is start investing early.

If you invest this much per week . . .	After 1 year, you'll have . . .	After 5 years, you'll have . . .	After 10 years, you'll have . . .
$10	$562	$3,295	$8,136
$20	$1,123	$6,589	$16,271
$50	$2,808	$16,473	$40,678

I didn't open an investment account until I was twenty-three, because I simply didn't know I should. And once I learned I should, I wasn't sure I had enough money to. Investing is for rich people, right? Not people going to college and earning less than $10 an hour, right? My other issue was that I didn't know what to do with the money even if I opened an account. I had no idea where to start, and as a (now recovering) perfectionist, the number of choices freaked me out.

—**SHANNON HULSEY, 26**

The Ladder of Personal Finance

These are the five systematic steps you should take to invest. Each step builds on the previous one, so when you finish the first, go on to the second. If you can't get to number 5, don't worry. You can still feel great, since most people never even get to the first step. In Chapter 5, I'll show you how to make this automatic, so your system runs itself with just a few hours of work *per year*—but remember, opening these accounts and getting started is the most important step.

Rung 1: If your employer offers a 401(k) match, invest to take full advantage of it and contribute just enough to get 100 percent of the match. A "401(k) match" means that for every dollar you contribute to your 401(k), your company will "match" your contribution up to a certain amount. For example, for easy math, let's assume you make $100,000. A "100 percent match up to 5 percent of your contribution" means that you'll contribute $5,000 and your company will match it with $5,000. This is free money and there is, quite simply, no better deal.

Rung 2: Pay off your credit card and any other debt. The average credit card APR is 14 percent, and many APRs are higher. Whatever your card company charges, paying off your debt will give you a significant instant return. For the best ways to do this, see page 40 in Chapter 1.

Rung 3: Open up a Roth IRA (see page 83) and contribute as much money as possible to it. (As long as your income is $101,000 or less, you're allowed to contribute up to $5,000 in 2009.)

Rung 4: If you have money left over, go back to your 401(k) and contribute as much as possible to it (this time above and beyond your employer match). The current limit is $15,500.

Rung 5: If you still have money left to invest, open a regular nonretirement account and put as much as possible there. For more about this, see the next page. Also, pay extra on any mortgage debt you have, and consider investing in yourself: Whether it's starting a company or getting an additional degree, there's often no better investment than your own career.

Remember, this ladder of personal finance only shows you *where* to invest your money. In Chapter 7, I'll show you *what* to invest in.

Mastering Your 401(k)

It is a universally acknowledged truth that girls named Nancy are never hot. But imagine that you met the hottest Nancy of your life on spring break in Cabo. Would you be willing to challenge your deep-seated worldview and hang out with her?

That's the trade-off you make with a 401(k): cryptic name, kinda boring, but huge . . . benefits. Here's how it works:

A 401(k) plan is a type of retirement account that many companies offer to their employees. (Note: Ask your HR representative if your company offers a 401(k). If not, skip ahead to the section on Roth IRAs on page 83.) It's a "retirement" account because it gives you large tax advantages if you agree not to withdraw your money from the account until your reach the retirement age of $59\frac{1}{2}$. (You don't actually have to start withdrawing your money until you're $70\frac{1}{2}$ years old, and even then there's an exception if you're still working. But don't worry about that now. By the time you're 70, we'll all have flying jet packs and robots to handle all our finances.) To set up your 401(k), you fill out a form authorizing part of each paycheck—you decide how much—to be sent to your account each month. The money goes straight from your employer to your 401(k), so you never see it in your paycheck. When you set the account up, you choose among some simple investment options, then let your money accumulate over time.

HOW A 401(K) GROWS

Age	Your contributions	Employer match	Balance without employer match	Balance with employer match
25	$5,000	$5,000	$5,214	$10,428
30	$5,000	$5,000	$38,251	$76,501
35	$5,000	$5,000	$86,792	$173,585
40	$5,000	$5,000	$158,116	$316,231
45	$5,000	$5,000	$262,913	$525,826
50	$5,000	$5,000	$416,895	$833,790
55	$5,000	$5,000	$643,145	$1,286,290
60	$5,000	$5,000	$975,581	$1,951,161
65	$5,000	$5,000	$1,350,762	$2,701,525

Let's dig deeper into the benefits of your 401(k).

401(k) Benefit 1: Using Pretax Money Means an Instant 25 Percent Accelerator: Retirement accounts offer you a deal: You promise to invest your money for the long term, and in exchange they give you huge tax advantages. Because the money you're contributing isn't taxed until you withdraw it many years later (this is called "pretax money"), you have much more money to invest for compound growth—usually 25 to 40 percent more.

Let's look at a regular account (a "nonretirement account") first. If you open one of these at any investment firm, you don't get many tax advantages: For every $100 you make, you'll be able to invest only about $75 of it because, depending on your tax rate, about 25 percent goes to pay income taxes.

A 401(k) is different. It's "tax-deferred," meaning you can invest the entire $100 and let it grow for about thirty-plus years. Sure, you'll pay taxes when you withdraw your money later, but that extra 25 percent turns out to make a huge difference as it gets compounded more and more.

401(k) Benefit 2: Your Employer Match Means Free Money: In many cases, your employer will match part of your contribution, meaning you get automatic free money for investing—a win-win situation. To find out if your company offers a 401(k) match, just ask your HR rep what the matching policy is.

How exactly does matching work? Here's an example: Again say your company offers a 1:1 ("one-to-one") match up to 5 percent. This means your company will match every dollar you invest up to 5 percent of your salary. For easy math, let's pretend you make $100,000 per year. You contribute $5,000 (5 percent of your salary) each year. Your employer then matches the $5,000, so your actual investment is $10,000 per year.

If you start at age twenty-five and earn 8 percent on your money, you'll have more than $2,700,000 with the 401(k) match when you retire—or just over $1,350,000 with no match. And each year you invest, the difference grows larger.

RETIREMENT VS. NONRETIREMENT ACCOUNT EARNINGS OVER TIME

(Assumes a 25% tax rate, $5,000 annual contribution ($3,750 after taxes) over 40 years, 8 percent rate of return)

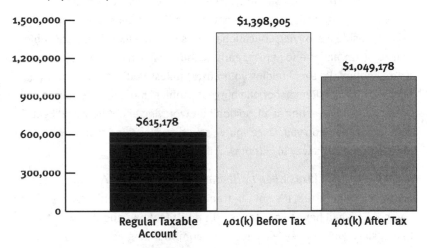

Calculate your own numbers at www.bloomberg.com/invest /calculators/401k.html.

401(k) Benefit 3: Automatic Investing: With a 401(k), your money is sent into your investment account *without you having to do anything.* If you don't see the money in your paycheck because it's automatically sent to your 401(k), you'll learn to live without it. This is an excellent example of using psychology to trick yourself into investing. In fact, there's an emerging body of literature on how powerful these effects are.

For example, some companies have begun offering "opt-out" 401(k)s rather than those that require you to opt in, meaning that you're automatically enrolled by default to contribute a certain percentage of your income. Sure, you're given the freedom to opt out, but automatic enrollment takes advantage of the fact that most people don't do anything active with their money. The results are dramatic: 401(k) participation was initially 40 percent in the companies that were studied, but after automatic enrollment it soared to more than 90 percent.

COMMON CONCERNS ABOUT 401(K)S

What happens if I really need my money? A 401(k) is a retirement account for long-term investments, not a checking or savings account. If you withdraw money before you're 59$^{1}/_{2}$ years old, you incur severe penalties, including income taxes and an early-withdrawal penalty of 10 percent. These punishments are intentional: This money is for your retirement, not to go out drinking on Saturday. That said, there are allowances for "hardship withdrawals," including paying medical expenses, buying a primary residence, paying educational costs, and the like. These are subject to income tax and the 10 percent early-withdrawal penalty, so they're not a great option (I'd avoid raiding your 401(k) unless you're truly desperate), but they do exist. Remember, the biggest problem most people have is not saving and investing at all, so don't let worrying about how you'll get your money out stop you. Once you've saved and invested money, you can always figure out a way to withdraw it if you really need to.

Will I have to pay taxes when I withdraw my money? Yes. Although your 401(k) is tax-deferred, it's not tax-free: When you start withdrawing after age 59$^{1}/_{2}$, you'll have to pay taxes. But don't feel bad about paying these taxes, since your money will have been compounding at an accelerated rate for the last thirty to forty years. Because you agreed to invest your money in a 401(k), you were able to put in about 25 percent more money to grow for you.

What if I switch jobs? The money in your 401(k) is yours, so if you move to another company, don't worry. You have a few options:

1. MOVE IT TO AN IRA. This option is preferred. It lets you "roll over" your 401(k) money into an IRA, which is great because an IRA lets you invest in virtually any kind of investment, including lifecycle funds and index funds, which we'll cover in Chapter 7. Call your discount brokerage, such as Vanguard, Fidelity, Schwab, or T. Rowe Price (You'll be signed up with one of these by the end of the chapter.), and ask for their help with a 401(k) rollover, including converting to a Roth IRA. It should take about ten minutes and it's free. Note that there may be a time limit on transferring the money to a new provider, so when you change jobs, you need to call your discount broker and ask them how to handle a rollover.

2. ROLL YOUR MONEY FROM THE OLD 401(K) TO THE NEW COMPANY'S 401(K). This is fine, but if you've already had a 401(k), you've probably noticed that their investing choices are limited. Plus, the main reason to contribute to a 401(k) is to take advantage of your employer's match, which won't apply to funds you roll into the new account. So, I prefer rolling 401(k) money into an IRA. If you really want to roll it over to the new 401(k), ask the HR person at your new employer for help.

3. LEAVE IT AT YOUR CURRENT COMPANY. This is almost always a bad move because you'll forget about it and certainly won't stay up to date on the investment options and changes offered through the plan.

4. CASH OUT THE MONEY AND PAY TAXES AND A 10 PERCENT EARLY-WITHDRAWAL PENALTY. This is the worst thing you could possibly do. Yet here's an astonishing fact: 78 percent of twentysomethings cash out their 401(k)s when they leave their jobs, taking a huge hit on taxes and fees. Don't be dumb.

SUMMARY OF 401(K) ADVANTAGES

We've covered this, but it bears repeating: 401(k)s are great because with virtually no effort on your part you get to put pretax money to work. What this means is that since you haven't paid taxes on the money yet, there's more of it to compound over time. On top of this, your company might offer a very lucrative 401(k) match, which amounts to free money that you'd be insane not to take. Remember to be aggressive with how much you contribute to your 401(k), because every dollar you invest now will likely be worth many more times that in the future.

DO IT NOW: SETTING UP YOUR 401(K)

To set up your 401(k), call your HR administrator and get the paperwork to open the account, which should take about thirty minutes to fill out. The forms will ask you to choose which funds you want to invest in. Before you make your choices, read through Chapter 7, where I cover your investment plan.

If you do have an employer match, calculate how much you need to contribute to your 401(k) to get the full match, and then have it automatically deducted from your paycheck. (The 401(k) paperwork you fill out will let you specify this.) For example, if your employer matches 5 percent of your salary and you make $50,000/year, you need to contribute about $208/month (that's $50,000 multiplied by 5 percent divided by twelve months). If that amount was automatically taken out of your paycheck and you never saw it, could you still live? Answer: Yes. If not, adjust the amount down until you're comfortable. Remember, investing 85 percent of the way is better than not doing it at all.

If your employer offers a 401(k) but doesn't offer a match, open up the 401(k) anyway (assuming there are no monthly fees), but don't contribute any money for now. Your first step will be to pay off debt and max out your Roth IRA.

Crush Your Debt

The second step on the Ladder of Personal Finance is addressing your debt. If you don't have any credit card debt, good for you! Skip this step and jump to the next page. Collect $200 as you pass Go. (Don't you wish that happened in real life?)

If you do have debt, it's time to pay it off. I know it's not sexy—or easy. Especially when we're talking about investing. It's a funny thing: Once people get their first taste of investing, setting up new accounts and learning phrases like *asset allocation* become way more exciting than paying off tired old debt. They say, "Why do we have to talk about debt? I'll make more from investing than paying off debt! I don't like this." Well, investing may sound hot, but you want to focus on being rich, which involves being debt-free. Because I want you to crush all the barriers that keep you from being rich, I encourage you to focus on paying off your loans, especially your credit card debt, which often comes with exorbitant interest rates. For the best ways to get rid of debt, revisit page 40.

The Beauty of Roth IRAs

Once you've set up your 401(k) and dispelled your debt, it's time to start funding a Roth IRA. A Roth IRA is another type of retirement account with significant tax advantages. It's not employer sponsored—you contribute money on your own. Every person in their twenties should have a Roth IRA, even if you're also contributing to a 401(k). It's simply the best deal I've found for long-term investing.

One of the benefits is that it lets you invest in whatever you want. Whereas a 401(k) has an array of funds that you must choose among, a Roth IRA lets you invest in anything you want: index funds, individual stocks, anything. A second difference has to do with taxes: Remember how your 401(k) uses pretax dollars and you pay taxes only when you withdraw money at retirement? Well, a Roth IRA uses after-tax dollars to give you an even better deal. With a Roth, you invest already-taxed income and you don't pay any tax when you withdraw it.

EVERY PERSON IN THEIR TWENTIES SHOULD HAVE A ROTH IRA, EVEN IF YOU'RE ALSO CONTRIBUTING TO A 401(K).

Let me put that into perspective: If Roth IRAs had been around in 1972 and you'd invested $10,000 after-tax dollars in LUV, Southwest Airlines' stock, you'd have hit a grand slam. Not only would the money have turned into about $10 million, but when you withdrew the money some thirty years later, you'd have paid no taxes. Although way back in 1972 you would have paid taxes on your initial $10,000 investment, the $9,990,000 you earned in the Roth IRA would have been tax-free. That's unbeatable.

Think about it. In a Roth IRA, you pay taxes on the amounts you contribute, but not the earnings. And if you invest well over thirty years, that is a stunningly good deal.

HOW MUCH WILL A ROTH IRA SAVE YOU?

Assumptions: 25 percent tax rate (now and at retirement), 8 percent annual rate of return, yearly contribution of $5,000 (that's $417/month). Notice how much taxes eat out of your returns.

	Roth IRA	Regular taxable investment account	Doing nothing
5 years	$31,680	$29,877	0
10 years	$78,227	$69,858	0
15 years	$146,621	$123,363	0
20 years	$247,115	$194,974	0
25 years	$394,772	$290,782	0
30 years	$611,729	$419,118	0

PROOF THAT A ROTH IRA WORKS

Ask your friends if they have a Roth IRA. Hint: They don't. If you sense derision in my voice, it's because I take a perverse pleasure in knowing how much you're going to dominate everyone else in the personal-finance arena. Because most people don't understand the benefits of a Roth IRA, they don't take the time to open an account. That's a costly mistake: Check out the table above to see the tax benefits of choosing a Roth IRA over a regular taxable account—or worse, doing nothing.

ROTH IRA RESTRICTIONS

As with a 401(k), you're expected to treat a Roth IRA as a long-term investment vehicle, and you're penalized if you withdraw your earnings before you're 59$\frac{1}{2}$ years old. Exception: Most people don't know this, but you can withdraw your principal, the amount you actually invested from your pocket, at any time, penalty-free. There are also exceptions for down payments on a home, funding education for you or your partner/children/grandchildren, and some other emergency reasons.

Important note: You qualify for the above exceptions only if your Roth IRA has been open for five years or more. This reason alone is enough for you to open your Roth IRA this week. Currently, the maximum you're allowed to invest in your Roth IRA is $5,000 a year. (Beginning in 2009, the limit will increase in $500 increments based on inflation, which means that at some future point the limit will be $5,500, then $6,000, and so on.)

One other important thing to know is that if you make more than $100,000 per year, there are restrictions on how much you can contribute to a Roth IRA (and over a certain income, you're not eligible to open one at all). These limits change each year, so when opening your Roth IRA, use Google or ask your broker about the current limits.

HOW TO OPEN A ROTH IRA

I don't care where you get the money to contribute to your Roth IRA, but get it (for ideas on reducing spending and increasing earnings so you can fund it, see Chapter 4). Contributing as much as possible is almost as important as starting early. I'm not going to belabor the point, but every dollar you invest now is worth much, much more later. Even waiting two

Growth Vs. Access

Q: *I don't want to lock my money up in a retirement account—I might need it soon. What should I do?*

A: Many people think of a retirement account as "locking" the money up, which is not entirely accurate. Remember that if you contribute to a Roth IRA, you can always withdraw the money you contribute ("the principal") at any time, penalty-free. With both Roths and 401(k)s, you can also access your money in cases of real need (like to pay medical expenses, prevent foreclosure, cover education costs, and so on). Nevertheless, unless you really have no other recourse, you should not withdraw money from your retirement account.

If you need your money in fewer than five years, put it in a high-interest savings account. But don't make the mistake of keeping your money in a savings account just because you're too lazy to take the time to learn how to invest it. If you'd invested ten years ago, wouldn't it feel good to have a lot more money right now? Well, the next best time to invest is today.

years can cost you tens of thousands of dollars. I want you to do your research and open your Roth IRA by the end of the week.

To start a Roth IRA, you're first going to open an investment brokerage account with a trusted investment company (see the table on next page). Think of the "investment brokerage account" as your house, and the Roth IRA as one of the rooms. Although this account will probably hold only your Roth IRA for now, you can expand it to host other accounts (such as taxable investment accounts or additional Roth IRAs for your future spouse and kids) as your needs change.

If this sounds complicated, don't worry. We're not going to pick the actual *investments* today—that comes in Chapter 7—but we are going to open your account and fund it with a little money, so that when you're ready to invest, you can.

We'll focus on discount brokerages like Vanguard and T. Rowe Price because they charge dramatically smaller fees than full-service brokerages like Morgan Stanley. Full-service brokerages offer so-called "comprehensive services," but they basically just charge you a lot of money to sell you useless research and let you talk to salesmen. Discount brokerages, on the other hand, let you make the choices, charge only small fees, and offer online access. Don't get fooled by smooth-talking salespeople: You can easily manage your investment account by yourself.

FACTORS TO CONSIDER WHEN CHOOSING YOUR INVESTMENT ACCOUNT

Frankly, most discount-brokerage investment accounts are pretty much the same. It's sort of like having the choice between two hot blonde twins—either one will do. Yes, I just compared investing accounts to choosing between two twins. My parents are going to kill me.

Minimums. Before you open your investment account, you'll want to compare minimum required investments. For example, some full-service brokerages will require you to have a hefty minimum amount to open an account. When I recently called Morgan Stanley, the rep I spoke to recommended a minimum balance of $50,000. "Technically, you could open an account with $5,000," she told me, "but the fees would kill you." This is why you use a discount brokerage. Most do require a minimum contribution of $1,000–$3,000 to open a Roth IRA, but they'll often waive it if you set up an automatic transfer. Even if

RECOMMENDED DISCOUNT BROKERAGES

Brokerage name	Minimum to open a Roth IRA	Things to know
Vanguard www.vanguard.com, (877) 662-7447	$3,000	Vanguard is great because of their low-cost funds. But they don't waive their minimums, even with automatic investing. If you want a Vanguard account but don't have $3,000, see page 106 to set it as a savings goal.
T. Rowe Price www.troweprice.com, (800) 541-6066	$1,000	Minimum is waived with $50 automatic monthly contribution. Great low-cost funds.
Schwab www.schwab.com, (866) 855-9102	$1,000	Minimum is waived with $100 automatic monthly contribution. If you set up a high-interest Schwab checking account from page 62, Schwab will automatically link a brokerage account to it. Handy for automatic investing.

it doesn't waive any minimums, I recommend setting up a monthly automatic transfer so your money will grow without you having to think about it. More on this in Chapter 5.

Features. You should also investigate the features your account offers. Will you have customer service via phone toll-free, 24/7? Is the online interface easy to use? Will your account allow easy automatic investing? Most of them do, but it is important to find out beforehand.

And that's it. Yes, you could spend hundreds of hours doing a detailed comparison of the total number of funds offered, frequency of mailings, and alternative-investment accounts available, but more is lost from indecision than bad decisions. As Benjamin Franklin said, "Don't put off until tomorrow what you can do today." And as Ramit Sethi said, "Let others debate minutiae—all you need to do is open an investment account at a discount brokerage. Sucka."

Keep Track of All Your Accounts

To help me manage all my accounts, I set up a free PBwiki (www .pbwiki.com) to store my account numbers and passwords on a private page. It's like an online notepad that you can keep private or public, and you can access it from wherever you can get on the web. My own wiki has a page to store my passwords, another to store future blog posts, and an entirely separate section to collaborate on marketing ideas I'm working on.

Full disclosure: I know it works, is secure, and that there are no gimmicks behind PBwiki because I'm a cofounder of the service.

Signing up should take about an hour. You can do it entirely online, or you can call the companies, and they'll mail or e-mail you the necessary documents. Remember to tell them that you want to open a Roth IRA so they give you the right paperwork. There will be a way to connect your checking account to your investment account so that you can regularly automatically transfer money to be invested. (Later, when we start investing in Chapter 7, I'll show you more about how companies waive minimum investing fees if you agree to automatically send $50 or $100 per month. But opening a Roth IRA is free.) Ideally you will be able to increase that amount—you'll learn exactly how much you're able to invest monthly after reading the next chapter.

I did not have much startup money since I am a graduate student. So saving even a thousand dollars to open an account would take a while, and those savings might be continually eaten up by general life emergencies like car repairs before I ever opened the account. I went with T. Rowe Price. It had no minimums with a fifty-dollar-a-month automatic contribution. Fifty dollars a month is easy to commit to, and from there raising my monthly contribution by ten bucks is easy to justify. No minimum meant I could open it immediately.

—HANNAH FLATH, 24

FEED YOUR INVESTMENT ACCOUNT

Okay, you have an investment account. Excellent! Since most of you set up automatic monthly contributions to waive the minimum, your money will be regularly sent to your Roth IRA. It will patiently wait for you to decide exactly how to invest it, which we'll cover in Chapter 7. If you didn't set up automatic contributions, do so now, even if it's just $50/month. It's a good habit to get into and will help you accrue any necessary minimum.

Hungry for Even More?

Let's say you've been kicking ass and you've maxed out your employer 401(k) match, paid off your credit card debt, and gotten your Roth IRA going. If you still have money to invest, it's time to look again at your 401(k). Remember, the maximum amount you can invest in a 401(k) is $15,500 per year. So far, you only invested enough to get your employer match, so you likely still have the ability to invest more in a 401(k) and reap the huge tax benefits. Cool thing to note: Your employer match isn't counted toward your contribution limit, so if you invest $5,000 and your employer matches $5,000, you can still invest $10,500 more for a total of $20,500 annually in your 401(k).

What should you do? Calculate how much you need to contribute each year: $15,500 minus the contribution you figured out on page 82. That gives you the amount you can still contribute. To break this amount down into a monthly contribution, divide that number by twelve.

Again, set your contributions so they happen automatically and you never even have to see the money.

BEYOND RETIREMENT ACCOUNTS

If you've taken full advantage of your 401(k) match, paid off all your credit card debt, topped out your Roth IRA, *and* gone back to max out the remainder of your 401(k), and you *still* have money to invest, there are even more choices to grow your money. In Chapter 7, we'll get into the best strategies and options. But right now, I want you to buy me something ornate because you have a lot of money.

Congratulations!

You've started up the Ladder of Personal Finance. Take a moment to pat yourself on the back. You now have a system set up to grow your money. This is so important. Having investment accounts means you're starting to think about rapid growth and distinguishing between short-term savings and long-term investing. And that $50 you sent may seem like a small step, but I believe it's the most significant $50 you'll ever invest.

WEEK THREE

1 **Open your 401(k) (three hours).** Get the paperwork from your HR manager and fill it out. Check to see if your employer offers a match. If it does, contribute enough to get the full match. If not, leave your 401(k) account open but contribute nothing.

2 **Come up with a plan to pay off your debt (three hours).** Get serious about getting out of debt. Run a calculation from www.dinkytown.net to see how much you could save by paying an extra $100 or $200 per month. Also revisit page 35 in Chapter 1 and see page 220 in Chapter 9 for details on how to pay off your credit card debt and student loans.

3 **Open a Roth IRA and set up automatic payment (one hour).** Send as much as you can, but even $50/month is fine. We'll dive into the details a little later.

Now that you've opened these accounts, let's figure out a way to get them as full as possible. In the next chapter, I'll show you how to get control of your spending to make your money go where you want it to go.

CHAPTER 4

CONSCIOUS SPENDING

How to save hundreds per month
(and still buy what you love)

I used to find it ridiculous when people said you could judge a person by their belt or shoes. Are you kidding me? Can I tell what kind of soup you like by the earrings you're wearing? Get the hell out of here.

Recently, however, I discovered I was wrong. It turns out there *is* one universal shortcut to discovering someone's true character: if they eat chicken wings like an immigrant.

Because I don't understand or care about sports, last Super Bowl Sunday I decided to go on a wing crawl. It's like a pub crawl, but with wings. I quickly realized that the most interesting part of eating wings with friends is seeing how much meat they leave on the bone. Some people leave half the chicken and move on to the next wing. These people are worthless, and I quickly distance myself from them. Then there are people who clean the bone so thoroughly, flawlessly ridding it of every last shred of meat and marrow, that you can conclude only two things: They will be stellar successes in all facets of life, and they must be from another country. You see, immigrants (like my parents) never leave a shred of meat on a chicken wing—we can all learn something from them.

I feel guilty about not having a budget. I have a hard time wrapping my brain around how to set a budget and then not actually spend more than the budget allows. I feel guilty that I'm a nerd in most other respects, but I just can't sit down and do the math about my spending.

—SARAH ROBESON, 28

That kind of economy is rare these days. (Although in the wake of the global financial crisis, frugality—or at least giving lip service to it— is becoming more common.) We spend more on our cell phones than most people in other countries do on their mortgages. We buy shoes that cost more than our grandparents paid for their *cars*. Yet we don't really know how much these individual costs add up to. How many times have you opened your bills, winced, then shrugged and said, "I guess I spent that much"? How often do you feel guilty about buying something—but then do it anyway? In this chapter, the antidote to unconscious spending, we're going to gently create a new, simple way of spending. It's time to stop wondering where all your money goes each month. I'm going to help you redirect it to the places *you* choose, like investing, saving, and even spending *more* on the things you love (but less on the things you don't).

Wait! Before you run away thinking this is a chapter on creating a budget, hang on a second. This isn't about creating a fancy budget that you'll have to maintain every day for the rest of your life. I hate budgeting. *Budgeting* is the worst word in the history of the world. I could be sitting on a golden throne surrounded by forty-three scantily clad models, and if I accidentally uttered the word *budget,* I sincerely believe they would all instantaneously look up (from feeding me grapes and fanning me, duh), open their jaws in shock, and then flee in horror. Nobody wants to budget.

I'm not finished. "Create a budget!" is the sort of worthless advice that personal-finance pundits feel good prescribing, yet when real people read about making a budget, their eyes glaze over faster than John Goodman's lips at Krispy Kreme. Who wants to track their spending? The few people who actually try it find that their budgets completely fail after two days because tracking every penny is overwhelming. Amusingly, in a 2007 survey by bankrate.com, 75 percent of Americans said they have a budget—which is complete nonsense. "There's probably a lot of wishful thinking in this response," says Jared Bernstein, director of the Living Standards Program of the Economic Policy Institute. "It's

HOW MANY TIMES HAVE YOU OPENED YOUR BILLS, WINCED, THEN SHRUGGED AND SAID, "I GUESS I SPENT THAT MUCH"?

probably more accurate to say that three-quarters *think* they should work on a monthly budget." My kind of man: exposing the delusions of people everywhere!

For the last fifty years, budgeting has been the battleground for snobby personal-finance writers who've tried to shove a daily tracking system down everyone's throats because it sounds logical: "Track your spending! It's so simple!" There's only one catch: NOBODY EVER DOES IT.

And I don't believe for a second that because times are tough, Americans are going to buckle down and stop consuming over the long term. Most people wouldn't know where to start if I told them to stop spending and start saving. I might as well try to convince an Ankylosaurus to dance a jig.

Many of my friends just throw up their hands when they have done something stupid with their money and don't learn from their mistakes. I see people get out of huge credit card debt and once their balances are wiped clean to zero, start the process of maxing out their cards again.

—FRANK WILES, 29

Because we know that budgets don't work, I'm not about to make the same mistake in recommending them to you.

Let's try something that actually works. Forget budgeting. Instead, let's create a Conscious Spending Plan. What if you could make sure you were saving and investing enough money each month, and then use the rest of your money guilt-free for whatever you want? Well, you can—with some work. The only catch is that you have to plan where you want your money to go *ahead of time* (even if it's on the back of a napkin). Would it be worth taking a couple of hours to get set up so you can spend on the things you love? It will automate your savings and investing, and make your spending decisions crystal clear. When your friends say, "I never have any money," you're going to wonder why they don't just spend a couple of hours to set things up right—like you did.

The Difference Between Cheap and Frugal

A while back, a couple of friends and I were talking about where we want to travel this year, and one of them said something that surprised me: "You probably wouldn't approve, but I want to go to the Caribbean."

Huh? Why wouldn't I approve?

I stared at him pensively for many moments, taking the form of Rodin's *Thinker* and wishing that I had a pipe and perhaps a tweed jacket. Then I figured it out. Apparently, he thought of me as a Finger-Wagging Money Judge, as if I silently disapproved of him for spending his money on something "frivolous." In other words, someone who writes about personal finance is automatically "the guy who tells me I can't do stuff because it costs too much money."

Nothing could be further from the truth. Now, I will call your ass out when you make mistakes (like one of my readers who wasn't worried about his cable bill increasing $5/month, yet complained every time the price of gas went up two cents a gallon). But I'm *not* the nagging parent who tells you not to spend money on lattes. I spend lots of money on eating out and traveling, but I never feel guilty. Instead of taking a simplistic "Don't spend money on expensive things!!!" view, I believe there's a more nuanced approach to spending.

Let's first dispense with the idea that saying no to spending on certain things means you're cheap. If you decide that spending $2.50 on Cokes when you eat out isn't worth it—and you'd rather save that $15 each week for a movie—that's not cheap. That's using frugality to drive conscious spending. Unfortunately, most Americans dismiss frugality because they confuse it with cheapness, thinking that frugality is all-or-nothing: "Frugal people don't spend money on anything! I'm never going to cut all my spending, so forget it." Furthermore, our parents never taught us how to be frugal, so not only have we confused frugality with cheapness, but we never really practiced it in the first place. As a country, we spend more than we make each year and virtually nothing seems to change our behavior. Even though we may tighten our wallets during a downturn, we soon return to our usual spending behaviors. And frankly, nobody's interested in changing the status quo: Consumer spending accounts for about 70 percent of the American economy.

Frugality isn't just about our own choices, though. There's also the social influence to spend. Call it the *Sex and the City* effect, where your friends' spending directly affects yours. Next time you go to the mall, check out any random group of friends. Chances are, they're dressed similarly—even though chances are good that they have wildly different incomes. Keeping up with friends is a full-time job. In fact, continuing the parallel between our attitudes toward money and food

> **TOO OFTEN, OUR FRIENDS INVISIBLY PUSH US AWAY FROM BEING FRUGAL AND CONSCIOUS SPENDERS.**

that I mentioned in the introduction, researchers found in a landmark 2007 study published in the *New England Journal of Medicine* ("The Spread of Obesity in a Large Social Network over 32 Years") that friends had a direct influence on one's likelihood of gaining weight. When a friend became obese, a person increased his or her chances of becoming obese by 57 percent. How do you think your friends' spending influences yours?

Too often, our friends invisibly push us away from being frugal and conscious spenders. Right around the time when the 3G iPhone came out, for example, I went to dinner with two friends. One of them was considering getting the new iPhone, and she pulled out her old phone to show us why she was thinking about buying a new one. My other friend stared in disbelief: "You haven't gotten a new phone in four years? What's wrong with you?" she asked. "You need to get the iPhone *tomorrow*." Even though it was only three sentences, the message was clear: There's something wrong with you for not getting a new phone (regardless of whether or not you need it).

CHEAP PEOPLE VS. FRUGAL PEOPLE

Cheap	Frugal
Cheap people care about the cost of something.	Frugal people care about the value of something.
Cheap people try to get the lowest price on everything.	Frugal people try to get the lowest price on most things, but are willing to spend on items they really care about.
Cheap people's cheapness affects those around them.	Frugal people's frugality affects only them.
Cheap people are inconsiderate. For example, when getting a meal with other people, if their food costs $7.95, they'll put in $8, knowing very well that tax and tip mean it's closer to $11.	Frugal people know they have to pick and choose where they spend their money. If they can spend only $10 on lunch, they'll order water instead of Coke.
Cheap people make you uncomfortable because of the way they treat others.	Frugal people make you feel uncomfortable because you realize you could be doing better with your money.
Cheap people keep a running tally of how much their friends, family, and coworkers owe them.	Some frugal people do this, too, but certainly not all.
Because of the fear of even one person suggesting they spent too much on something, cheap people are not always honest about what they spend.	Neither are frugal people.
Cheap people are unreasonable and cannot understand why they can't get something for free. Sometimes this is an act, but sometimes it's not.	Frugal people will try as hard as cheap people to get a deal, but they understand that it's a dance, and in the end, they know they don't intrinsically *deserve* a special deal.
Cheap people think short term.	Frugal people think long term.

Spend on What You Love

Frugality isn't about cutting your spending on everything. That approach wouldn't last two days. Frugality, quite simply, is about choosing the things you love enough to spend extravagantly on— and then cutting costs mercilessly on the things you don't love.

The mind-set of frugal people is key to being rich. Indeed, as the researchers behind the landmark book *The Millionaire Next Door* discovered, 50 percent of the more than one thousand millionaires surveyed have never paid more than $400 for a suit, $140 for a pair of shoes, and $235 for a wristwatch. Again, frugality is not about simply cutting your spending on various things. It's about making your own decisions about what's important enough to spend a lot on, and what's not, rather than blindly spending on *everything*.

THE PROBLEM IS THAT HARDLY ANYONE IS DECIDING WHAT'S IMPORTANT AND WHAT'S NOT, DAMMIT! That's where the idea of conscious spending comes in.

How My Friend Spends $21,000 Per Year Going Out—Guilt-Free

I want you to consciously decide what you're going to spend on. No more "I guess I spent that much" when you see your credit card statements. No. Conscious spending means you decide exactly where you're going to spend your money—for going out, for saving, for investing, for rent—and you free yourself from feeling guilty about your spending. Along with making you feel comfortable with your spending, a plan keeps you moving toward your goals instead of just treading water.

The simple fact is that most young people are not spending consciously. We're spending on whatever, then reactively feeling good or bad about it. Every time I meet someone who has a Conscious Spending Plan ("I automatically send money to my investment and savings accounts, then just spend the rest"), I'm so enchanted that my love rivals Shah Jahan's for his wife, Mumtaz Mahal (look it up).

I'm going to tell you about three friends who are spending lots and lots of money on things you might consider frivolous—like shoes and going out—but whose actions are perfectly justified.

THE SHOE LOVER

My friend "Lisa" spends about $5,000/year on shoes. Because the kind of shoes she likes run more than $300, this translates to about fifteen pairs of shoes annually. "THAT'S RIDICULOUS!!!" you might be saying. And on the surface, that number is indeed large. But if you're reading this book, you can look a little deeper: This girl makes a very healthy six-figure salary, has a roommate, eats for free at work, and doesn't spend much on fancy electronics, gym membership, or fine dining. In fact, her job provides many of the amenities that other people pay for.

Lisa loves shoes. A lot. She's funded her 401(k) and a taxable investment account (she makes too much for a Roth). She's putting away money each month for vacation and other savings goals, and giving some to charity. And she still has money left over. Now here's where it's interesting. "But Ramit," you might say, "it doesn't matter. Three-hundred-dollar shoes are ridiculous. Nobody needs to spend that much on shoes!"

Before you chastise her for her extravagance, ask yourself these questions: Have you funded your 401(k) and opened additional investment accounts? Are you fully aware of where your spending money is going? And have you made a strategic decision to spend on what you love? Very few people decide how they want to spend their money up front. Instead they end up spending it on random things here and there, eventually watching their money trickle away. Just as important, have you decided what you *don't* love? For example, Lisa doesn't care about living in a fancy place, so she has a tiny room in a tiny apartment. Her decision to live in a small place means she spends $400 less every month than many of her coworkers.

After planning for her long-term and short-term goals, she has money left over to spend on the things she loves. I think she's right on.

THE PARTYER

My friend "John" spends more than $21,000 a year going out. "OMG, THAT'S SO MUCH *#%#%#% MONEY!" you might say. Well, let's break it down. Say he goes out four times a week—to dinners and bars—and spend an average of $100/night. I'm being conservative with the numbers here, because a dinner can run $60/person and drinks could be $12 each.

So You Want to Judge Your Friends' Spending?

When it comes to judging our friends' spending, we look at surface characteristics and make snap judgments. "You spent $300 on jeans!" "Why do you shop at Whole Foods?" "Why did you decide to live in that expensive area?" I know we all wonder these things about our friends because I do, too.

And, in fact, most of our judgments are right: Because young people are not carefully considering their financial choices in the context of their long-term goals—we're not paying ourselves first and we're not developing an investment/savings plan—you're probably right when you think your friend can't afford those $300 jeans.

I've been trying to be less judgmental about this. I'm not always successful, but I now focus on the fact that the sticker price doesn't matter—it's the context around it. You want to buy a $1,000 bottle of wine? And you already saved $20,000 this year at age twenty-five? Great! But if your friends are going out four times a week on a $25,000 salary, I bet they're not consciously spending.

So although it's fun to judge your friends, keep in mind that the context matters.

(Warning: If you want to judge your significant other, tread lightly: Check page 225 for my breakup-prevention financial advice.)

I'm not including bottle service, which might cost $800 or $1,000. (He lives in a big city.) That's easily $400/week.

Now, John also makes a healthy six-figure salary, so he's been able to make a Conscious Spending Plan without much difficulty. But even he has to decide what he doesn't want to spend on. For example, when his coworkers took a weekend trip to Europe (I am not kidding), he politely passed. In fact, because he works so hard, he almost never takes vacations. Similarly, because he's always at work, he doesn't care about decorating his apartment at all, so he's skipped virtually all decoration costs: He still has wire hangers holding up the few bargain suits that he wears, and he doesn't even own a spatula.

(continued on page 102)

Use Psychology Against Yourself to Save

One of my readers makes $50,000/year and, after working through some of my suggestions, realized she's paying 30 percent of her after-tax income for subscriptions. That's a truly shocking figure, so I want to share a method to dramatically cut down on unneeded subscriptions that you currently pay for. Subscriptions can be anything from Netflix to cell phone plans to your cable bill. They are a business's best friend: They let companies make a reliable, predictable income off of you—*with no action on your part.* There's a convenience to this, of course—but there's a significant cost: When was the last time you scrutinized your monthly subscriptions and canceled one? Probably never. Yet compare this with any recent time you went shopping. When was the last time you saw something you liked but decided not to buy it?

THE À LA CARTE METHOD. The À La Carte Method takes advantage of psychology to cut our spending. Here's how it works: Cancel all the discretionary subscriptions you can: your magazines, TiVo, cable—even your gym. (It would be totally ridiculous to cancel your Internet, though. I'd cry like a little girl if I couldn't get online from my house.) Then, buy what you need à la carte:

- Instead of paying for a ton of channels you never watch on cable, buy only the episodes you watch for $1.99 each off iTunes.

- Buy a day pass for the gym each time you go (around $5–$10).

- Buy songs you want for $0.99 each from Amazon or iTunes.

The À La Carte Method works for three reasons:

1. You're probably overpaying already. Most of us dramatically overestimate how much value we get from subscriptions. For example, if I asked you how many times a week you go to the gym, chances are you'd say, "Oh . . . two or three times a week." That's B.S. In fact, one 2006 study showed that gym members overestimate how much they'll use their membership by more than 70 percent. Members who chose a monthly fee of about $70 attended an average of 4.3 times per month.

That comes out to more than $17/gym visit—when in reality they'd have been better off buying pay-as-you-go passes for $10 each.

2. You're forced to be conscious about your spending. It's one thing to passively look at your credit card bill and say, "Ah, yes, I remember that cable bill. Looks like a valid charge. Tallyho!" It's quite another to spend $1.99 each time you want to buy a TV show—and when you actively think about each charge, you *will* cut consumption.

3. You value what you pay for. You place a higher premium on the things you pay for out of your pocket than those that come via subscription.

THE DOWNSIDE OF THE À LA CARTE METHOD. The big downside is that this method requires you to de-automate your life. This is the price you pay for saving money. Give it a shot for two months and see how it feels. If you don't like it, go back to your old subscriptions.

HOW TO IMPLEMENT THE À LA CARTE METHOD:

1. Calculate how much you've spent over the last month on any discretionary subscriptions you have (for example, music subscriptions, Netflix, and the gym).

2. Cancel those subscriptions and begin buying these things à la carte. (But don't let losing the gym membership be your excuse to become a fat ass.)

3. In exactly one month, check and calculate how much you spent on these items over the last month. That's the *descriptive* part.

4. Now, get *prescriptive*. If you spent $100, try to cut it down to $90. Then $75. Not too low—you want your spending to be sustainable, and you don't want to totally lose touch with what's going on in the world. But you can control exactly how many movies you rent or how many magazines you buy, because each one comes out of your pocket.

Remember, this isn't about depriving yourself. The ideal situation is that you realize you were spending $50/month in subscriptions for stuff you didn't really want—now you can consciously reallocate that money into something you love.

(continued from page 99)

For John, the limiting factor is *time*. He knows he'll never send money regularly anywhere, so he's set up his investment accounts to automatically withdraw money before he ever sees it. The key here is that John knows himself and has set up systems to support his weaknesses. In terms of spending, he works hard and plays hard, going out twice during the week and twice on the weekends, when he causes some real damage. Yet, despite spending ungodly amounts going out each week, in just a couple of years John has saved more than almost any of my friends. And although $21,000 sounds outrageous on the surface, you have to take the context of his salary and priorities into consideration. Whereas other friends might spend thousands decorating their apartments or taking vacations, John, after meeting his investment goals, chooses to spend that money going out.

The point here is that whether or not I agree with his choices, he's thought about it. He sat down, considered what he wanted to spend on, and is executing that plan. He's doing more than 99 percent of the young people I've talked to. If he had decided he wanted to spend $21,000/year on furry donkey costumes and Fabergé eggs, that would have been great, too. At least he has a plan.

THE NONPROFIT EMPLOYEE

You don't have to make a six-figure salary to be a conscious spender. My friend "Julie" works at a nonprofit firm in San Francisco, making about $40,000 per year, but she saves more than $6,000 per year—far more than most Americans.

She does this by being extremely disciplined: She cooks at home, shares rent in a small apartment, and is reimbursed for her driving by her office. When she's invited out to eat, she checks her envelope system (more on that on page 115) to see if she can afford it. If not, she politely declines. But when she *does* go out, she never feels guilty about spending because she *knows* she can afford it. Yet it's not enough to save money on just rent and food. She also chooses to save aggressively, maxing out her Roth IRA and putting aside extra money for traveling. Each month, that money is the first to be automatically transferred out.

From talking to Julie at a party or over dinner, you would never know that she saves more than most Americans. We glibly make snap decisions about people's spending using the most cursory data: Their job and their clothes give us most of what we think we need to know to understand someone's financial situation. But Julie proves that the surface data isn't always enough. Regardless of her situation, she's chosen to put her investing and saving priorities first.

WHAT THEY'RE DOING RIGHT

The friends I wrote about above are exceptions to most people our age.

They have a plan. Instead of getting caught on a spending treadmill of new phones, new cars, new vacations, and new everything, they plan what's important to them and save on the rest. My shoe friend lives in a microscopic room because she's hardly home, saving her hundreds per month. My partyer friend uses public transportation and has exactly zero décor in his apartment. And my nonprofit friend is extraordinarily detailed about every aspect of her spending.

Each of them pays themselves first, whether it's $500/month or $2,000/month. They've built an infrastructure to do this automatically so that by the time money ends up in their checking account, they know they can spend it guilt-free. They spend less time worrying about money than most people! They already know about online savings accounts and credit cards and basic asset allocation. They're not experts—they've just got a head start.

To me, this is an enviable position to be in, and it's a big part of what *I Will Teach You to Be Rich* is about: automatically enabling yourself to save, invest, and spend—enjoying it, not feeling guilty about those new jeans, because you're spending only what you have.

You can do it. It takes a plan. And it's really as simple as that.

The *I Will Teach You to Be Rich* Conscious Spending Plan

Clearly, budgeting sucks. But agreeing that conscious spending is good is like forming a group called "Americans for Babies and Lovable Koala Bears." Who would ever disagree with you? The real challenge, of course, is doing something about it.

Let's get on with the specifics of how you can make your own Conscious Spending Plan. I'm not going to lie to you: The most difficult thing in this book is not structuring your tax-deferred accounts or understanding the difference between APR and APY, it's this section right here. But I'll try to make it as painless as possible. Whatever you do, don't get overwhelmed by the idea that you need to create a massive budgeting system. All you need is to just get a simple version ready today and work to improve it over time.

Here's the idea: A Conscious Spending Plan involves four major buckets where your money will go: Fixed Costs, Investments, Savings, and Guilt-free Spending Money.

CATEGORIES OF SPENDING

Fixed costs Rent, utilities, debt, etc.	50–60% of take-home pay
Investments 401(k), Roth IRA	10%
Savings Vacations, gifts, house down payment, unexpected expenses	5–10%
Guilt-free spending money Dining out, drinking, movies, clothes, shoes	20–35%

MONTHLY FIXED COSTS

Fixed costs are the amounts you must pay, like your rent/mortgage, utilities, cell phone, and student loans. A good rule of thumb is that fixed costs should be 50–60 percent of your take-home pay. Before you can do anything else, you've got to figure out how much these add up to. You'd think it would be easy to figure this out, right?

Ha! It turns out this is one of the toughest questions in personal finance. Luckily, my way of answering this question is far faster and easier than most other methods.

Okay, let's walk through this step by step. Check out the chart on the next page with common basic expenses (the bare minimum that any ordinary person would use to live). If you see any glaring omissions for major spending categories, add them. Notice that I didn't include "eating out" or "entertainment," as those come out of the guilt-free spending category.

Category	Monthly Cost
Rent/mortgage	
Utilities	
Cell phone, landline	
Medical insurance, bills	
Car payment	
Public transportation	
Loans	
Groceries	
Clothes	
Internet/cable	

Fill in the dollar amounts you know offhand.

Now, to fill in the costs and categories you haven't yet accounted for, you're going to have to dive a little deeper. You'll need to look at your past spending to fill in all the dollar amounts, and to make sure you've covered every category. Limit this to the past month to keep things simple. The easiest way to get an idea of what you've spent where is to look at your credit card and banking statements or, if you're old-fashioned, review your receipts. Sure, you may not capture every last expense doing it this way, but it's probably good enough.

Finally, once you've gotten all your expenses filled in, add 15 percent for expenditures you haven't counted yet. Yes, really. For example, you probably didn't capture "car repair," which can cost $400 each time (that's $33/month). Or dry cleaning or emergency medical care or charitable donations. A flat 15 percent will cover you for things you haven't figured in, and you can get more accurate as time goes on.

(I actually have a "Stupid Mistakes" category in my money system. When I first started this, I saved $20/month for unexpected expenses. Then, within two months, I had to go to the doctor for $600 and I got a traffic ticket for more than $100. That changed things quickly, and I currently save $150/month for unexpected expenses.)

Once you've got a fairly accurate number here, subtract it from your take-home pay. Now you'll know how much you'll have left over to spend in other categories like investing, saving, and guilt-free spending. Plus, you'll have an idea of a few targeted expense areas that you can cut down on to give yourself more money to save and invest.

LONG-TERM INVESTMENTS

This bucket includes the amount you'll send to your 401(k) and Roth IRA each month. A good rule of thumb is to invest 10 percent of your take-home pay (after taxes, or the amount on your monthly paycheck) for the long term. Your 401(k) contributions count toward the 10 percent, so if you already participate in a 401(k), you'll need to add that amount to your take-home money to get a total monthly salary.

If you're not sure how much to allot to your investing bucket, open up an investment calculator from www.dinkytown.net (try the "Investment Returns" calculator) and enter some numbers. Experiment with contributing $100/month, $200/month, $500/month, or even $1,000/month. Assume an 8 percent return. You'll see dramatic differences over forty years.

Because most of your investments will be in tax-advantaged retirement accounts, which we'll cover in Chapter 7, remove the taxes to get a back-of-the-napkin calculation. Just understand that taxes ultimately will take a chunk out of your 401(k) returns. Remember, the more aggressively you save now, the more you'll have later.

SAVINGS GOALS

This bucket includes short-term savings goals (like Christmas gifts and vacation), midterm savings goals (a wedding in a few years), and larger, longer-term goals (like a down payment on a house).

To determine how much you should be putting away each month, check out these examples. They'll shock you:

GIFTS FOR FRIENDS AND FAMILY. In 2007 Americans spent around $900 on Christmas gifts, according to the American Research Group. In 2008 it was about half of that. If you're an average consumer and want to

The 60 Percent Solution

You've heard me talk about the 85 Percent Solution, which focuses on getting most of the way there rather than 100 percent and ending up doing nothing at all. Well, Richard Jenkins, the editor-in-chief of MSN Money, wrote an article called "The 60 Percent Solution," which suggested that you split your money into simple buckets, with the largest being basic expenses (food, bills, taxes) making up 60 percent of your gross income. The remaining 40 percent would be split four ways:

1. Retirement savings (10 percent)

2. Long-term savings (10 percent)

3. Short-term savings for irregular expenses (10 percent)

4. Fun money (10 percent)

The article has been widely distributed, although curiously, none of my friends had heard of it. My Conscious Spending Plan relates to Jenkins's 60 percent solution, but it's more focused toward young people. We spend a huge amount on eating out and going out, whereas our housing costs are lower because we can share apartments and rent more comfortably than older people with families.

pay for your gifts without going into debt, that means you need to save $75/month for your Christmas gifts. (And what about birthday gifts?) Check out my site nochristmasgiftsthisyear.com.

YOUR WEDDING (WHETHER YOU'RE ENGAGED OR NOT). The average wedding costs about $28,000. Because we know the average wedding age is twenty-seven for men and twenty-six for women, you can figure out exactly how much you need to be saving, assuming you want to pay for it without help or debt: If you're twenty-five years old, you need to be saving more than $1,000/month for your wedding. If you're twenty-six, you should be saving more than $2,300/month. (I cover financing weddings in detail on page 229.)

BUYING A HOUSE. If you're thinking about buying a house in a few years, log on to www.zillow.com and check home prices in your area. Let's just say the average house in your neighborhood costs $300,000 and you want to do a traditional 20 percent down payment. That's $60,000, so if you want to buy a house in five years, you should be saving $1,000/month.

Crazy, right? Nobody thinks like this, but it's truly eye-opening when you plot out your future spending for the next few years. It can almost seem overwhelming, but there's good news: First, the longer you have to save for these things, the less you have to save each month. (For example, if you started saving for an average wedding at age twenty, you would have to save about $333/month. By age twenty-six, however, you'd have to save $2,333/month.) Second, we often get help: Our spouse or parents may be able to chip in a little, but you can't count on someone else coming to rescue you. Third, theoretically you could use some of your investment money from Step 2 to pay for these savings goals. It's not ideal, but you can do it.

Regardless of exactly what you're saving for, a good rule of thumb is to save 5 to 10 percent of your take-home pay to meet your goals.

GUILT-FREE SPENDING MONEY

After all that spending, investing, and saving, this bucket contains the fun money—the stuff you can use for anything you want, guilt-free. Money here covers things like going out to restaurants and bars, taxis, movies, and vacations.

Depending on how you've structured your other buckets, a good rule of thumb here is to use 20 percent to 35 percent of your take-home income for guilt-free spending money.

Optimizing Your Conscious Spending Plan

Now that you've worked out the basics of your Conscious Spending Plan, you can make some targeted improvements to tweak your spending and make your money go where you want it to go. Instead of having this dull, throbbing cloud of worry over your head—"I know I'm spending too much"—your plan will serve as a living, breathing

Tools of the Trade

Q: *What do you use to manage your finances?*

A: For budgeting, I use a combination of mint (www.mint.com), Excel, and plain paper. I enter expenses into my system within two days. Otherwise, I forget.

For investing, I use Instant X-Ray (www.morningstar.com/Cover /Tools.html) to make sure my asset allocation makes sense.

For other money management, I've opted out of credit card offers at www.optoutprescreen.com. I use www.myfico.com to get my credit score and report each year. (Yes, I could get it for free, but this is more convenient for me.) I use a service called Catalog Choice (www.catalogchoice.org) to keep from getting unwanted catalogs in the mail. And when I can't figure out calculations, I use the financial calculators at www.dinkytown.net.

system that signals you when something's broken. If the alarm bells aren't going off, you don't need to waste time worrying.

GO FOR BIG WINS

Optimizing your spending can seem overwhelming, but it doesn't have to be. You can do an 80/20 analysis, which often reveals that 80 percent of what you overspend is used toward only 20 percent of your expenditures. That's why I prefer to focus on one or two big problem areas and solve those instead of trying to cut 5 percent out of a bunch of smaller areas. To run an 80/20 analysis yourself, do a Google search for "conducting a Pareto analysis."

Let's take an example: Brian takes home $48,000 per year after taxes, or $4,000/month. According to his Conscious Spending Plan, here's how his spending *should* look:

- *Monthly fixed costs (60 percent): $2,400*
- *Long-term investments (10 percent): $400/month*
- *Savings goals (10 percent): $400/month*
- *Guilt-free spending money (20 percent): $800/month*

Big Win: No More Fees

I recently had breakfast with someone who told me the most interesting story. He'd been dating his girlfriend for two years before they talked about finances. "It took me that long to gain her trust," he said. She was a public school teacher, so she didn't make much money. When he looked at her finances, he noticed that she had a lot of overdraft fees. He asked her to estimate how much she had spent in overdraft fees. "About $100 or $200?" she guessed.

It turns out that her overdraft fees totaled $1,300 in the last year.

Did he freak out or start yelling about how to negotiate out of bank fees? No, he simply pointed out something very gently: "What if you focused on your overdrafts? If you eliminated *just* that category of fee, you'd be so much better off." Simply avoiding overdraft fees was a big win for her.

Brian's problem is that $800 isn't enough for his spending money—this plan leaves him $250 short each month. What should he do?

Bad answer: The superficial answer is that Brian can decrease his contributions to his long-term investments and savings goals. Sure, he could do that, but it will cost him down the line.

A better way is to tackle the two most problematic areas on his monthly spending: *monthly fixed costs* and *guilt-free spending money*.

Good answer: Brian decides to pick his three biggest expenses and optimize them. First, he looks at his *monthly fixed costs* and realizes that because he's been consistently paying the minimum monthly payment on his credit card debt at 18 percent, he has $3,000 of debt left. Under his current plan, it will take him about twenty-two years and cost him $4,115 in interest to pay off his debt. But he can call his credit card to request a lower interest rate (see page 42 for details). With his new lower credit card APR of 15 percent, it will take him eighteen years and he'll pay $2,758 in interest. He saves fifty-three months and $1,357 of payments. That's only $6/month, but over eighteen years it adds up to a lot.

Next, he checks his subscriptions and realizes he's been paying for a Netflix account and a Star Wars membership site, both of which he rarely uses. He cancels them, saving $60/month and increasing his chances of getting a girlfriend.

Finally, he logs in to his money-management account at www.mint.com and realizes that he's spending $350 eating out each month, plus $250 at bars, or $600 in total. He decides that over the next three months, he'll slowly ratchet that amount down to $400/month, saving him $200/month.

Total amount saved: $266/month. By adjusting his spending, Brian is able to create a Conscious Spending Plan that works for him.

Brian was smart to focus on changing the things that mattered. Instead of promising that he'd stop spending money on Cokes every time he ate out, he picked the big wins that would really make an impact on his total dollar amount. You'll see this a lot: People will get really inspired to budget and decide to stop spending on things like appetizers with dinner. Or they'll buy generic cookies. That's nice—and I definitely encourage you to do that—but those small changes will have very little effect on your total spending. They serve more to make people feel good about themselves, which lasts only a few weeks once they realize they still don't have any more money.

Try focusing on big wins that will make a large, measurable change. In fact, I focus on only one or two big wins each month: eating out, and buying books because I am a huge, huge dork. You probably know what your big wins are. They're the expenses you cringe at, the ones you shrug and roll your eyes at, and say, "Yeah, I probably spend too much on ____." For most of my friends, these big wins are eating out and drinking.

SET REALISTIC GOALS

Last year, a friend of mine started getting really into fitness. I think it was because of his laudable goal of "getting some girls." Kudos, sir. Anyway, he started working out a lot: going to the gym in the morning, running during the day, then hitting the gym *again* at night. Needless to say, this fitness program didn't last long. Do you know people who get so into their idea du jour that they go completely overboard and burn out? I would rather do less but make it sustainable. The problem is that that's rarely sexy.

This idea of sustainable change is core to personal finance. Sometimes I get e-mails from people who say things like, "Ramit! I started managing my money! Before, I was spending $500 a week! Now I'm saving $495 of it and

(continued on page 114)

DON'T JUST SAVE— SAVE FOR A GOAL

It's Hard to Save Unless There's a Reason

by Jim Wang of www.pfblueprint.com

My friend and I are the same age, make roughly the same amount, and have similar lifestyles. So, over five years, why was I able to save $20,000 for a down payment and buy a house . . . and he ended up with hardly anything? He came to talk to me about it one day.

We soon sorted out that the key difference was that we had a different approach to saving money. In his mind, he was simply "saving." I, on the other hand, was "saving for a down payment." Though it might not seem like a big deal, that small distinction makes all the difference in the world. I brought in a bag lunch because I was saving toward a house, he brought in a bag lunch because he was simply saving. When it came time for lunch, his was merely a decision between whether he wanted his sandwich or something different. For me, it was whether I was willing to sacrifice that $5 or $10 that could be going toward a house on something more interesting to eat that day. Saving with a goal—whether it's tangible like a house or intangible like your kid's education—puts all your decisions into focus.

MAKE THE TRADEOFFS WORTHWHILE. Having a goal means that you are working toward something concrete. It gives you a reason to make those tradeoffs. You don't just think of that $5 saved as $5—instead it is something that gets you closer to your goal of having $20,000 for a down payment on a home. It changes the entire motivation for saving.

Spending less isn't always easy, but with this newfound motivation, it's much easier to make and justify your decisions. For a while, I was only going out with my friends one night a week, rather than the two or three times we normally did. This still gave me a chance to hang out with my buddies, but I was spending one-third less than I used to! When my friends asked, I told them I couldn't go out because I was saving up for a down payment. They accepted this as a pretty good reason not to go out all the time. My friends might give me grief if I was simply being lazy, or lame, but because I had a concrete goal—and one that they could identify with—they became supporters of my cause rather than unwitting detractors.

SET UP A SPECIFIC ACCOUNT. *Another key difference was how I was saving. I opened up an ING Direct savings account and named it "Down Payment," regularly transferring in the amount I had determined I wanted to save. As the months passed, the amount in that account grew larger and larger, and I felt as though I was making progress toward my goal.*

My friend never set aside an account, so his regular checking account was one big pot of money mentally "earmarked" for various things. His account balance grew but he had no pride of achievement or sense of closing in on his goal (because he didn't have a goal). It's possible that he could have saved as much as I had and just not have known it!

> Saving with a goal—whether it's tangible like a house or intangible like your kid's education—puts all your decisions into focus.

That second difference was psychological. Rather than being motivated to save, he developed a feeling of despair about it. Trying to save $20,000 sounds daunting until you spread it out over three years—then it's $555 a month. Spread it out over five years and it's only $333 a month (not including interest earned). That's certainly doable if you make sacrifices and track your progress. After my friend opened a separate account, he told me that this step alone changed his whole perspective about saving money for his down payment (once he accomplished that goal, he planned to use the account to save for his annual vacations and his emergency fund).

ENJOY LUNCH! *Don't listen to experts telling you that you should stop buying CDs or how you should brown bag a lunch. Think about your goals. Ask yourself if you'd rather spend $10 on lunch or save $10 toward a house or a car. If you would rather spend the money on lunch, by all means enjoy lunch! You save money so that you can spend it later on the things that make you happy. You don't save money just to watch your account balance grow. Once you list your goals and start making those trade-offs, you'll realize that saving money becomes far easier.*

Jim Wang writes about personal finance and money management at www.pfblueprint.com.

(continued from page 111)

putting it into a bank account!" I read this and just sigh. Although you might expect me to get really excited about someone contributing $495/month to their savings, I've come to realize that when a person goes from one extreme to another, the behavioral change rarely lasts.

When I make a change, I almost always make it bite-sized in an area that matters (see my previous discussion of big wins) and work in increments from there. This is why I just shake my head when I see personal-finance pundits giving families advice to go from a zero percent savings rate to a 25 percent savings rate ("You can do it!!!"). Giving that kind of advice is not useful. Habits don't change overnight, and if they do, chances are it won't be sustainable.

For example, if I started keeping track of my expenses and discovered I was short $1,000/month (this happens more than you think), I'd pick the two big wins—two items that I spend a lot on, but know I could cut down with some effort—and focus my efforts on them. Say I was spending about $500/month eating out, here's how it would look:

Month 1: .... $475 on eating out

Month 2: .... $450 on eating out

Month 3: .... $400 on eating out

Month 4: .... $350 on eating out

Month 5: .... $300 on eating out

Month 6: .... $250 on eating out

It's not a race, but within six months, I'd have cut my eating out budget *in half*. And it'd be much more likely to be sustainable.

The other way to do it is to look at your current spending, freak out, and cut half your total spending. Then you're suddenly forced to spend in a completely different way, without the means to cope. How long do you think your ambitious spending goal will last?

How many times have you heard friends say something like, "I'm not going to drink for a month"? I don't understand the point of short-term whims like that. A month from now, okay, you spent only 50 percent of what you normally do. And . . . then what? If you can't keep it up and you bounce right back to your normal spending habits, what did you really

Join the "Save $1,000 in 30 Days" Challenge

Last year, I got sick of reading the same old frugality tips, so I launched this challenge to help people save $1,000 in thirty days. I wrote thirty tips, including how to negotiate your car insurance, save $2,000/a year eating out, and how to optimize your cell phone bill. Tens of thousands of people joined and they saved over $500,000 in thirty days. Check it out at www.iwillteachyoutoberich.com/30daychallenge.

accomplish? I'd rather have people cut their spending by 10 percent and sustain it for thirty years than cut 50 percent for just a month.

Whether you're implementing a change in your personal finances, eating habits, exercise plan, or whatever . . . try making the smallest change today. Something you won't even notice. And follow your own plan for gradually increasing it. In this way, time is your friend because each month gets better than the one before it, and it adds up to a lot in the end.

USE THE ENVELOPE SYSTEM TO TARGET YOUR BIG WINS

All this conscious spending and optimizing sounds nice in theory, but how do you do it? I recommend the envelope system, in which you allocate money for certain categories like eating out, shopping, rent, and so on. Once you spend the money for that month, that's it: You can't spend more. If it's really an emergency, you can dip into other envelopes at the cost of spending in *that* category. These "envelopes" can be figurative (like in Mint or Excel) or literally envelopes that you put cash in. This is the best system I've found for keeping spending simple and sustainable.

One of my friends, for example, has been carefully watching her spending for the last few months. When she started tracking her spending, she noticed that she was spending an unbelievable amount going out every week. So she came up with a clever solution to control her discretionary spending. She set up a separate bank account with a debit card. At the beginning of each month, she transfers, let's say, $200, into it. When she goes out, she spends that money. And when it's gone, it's gone.

The Envelope System

1. Decide how much you want to spend in major categories each month. (Not sure? Start with one: Eating out.)

2. Put money in each envelope (category):

$200	$150	$60
Groceries	**Eating out**	**Entertainment**

3. You can transfer from one envelope to another . . .

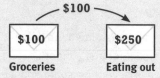

$100	$250
Groceries	**Eating out**

. . . but when the envelopes are empty, that's it for the month.

Tip: If you set up a debit account like this, call your bank and tell them you don't want them to allow you to spend more than you have in your account. Tell them, "If I have only thirty dollars in my account and I try to charge thirty-five dollars on my debit card, I don't want your system to let me." Some banks can handle this request. (Schwab Checking can do this by turning off overdraft/margin protection, whereas Wells Fargo can't because they are useless.) If you don't do this, you'll likely run up tons of overdraft fees.

Whatever system you want to use to divvy up the money is fine. Just decide how much you want to spend in major categories each month. (Pick your big wins to start.) Put the allotted money in each "envelope." When the envelopes are empty, that's it for the month. You can transfer from one envelope to another . . . but that money is coming out of another category, so your total spending doesn't actually increase.

Some of my nerdier friends even get more detailed with their system. One of my readers created this table:

	Eating out	Taxis	Books
Times per month	12	8	5
Amount per event	$23	$9	$17

"Each month, I try to cut the quantity and amount I spend on something," he told me. I looked at him in shock, but how can I argue? In less than eight months, he cut his spending by 43 percent (he knew the exact figure, of course). In my opinion, that level of analysis is overkill for most people, but it shows how detailed you can get once you set up a Conscious Spending Plan.

What If You Don't Make Enough Money?

Depending on your financial situation, setting up a workable Conscious Spending Plan may seem out of reach for you. Some people have already cut their spending to the bone and still don't have any extra money. For me to suggest that they put away 10 percent for retirement is, frankly, insulting. How can they be expected to contribute 10 percent toward long-term savings when they don't have enough to fill the car with gas?

Sometimes this is reality, and sometimes it's perception. Many of the people who've written me saying they live paycheck to paycheck actually have more wiggle room in their budgets than they think (cooking instead of eating out, for example, or not buying a new cell phone every year). They just don't *want* to change their spending.

However, it's true that many people really cannot afford to cut more spending and really are living check to check. If you simply can't cut more out of your budget, this spending plan may be a useful theoretical guide, but you have more important concerns: making more money. Once you increase your earnings, you can use the Conscious Spending Plan as your guide. Until then, here are three strategies you can use to earn more.

NEGOTIATE A RAISE

If you already have a job, it's a no-brainer to negotiate for a raise. A recent study by NACE, the National Association of Colleges and Employers, showed that companies pay more than $5,000 to hire the average college graduate. If you've been out of school for a few years, it's even more expensive. If they've already spent $5,000 recruiting you, and thousands more training you, would they really want to lose you?

Asking for a raise takes careful planning. Don't do what my friend "Jamie" did. When he realized he was being drastically underpaid for his contributions, he seethed without taking any action for more than two months. When he finally got up the courage to ask his boss for a raise, he said it in the most timid way: "Do you think I might possibly ask you about a raise?" If you're a manager, the first thing you'd think is, "Oh God, not another thing in my day." My friend's boss brushed him off, leaving Jamie, who's still at the company, frustrated and underpaid.

REMEMBER THAT GETTING A RAISE IS NOT ABOUT YOU. IT'S ABOUT YOU DEMONSTRATING YOUR VALUE TO YOUR EMPLOYER.

Remember that getting a raise is not about you. It's about you demonstrating your value to your employer. You can't tell them you need more money because your expenses are higher. Nobody cares. You *can,* however, show how your work has been clearly contributing to the company's success, and ask to be compensated fairly. Here's what you need to do:

Three months before you ask for a raise, start tracking everything you do at work *and the results you get.* If you were on a team that sold 25,000 widgets, figure out what you did to help make that happen and, as much as possible, quantify it. If you can't figure out the exact results you're causing, ask someone at work who's more experienced. This is a classic question that new employees have, and many experienced coworkers would be happy to help you.

At the same time, ask your boss if you can sit down and discuss ways you can excel at work. Make it clear you want to exceed expectations, and ask what that would entail. If you're really clever, you can hint about discussing compensation in the future.

Two months before you ask for a raise, meet with your boss again and show him your tracking from the previous month. Ask what you could do better. You want to know if you're on the right track with your work and, more important, the way you're communicating it.

One month before the big event, mention to your boss that because you've been doing so well, you'd like to discuss compensation at a meeting the next month. Ask what you'll need to bring to make it a fruitful discussion. Listen very carefully to what he says.

Around this time, it wouldn't hurt to ask your fellow coworkers to put in a good word with the boss. This assumes, of course, that you've been exceeding expectations and driving concrete results.

Two weeks before you ask for a raise, ask a couple of friends to role-play your job negotiation. This seems really weird, but negotiating is *not* a natural behavior. It will feel extremely odd and uncomfortable the first couple of times you do it. Better to do it with friends than your boss. And pick good friends, people who have business experience and will give you feedback on how you performed.

On the day you negotiate, come in with your salary, a couple of competitive salaries from www.salary.com and www.payscale.com, and your list of accomplishments, and be ready to discuss fair compensation. Remember, you're not asking your mommy for lemonade, you're a professional who's asking to be compensated fairly. You want to proceed as partners, as in "How do we make this work?"

If you get the raise you were looking for, congratulations! That was a huge first step toward increasing your income. If you don't, ask your boss

Cool Trick: Quickly Discover How Much You Make

To find your annual salary, just take your hourly rate, double it, and add three zeros to the end. If you make $20/hour, you make approximately $40,000/year. If you make $30/hour, you make approximately $60,000/year.

This also works in reverse. To find your hourly rate, divide your salary by two and drop the three zeros. So $50,000/year becomes approximately $25/hour.

This is based on a general forty-hour workweek and doesn't include taxes, but it's a good general back-of-the-napkin trick. And it's most useful when you're deciding whether to buy something or not. If that pair of pants is going to cost you eight hours of work, is it worth it?

When I was in college, I used to measure those decisions by the number of quarters I'd have to trade away from my laundry stash. Those may have been the most intellectually rigorous years of my life.

what you can do to excel in your career, or consider leaving to find another company that will give you greater room to grow.

GET A HIGHER-PAYING JOB

This takes us to the second way to increase your income. If you find that your existing company doesn't offer you growth potential, or you're in the process of getting a new job, negotiating your salary will never be easier. During the job-hiring process, you have more leverage than you'll ever have.

I cover negotiating a new salary in detail on page 234.

DO SOME FREELANCE WORK

Freelancing can be a relatively easy way to earn some extra money. Think about what skills or interests you have that others could use. You don't necessarily have to have a technical skill. Babysitting is freelancing (and it pays very well). If you have free time at home (or don't have a car), you can sign up to be a virtual assistant on sites like www.elance.com and www.odesk.com. Tutoring is also a simple, profitable way to make some extra side cash: You might be able to moonlight at a company like Kaplan and help kids with test prep, or you can post a notice at your neighborhood library and offer to teach English, math, or anything. What about dog walking? Remember, busy people want others to help them with their lives. A great place to start is www.craigslist.org's "Help Wanted" section for your city.

> **YOU DON'T NECESSARILY HAVE TO HAVE A TECHNICAL SKILL TO FREELANCE. BABYSITTING IS FREELANCING (AND IT PAYS VERY WELL).**

If you have expertise in something, reach out to companies who'd need someone like you. For example, when I was in high school, I e-mailed fifty websites from all different industries that looked interesting but had poor marketing and copywriting. I offered to help them rewrite their websites. About fifteen responded, and I ended up editing copy for one company that eventually promoted me to run their sales department.

Later, during college, I consulted for venture capitalists, teaching them about Web 2.0 technologies, like YouTube, Facebook, and Flickr. This is stuff you and I know like the back of our hand, but it was new to these VCs—and valuable enough that they paid a great consulting fee.

Maintaining Your Spending Plan

Once you've done what you can to design and implement a Conscious Spending Plan that you're comfortable with, give yourself some time to settle into a rhythm with it. Sure, eventually you can spend your time on strategic money decisions—"Should I be contributing 10 percent or 12 percent to my monthly savings goals?"—but first, you've got to get the basics down. As you go along from month to month with this new system, you'll discover some surprises you hadn't anticipated.

You'll always have unexpected cash expenses like cabs or an umbrella when you forgot yours. And don't flip out if you miss tracking a few dollars here or there—the minute your system becomes too oppressive for you to use is the minute you stop using it. I try to make as many purchases on my credit card as possible, so my software can automatically download my transactions. For cash spending, try to get the receipts and enter them into your system within seven days. After that, I tend to lose receipts or let them build up so much that I forget what some of the receipts were for. Make tracking your spending a weekly priority. For example, set aside thirty minutes every Sunday afternoon.

HOW TO HANDLE UNEXPECTED AND IRREGULAR EXPENSES

It can be frustrating to have a spending plan that keeps getting disrupted by surprise expenses like wedding gifts, car repairs, and late fees. So another key to having a plan you'll use is to account for the unexpected and build in a bit of flexibility.

Known irregular events (vehicle registration fees, Christmas gifts, vacations). There's an easy way to account for this type of irregular event. In fact, this is already built into your spending plan: Under *Savings Goals,* you allocate money toward goals where you have a general idea of how much it will cost. It doesn't have to be exact, but try to get a rough ballpark figure and then save every month toward that goal. For example, if you know you'll have to spend about $500 on Christmas gifts, start saving $42/month (that's $500 divided by twelve months) in January. By the time December rolls around, you won't have to take a huge hit on your spending.

Unknown irregular events (surprise medical expenses, late fees for your library card, or $100 flowers to make up to your girlfriend for something stupid you did last night). These types of surprises fall under your *Monthly Fixed Expenses* because no matter how hard you try to avoid them, there will always be unexpected expenses. Earlier, I suggested that you add about 15 percent to your estimate of your fixed costs to accommodate these surprises. In addition, I recommend starting by allocating $50/month for unexpected expenses. You'll soon realize that this cartoonishly low figure is not enough. But with some time, you'll have a better idea of what the figure should actually be and can change the amount accordingly.

> **ADD ABOUT 15 PERCENT TO YOUR ESTIMATE OF YOUR FIXED COSTS TO ACCOMMODATE SURPRISE EXPENSES.**

Fortunately, with each month that goes by, you'll get a more accurate picture of your spending. After about a year or two (remember, think long term), you'll have a very accurate understanding of how to project. The beginning is the hard part, but it only gets easier.

THE "PROBLEM" OF EXTRA INCOME

Just as there are surprise expenses, there is also surprise income. It's tempting to take a windfall and blow it all on something fun, but I urge you not to follow that instinct. Instead, work within your Conscious Spending Plan.

Unexpected onetime income. Sometimes money unexpectedly falls in your lap, like a birthday gift or from selling something on eBay. Believe it or not, I don't encourage you to save all this money. Instead, whenever I make money I didn't expect, I use 50 percent of it for fun—usually buying something I've been eyeing for a long time. Always! This way, I keep motivating myself to pursue weird, offbeat ideas that may result in some kind of reward. The other half goes to my investing account. Compare this with not having a plan and letting your money "just sort of" get spent.

Raises. A raise is different from onetime income because you'll get it consistently, and it's therefore much more important to do the right thing financially. There's one important thing to remember when you get a raise:

Maintain your current standard of living. Too many people get a raise at work and say, "Great! I'll go on that vacation!" Sure, you can do that. Then, "I'll buy that new sofa I've been wanting!" Uh oh. And then, "I think I need those new shoes. What? I've been working hard!" And then you want to kill yourself because you're swirling into a downward spiral of spending.

If you get a raise, be realistic: You earned it, and you should enjoy the results of your hard work. Buy yourself something nice that you've been wanting for a long time, and make it something you'll remember. After that, however, I strongly encourage you to save and invest as much of it as possible, because once you start getting accustomed to a certain lifestyle, you can never go back. After buying a Mercedes, can you ever drive a Toyota Corolla again?

Working retail for five years I made a goal out of saving up 10K to be able to invest in the stock market. I decided everything I saved before the age of twenty-eight was available for me to fiddle with stocks; everything after twenty-eight was to be put in a blend of investment funds safe from my amateur investing styles. I was able to accomplish saving up 10K on a meager retail wage by putting half of every raise into my 401(k) plan. Every 4 percent raise was a 2 percent raise to my retirement plan.

—JASON HENRY, 33

The best part about setting up a strategic budget is that *it* guides your decisions, letting you say no much more easily—"Sorry, it's not in my plan this month"—and freeing you up to enjoy what you do spend on. This is guilt-free spending at its best. Sure, there will be tough decisions. Deciding to change the way you spend is the most difficult part of this book. It involves making choices and saying no to certain things. Your system, however, makes this much less painful. If a friend asks you out to dinner and you don't have enough spending money left, it will be easier to politely pass. After all, it's not personal—it's just your *system*. Remember that most people are, by definition, ordinary. They go through their twenties and thirties feeling a gnawing sense that they "should" do something about their money—tomorrow. They don't think about saving until their mid-forties. And yet, you are now extraordinary, because you see that setting up a simple system will let you make the tough decisions up front and spend your money guilt-free.

ACTION STEPS

WEEK FOUR

1 **Get your paycheck, determine what you've been spending, and figure out what your Conscious Spending Plan should look like (thirty minutes).** Do this now and don't overthink it. Just break your take-home income into chunks of fixed costs (50–60 percent), long-term investments (10 percent), savings goals (5–10 percent), and guilt-free spending money (20–35 percent). How does it fit?

2 **Optimize your spending (two hours).** Dig in deeper to your savings goals and monthly fixed costs. Try the À La Carte Method. How much does your insurance actually cost—can you improve on that? How much will you spend for Christmas gifts and vacation this year? Break these expenses down into monthly chunks, then recalculate your plan.

3 **Pick your big wins (five hours).** Open an account at Mint or Quicken Online. Assuming you want to cut your spending by $200/month, what one or two big wins will you target? Start using the envelope system.

4 **Maintain your Conscious Spending Plan (one hour per week).** Enter any cash receipts into your system each week. Tweak the percentages you send to each part of your spending plan (we'll cover this in detail in the next chapter). And most important, make sure your system is realistic enough that you'll stick with it for the long term.

All right, deep breath. You did it. You made it through the most difficult part of the book! Now you've got a strategic spending plan. You no longer have to constantly worry about how much money you're spending. Phrases like "Can I afford this?" and "I know I'm going to worry about this later, but for now . . ." will be erased from your vocabulary. Now we're going to automate this system so each new dollar that comes into your system gets instantly sent to the right area, whether it's investments, savings, fixed costs, or guilt-free spending.

CHAPTER 5

SAVE WHILE SLEEPING

Making your accounts work together—automatically

I want to be clear about something: I plan to do less and less work as I go through my life. When I meet people on a career path that will have them working *more,* not less, I'm always puzzled. That's like being a real-life Mario Brother, where every level you beat means your life gets progressively more difficult. Why would you want that?

Managing money is no different: By investing a little now, we don't have to invest *a lot* later. Of course, that's easier said than done. Somehow we just never get around to consistently managing our money—and let's be honest: That will never change. Because who really cares about managing money? It's about as appealing as cleaning the garage . . . every week for the rest of your life. We dream of having an automated system that handles most of the work for us, something that *just works.*

In the last chapter, you set up a Conscious Spending Plan to determine how much you want to spend in each category (fixed costs, investments, savings goals, and guilt-free spending money). You didn't think you'd have to manually transfer money each month, did you? Not a chance.

In this chapter, we'll create an Automatic Money Flow to manage your money for you. It will take the accounts you've set up—your credit cards, checking, savings, and investment accounts—and create automatic transfers so your money goes where it needs to go.

I call it my "finance assembly line." Before I even see a paycheck I automatically give the maximum amount to my company's 401(k). The remainder of my pay is direct-deposited into a checking account. Then part of it is automatically transferred to a high-interest online savings account, and another part goes to my discount brokerage account. My rent is paid automatically on the 1st of every month and I pay my credit card bill online on the 15th. I never miss the money I invest because I never see it. In total I spend about thirty minutes a month on my finances.

—**MARK LAURENZ, 22**

DO MORE BEFORE DOING LESS

Some people just seem to have a magical ability to manage money. They enrolled in their 401(k) years ago, they always know how much money they have, and they seem to relish tweaking their system to optimize it. Usually, these people are extremely annoying and unattractive. But that doesn't mean we can't learn something from them. You see, they don't spend more time on day-to-day money management than most average people. In fact, they spend *less* time thinking about their money because they've set up an automated system that frees them from having to worry. These people don't work harder, they just work smarter.

You can become one of these people (only you'll be very attractive and not at all annoying) if you follow my advice about automating. This is all driven by a principle I'll call The Curve of Doing More Before Doing Less:

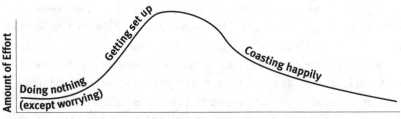

This is as much about where to invest your time as it is about where to put your money. Sure, setting up an Automatic Money Flow will take you a few hours. It would be easier to do nothing—but that would mean you'll have to manage your money constantly for the rest of your life. By spending a few hours up front, you'll end up saving huge amounts of time over the long term. Your money flow will be automatic, and each dollar that comes in will be routed to the right account in your Conscious Spending Plan from Chapter 4 without you really having to think about it.

The payoff for these few hours is huge because this automatic system will let you focus on the fun parts of life. No more worrying about whether you paid that bill or if you're going to overdraft again. You'll start to see money as a tool for getting what you want without the manual drudgery of tracking categories and transferring money from one account to another each week.

I spend an hour per month managing my money, perhaps. Paying bills, checking the balance on my credit card and my bank accounts, and watching a few holdings in my portfolio (but I'm not an active trader—just maintaining situational awareness). Once a month, I might evaluate my savings plan to see if I can plan a vacation or make a larger purchase.

—JENNIFER CHANG, 32

THE POWER OF DEFAULTS

We know people are incredibly lazy and will do whatever requires no work—often at their own financial expense. Think about how many people lose thousands of dollars per year by not taking advantage of 401(k) matches alone. How much more money do we lose from inaction overall?

The key to taking action is, quite simply, making your decisions automatic. You think you'll actually do the work each week? No, you won't. You don't care. Sure, you might care right now, but in two weeks it'll be back to Twitter and Perez Hilton. Nobody really cares about managing their money. Hell, I don't even care. Get away from me, endless mailings from banks and investment accounts. (That's the line I will use as a bedtime story to soothe my future children. I know, I know. My future wife is a lucky woman.)

Your money management must happen by default. We've already talked about it in reference to 401(k)s, but now we're going to apply that to every dollar you make. You'll be making your contributions to your savings and investing accounts grow passively—with no action required. In fact, by setting up an automatic payment plan you actually make it difficult to *stop* the contributions to your retirement account! Not because you can't—you can adjust your system any time—but because you're lazy and you won't. Hey, I'm lazy, too. You just have to know how to take advantage of it. Once it's set up, this system is so hands-off that if you got eaten alive by a Komodo dragon, your money system would continue transferring money from account to account by default, a ghostlike reminder of your financial prescience. Haunting, but cool.

If you want to build wealth over your lifetime, the only sure way to do it is to get your plan on autopilot and make everything that's financially important in your life automatic. . . . I recommend that people automate a handful of things in their financial lives. You can set it up once in less than an hour and then go back to your life.

—**DAVID BACH, AUTHOR OF** *THE AUTOMATIC MILLIONAIRE*

How to Spend Only Three Hours a Month Managing Your Money

I hope I've convinced you by now that automation is the way to go. In Chapter 4, you set up a basic system—the Conscious Spending Plan—that gave you an idea of where you're going to distribute your money. As a refresher, check out the rough percentages to assign to the four categories (or buckets) in the table on the next page:

Now, let's take your Conscious Spending Plan and make it automatic. To do this, I use a concept called "The Next $100." This means, simply, where will the next $100 you make go? Will it all go to your investment account? Will you allocate 10 percent to your savings account? Most people just shrug and don't take any time to think about how their money

CATEGORIES OF SPENDING

Fixed costs Rent, utilities, debt, etc.	50–60% of take-home pay
Investments 401(k), Roth IRA	10%
Savings goals Vacations, gifts, house down payment, cash for unexpected expenses	5–10%
Guilt-free spending money Dining out, drinking, movies, clothes, shoes	20–35%

will be allocated—which means it gets thoughtlessly spent and I sob uncontrollably.

But there's a better way! It involves actually using the guidelines you established in your Conscious Spending Plan. If you did things right in Chapter 4, you already know how much money you want to contribute to your fixed costs, investments, savings, and spending money. So, if you made $100, and your plan resembled the example above, you'd put $60 toward your fixed costs, $10 into your investment account, $10 into savings, and then you'd spend the remaining $20 on whatever you felt like. Pretty cool, right? Well, it gets even better, because once everything is automated, that money will be shunted from your checking account right into the appropriate accounts without you even thinking about it.

To see how it works, let's use Michelle as an example:

Michelle gets paid once a month. Her employer deducts 5 percent of her pay automatically and puts it in her 401(k). The rest of Michelle's paycheck goes to her checking account by direct deposit.

About a day later, her Automatic Money Flow begins transferring money out of her checking account. Her Roth IRA retirement account will pull 5 percent of her salary for itself. (That combines with the 401(k) contribution to complete the 10 percent of take-home pay for investing.) Her savings account will pull 5 percent, automatically breaking that money into chunks: 1 percent for a wedding sub-account and 4 percent to a house down-payment sub-account. (That takes care of her monthly savings goals.)

Her system also automatically pays her fixed costs. She's set it up so that most of her subscriptions and bills are paid by her credit card. Some of her bills can't be put on credit cards—for example, utilities and loans—so they're automatically paid out of her checking account. Finally, she's automatically e-mailed a copy of her credit card bill for a five-minute review. After she's reviewed it, the bill is also paid from her checking account.

The money that remains in her account is used for spending money.

IT'S WELL WORTH TAKING AN HOUR TO GET ALL YOUR ACCOUNT NUMBERS IN ONE PLACE.

To make sure she doesn't overspend, she's focused on two big wins: eating out and spending money on clothes. She sets alerts in her Mint account if she goes over her spending goals, and she keeps a reserve of $500 in her checking account just in case. (The couple of times she went over her spending, she paid herself back using her "unexpected expenses" money from her savings account.) To track spending more easily, she uses her credit card as much as possible to pay for all of her fun stuff. If she uses cash for cabs or coffee, she keeps the receipts and tries to enter them into Mint as often as possible.

In the middle of the month, Michelle's calendar reminds her to check her Mint account to make sure she's within her limits for her spending money. If she's doing fine, she gets on with her life. If she's over her limit, she decides what she needs to cut back on to stay on track for the month. Luckily, she has fifteen days to get it right, and by politely passing on an invitation to dine out she gets back on track.

My savings accounts and investment account all have auto draft on the first of every month. I figure pay yourself first, then plan to play with what's left. I use Quicken to track all of my bills, incomes, and expenses along with keeping track of my budget. Three clicks and I have all the information I need to see on how my budget/savings goals are coming along. It's also incredibly easy to see where all my money is going.

—JONATHAN ROTH, 24

By the end of the month, she's spent less than two hours monitoring her finances, yet she's invested 10 percent, saved 5 percent (in sub-buckets for her wedding and down payment), paid all of her bills on time, paid off her credit card in full, and spent exactly what she wanted to spend. She had to say "no" only once, and it was no big deal. In fact, none of it was.

Create Your Automatic Money Flow

Now that you see how it works, it's time to implement your Automatic Money Flow. You'll start by linking all your accounts together. Then, you'll set up automatic transfers to happen on various days. Below, I'll assume that you're paid once per month, but I'll also cover slight tweaks to implement if you're paid biweekly or if you're a freelancer who's paid irregularly.

To get set up, you'll need a complete list of all your accounts, their URLs, and the login/passwords. Make a chart that looks something like this.

Account	URL	Login	Password
checking account			
savings account			
credit card(s)			
401(k)			
Roth IRA			
any regular bills*			

*e.g., rent, student loans, car payments, utilities, Netflix, etc.

Alternatively, remember that on page 88 I mentioned that I use a PBwiki account to store all of this information. It's well worth taking an hour to get all these handy account numbers in one place so you never have to do this again.

Also, before you start linking your online accounts, you may need to work with your employer to get your paycheck going to the proper places. If you don't already have it, talk to your HR rep and set up direct deposit into your checking account. (This is easy. It basically entails giving your checking account number to your employer.) In addition, you need to get everything squared away with your 401(k) contribution. Ideally you already set up your 401(k) way back in Chapter 3, but if not, DO IT NOW! Even if you already have a 401(k) going, you may have to adjust the amount you contribute every month based on your shiny new Conscious Spending Plan.

LINK YOUR ACCOUNTS

First, you'll need to log in to each account and link your accounts together so you can set up automatic transfers from one account to another. When you log in to any of your accounts, you'll usually find an option called something like "Link Accounts," "Transfer," or "Set Up Payments."

These are all the links you need to make:

- If you haven't already done this, connect your paycheck to your 401(k), so it's automatically funded each month. (I cover this on page 82.).

- Connect your checking account to your savings account.

- Connect your checking account to your investment account/ Roth IRA. (Do this from your investment account.)

- Connect your credit card to any bills you've been paying by using your checking account. (If you've actually been paying bills by writing checks with a pen, please understand that man has discovered fire and combustible engines and join our modern times.) For example, if you've been paying your cable bill by check each month, log in and switch it so that the bill is paid by your credit card instead.

- Some bills can't be paid using a credit card, like rent and loans. For these regular bills, link them to your checking account. (Do this by logging in to the company's website, and initiating the transfer there.)

- Set it up so that all your credit card accounts are paid from your checking account. (This is set up from your credit card's "Transfer" or "Link Accounts" page.)

Finally, there are payments that simply can't be automatically drawn from your checking account. For example, if you're renting from a little old lady, she may not have a sophisticated financial infrastructure including a website where you can enter your checking account information and automatically transfer money each month. Sigh. Get it together, Mildred. Anyway, you can still automate payment using your checking account's bill-pay feature, which is free with nearly every account. Example: If you pay rent by writing a check and sticking it in an envelope each month, log in to your checking account and set up automatic bill pay for your rent. Your bank will then write a check for you each month and mail it to your landlord. Just make sure you schedule it so that it has enough time to reach your landlord in the mail.

WHERE THE MONEY FLOWS

This account . . .	. . . Should fund this account
Paycheck	■ 401(k) ■ Checking account (direct deposit)
Checking account	■ Roth IRA ■ Savings account (which is sub-divided into savings goals) ■ Credit card ■ Fixed costs that don't allow credit card payment (like rent) ■ Occasional spending cash
Credit card	■ Fixed costs ■ Guilt-free spending

SET UP YOUR AUTOMATIC TRANSFERS

Now that all your accounts are linked, it's time to go back into your accounts and automate all transfers and payments. This is really simple: It is just a matter of working with each individual account's website to make sure your payment or transfer is set up for the amount you want and on the date you want.

One thing you want to pay attention to is picking the right dates for your transfers. This is key, but people often overlook it. If you set automatic transfers at weird times, it will inevitably necessitate more work. For example, if your credit card is due on the 1st of the month, but you don't get paid until the 15th, how does that work? If you don't

(continued on page 136)

SET IT AND FORGET IT

Automate Your Finances to Focus on Long-Term Goals

by Gina Trapani of Lifehacker.com

Tech-savvy folks who want to get more done in less time don't want to fuss with tedious money tasks like writing checks and transferring funds, so financial automation is very popular among the Lifehacker readership. Personally, I'm right there: "Set it and forget it" is my guiding personal finance system principle. Well, not exactly "forget it," but I set up my accounts to run themselves to the extent they can, and check in on things monthly to make sure all the gears are turning as I intended.

I'm a busy person who doesn't want to think about money matters any more than I need to, so I rely heavily on automated transfers, deposits, and e-mail notifications to keep my dollars and cents where they need to be. Most good banks these days offer electronic bill pay, direct deposit, recurring savings account transfers, and some even offer e-mail notifications if an account balance goes above or below a certain threshold. I use all these tools. My income goes in, bill payments go out, and my credit card gets paid in full with minimal intervention. If my credit card debt in a given month goes above a certain threshold—like $3,000—I get an e-mail letting me know so I can make sure I've got that cash ready in my checking account. For week-to-week money tasks, this all works like a charm.

TOOLS OF THE TRADE. For a longer, bird's-eye view of my finances, I use a desktop copy of Quicken to suck in all my account transactions and make me pretty charts. Using Quicken, I check in on my net worth over time and see if there are any expenses that I can cut down. This kind of overview work is where I spend the most time—deciding on my savings goals, tracking them, seeing where I was at the same time last year, plotting where I want to be at the same time next year. Being a personal productivity obsessive, I'm big on having goals and using checkpoints along the way to get there. I use Google Calendar to set twelve savings goals throughout the year, with an e-mail reminder for each one. At the end of each month

I get an e-mail from my calendar saying something like, "It's October! Should be $X in the nest egg account by now!" That really keeps me on track when life has swept me away and I'm thinking about other things.

As a freelancer, things get tricky around tax time—and tax time happens four times a year for self-employed folks. I use automated monthly transfers into an income tax holding account so I can pay my quarterly estimated taxes without feeling like I just lost my shirt. (That's not a good feeling, ever—so do whatever you have to do to avoid it. In fact, keeping an attitude of confidence and prosperity is one of the best financial moves you can make, regardless of what your account balance is.) I use a simple spreadsheet to track deductions, and a big manila envelope to keep original receipts—one envelope per year.

Being a personal productivity obsessive, I'm big on having goals and using checkpoints along the way to get there. I use Google Calendar to set twelve savings goals throughout the year, with an e-mail reminder for each one.

STRATEGIES FOR DEBT. *Some of the best debt reduction strategies we've gotten from Lifehacker readers involve tricking yourself into putting money aside, and making it hard to spend. Many endorse the old-fashioned way: Cut up the credit cards, and pay down the ones with the highest interest rates most aggressively. Another strategy to avoid impulse buying is filling up online shopping carts or wishlists and then making yourself wait a week or two before you pull the trigger and hit the "Check out" button. I use this method a lot: Usually, impulse buys make much less sense when you've had some time to think about it.*

In the end, managing your finances well is a lot like developing a strong personal productivity system: You keep track of everything without making it your full-time job; you set goals; you break them down into small bite-size tasks; you save yourself time by automating manual work; and you spend your time and brainpower focusing on the big picture. That's what I try to do with my time and money.

Gina Trapani is the founding editor of Lifehacker.com, a daily weblog on software and personal productivity.

(continued from page 133)

synchronize all your bills, you'll have to pay things at different times and that will require you to reconcile accounts. Which you won't do.

The easiest way to avoid this is to get all your bills on the same schedule. To accomplish this, gather all your bills together, call the companies, and ask them to switch your billing dates. Most of these will take five minutes each to do. There may be a couple of months of odd billing as your accounts adjust, but it will smooth itself out after that. If you're paid on the 1st of the month, I suggest switching all your bills to arrive on or around that time, too. Call and say this: "Hi, I'm currently being billed on the 17th of each month, and I'd like to change that to the 1st of the month. Do I need to do anything besides ask right here on the phone?" Of course, depending on your situation, you can request any billing date that will be easy for you.

> **GET ALL YOUR BILLS ON THE SAME SCHEDULE BY CALLING THE COMPANIES AND ASKING TO SWITCH YOUR BILLING DATES.**

Now that you've got everything coming at the beginning of the month, it's time to actually go in and set up your transfers. Here's how to arrange your Automatic Money Flow, assuming you get paid on the 1st of the month.

2nd of the month: Part of your paycheck is automatically sent to your 401(k). The remainder (your "take-home pay") is direct-deposited into your checking account. Even though you're paid on the 1st, the money may not show up in your account until the 2nd, so be sure to account for that. Remember, you're treating your checking account like your e-mail inbox—first, everything goes there, then it's filtered away to the appropriate place. Note: The first time you set this up, leave a buffer amount of money—I recommend $500—in your checking account just in case a transfer doesn't go right. And don't worry: If something *does* go wrong, use the negotiation tips on page 24 to get any overdraft fees waived.

5th of the month: Automatic transfer to your savings account. Log in to your savings account and set up an automatic transfer from your checking account to your savings account on the 5th of every month. Waiting until the 5th of the month gives you some leeway. If, for some reason, your paycheck doesn't show up on the 1st of the month, you'll have four days to correct things or cancel that month's automatic transfer.

Don't just set up the transfer. Remember to set the amount, too. Use the percentage of your monthly income that you established for savings in your Conscious Spending Plan (typically 5 to 10 percent). But if you can't afford that much right now, don't worry—just set up an automatic transfer for $5 to prove to yourself that it works. The amount is important: $5 won't be missed, but once you see how it's all working together, it's much easier to add to that amount.

5th of the month: Automatic transfer to your Roth IRA. To set this up, log in to your investment account and create an automatic transfer from your checking account to your investment account. Refer to your Conscious Spending Plan to calculate the amount of the transfer. It should be approximately 10 percent of your take-home pay, minus the amount you send to your 401(k).

WHEN THE MONEY FLOWS

On this date . . .	. . . these actions happen
2nd of the month	■ Part of your salary goes into your 401(k) ■ The rest of your salary is direct-deposited into your checking account
5th of the month	■ Automatic transfer from checking to savings account ■ Automatic transfer from checking account to Roth IRA
7th of the month	■ Automatic payment of bills from checking account and credit card ■ Automatic transfer from checking account to pay off credit card bill

7th of the month: Auto-pay for any monthly bills you have. Log in to any regular payments you have, like cable, utilities, car payments, or student loans, and set up automatic payments to occur on the 7th of each month. I prefer to pay my bills using my credit card, because I earn points, I get automatic consumer protection, and I can easily track my spending on online sites like www.mint.com, www.quicken.com, or www.wesabe.com.

But if your merchant doesn't accept credit cards, they should let you pay the bill directly from your checking account, so set up an automatic payment from there if needed.

7th of the month: Automatic transfer to pay off your credit card. Log in to your credit card account and instruct it to draw money from your checking account and pay the credit card bill on the 7th of every month—in full. (Because your bill arrived on the 1st of the month, you'll never incur late fees using this system.) If you have credit card debt and you can't pay the bill in full,

> ## GET YOUR CREDIT CARD TO EMAIL YOU A MONTHLY LINK TO YOUR BILL, SO YOU CAN REVIEW IT BEFORE THE MONEY IS AUTOMATICALLY TRANSFERRED OUT OF YOUR CHECKING ACOUNT.

don't worry. You can still set up an automatic payment; just make it for the monthly minimum or any other amount of your choice. (See page 39 to learn why this is a very good idea.)

By the way, while you're logged in to your credit card account, also set up an e-mail notification (this is typically under "Notifications" or "Bills") to send you a monthly link to your bill, so you can review it before the money is automatically transferred out of your checking account. This is helpful in case your bill unexpectedly exceeds the amount available in your checking account—that way you can adjust the amount you pay that month.

TWEAKING THE SYSTEM

That's the basic Automatic Money Flow schedule, but you may not be paid on a straight once-a-month schedule. That's not a problem. You can just adjust the above system to match your payment schedule.

If you're paid twice a month: I suggest replicating the above system on the 1st and the 15th—with half the money each time. This is easy enough, but the one thing to watch with this is paying your bills. If the second payment (on the 15th) will miss the due dates for any of your bills, be sure that you set it so that those bills are paid in full during the payment on the 1st. Another way to work your system is to do half the payments with one paycheck (retirement, fixed costs) and half the

Review Your Credit Card Bill

I pay with my credit card as much as possible because it lets me automatically download my transactions and categorize my spending. Plus, I get travel points and extra consumer protection, like a free additional warranty for any electronic device (for more on this, see page 31).

Once a week, I take five minutes and review all the charges on my card, and once a month I get an e-mail to review my entire bill. If I take no action, my credit card reaches into my checking account and pays the full amount automatically. No late fees, no worries. If I do see an error, I just call my credit card company anytime twenty-four hours a day and get it fixed.

Let's talk about those weekly reviews for a second. I do like to keep an eye on my credit card charges whenever there's a human involved, so I keep my receipts whenever I go to restaurants, and store them in a folder on my desk.

Every Sunday night, I open the folder and spend about five minutes comparing my receipts with what my credit card's website says. I just do a "ctrl-f" for the amount (for example, $43.35) and confirm that it's correct. If I wrote down $43.35 as the full amount, but instead saw that the restaurant had charged me $50, someone's trying to make a quick buck off me. And in that case, you need to ask yourself one question:

WWAID?

(What would an Indian do?)

Answer: A quick call to my credit card company will resolve this.

The most important thing is keeping your receipt folder *on your desk.* If you have to get up to get it—even a few steps away—that's a huge barrier to getting this done consistently.

payments with the second paycheck (savings, guilt-free spending), but that can get clunky.

If you have irregular income: Irregular incomes, like those of freelancers, are difficult to plan for. Some months you might earn close to nothing, others you're flush with cash. This situation calls for some changes to

Living for Today, Too

Q: *When do I get to spend my money?*

A: Okay. You've got your automatic infrastructure set up. Each month, you've got money flowing automatically to your investing accounts and savings accounts. You've even cut your spending by focusing on a couple of big wins. So when do you get to spend all this money?

What a great question. The only people who've ever asked me this are actually concerned about saving *too much*.

The answer is simple: Once you've gotten your money under control and you're hitting your targets, you absolutely should spend your leftover money. Look to your savings goals. If you don't have something in there for "vacation" or "new snowboard," maybe you should. Otherwise, what is all this money for?

Money exists for a reason—to let you do what you want to do. Yes, it's true, every dollar you spend now would be worth more later. But living only for tomorrow is no way to live. Consider one investment that most people overlook: *yourself*. Think about traveling—how much will that be worth to you later? Or attend that conference that will expose you to the top people in your field. My friend Paul has a specific "networking budget" that he uses to travel to meet interesting people each year. If you invest in yourself, the potential return is limitless.

If you're meeting your goals, another route you could take is to start saving less and increase the amount you allocate to your guilt-free spending money.

One final thing: I hope this doesn't sound too cheesy, but one of the best returns I've ever gotten has been with philanthropy. Whether it's your time or your money, I can't emphasize enough how important it is to give back, be it to your own community or to the global community. Volunteer your time at a local school or youth organization, or help teachers get the tools they need by giving to DonorsChoose.org. For more on giving back, see page 215.

Saving too much is a good problem to have. Fortunately, there are great solutions, too.

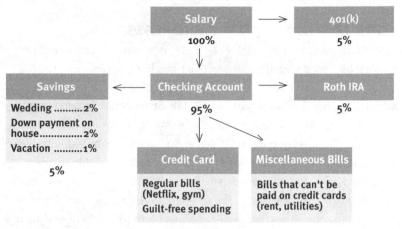

AUTOMATING YOUR MONEY: HOW IT WORKS

- Salary — 100%
- 401(k) — 5%
- Checking Account — 95%
- Savings — 5%
  - Wedding 2%
  - Down payment on house...............2%
  - Vacation 1%
- Roth IRA — 5%
- Credit Card
  - Regular bills (Netflix, gym)
  - Guilt-free spending
- Miscellaneous Bills
  - Bills that can't be paid on credit cards (rent, utilities)

Note: For simplicity, this diagram does not include taxes.

your spending and savings. First—and this is different from the Conscious Spending Plan—you'll need to figure out how much you need to survive on each month. This is the bare minimum: rent, utilities, food, loan payments—just the basics. Those are your bare-bones monthly necessities.

Now, back to the Conscious Spending Plan. Add a savings goal of three months of bare-bones income before you do any investing. For example, if you need at least $1,500/month to live on, you'll need to have $4,500 in a savings buffer, which you can use to smooth out months where you don't generate much income. The buffer should exist as a sub-account in your savings account. To fund it, use money from two places: First, forget about investing while you're setting up the buffer, and instead take any money you would have invested and send it to your savings account. Second, in good months, any extra dollar you make should go into your buffer savings.

Once you've saved up three months of money as a cushion, congratulations! Now go back to a normal Conscious Spending Plan where you send money to investing accounts. Because you're self-employed, you probably don't have access to a traditional 401(k), but you should look into a Solo 401(k) and SEP-IRA, which are great alternatives. Just keep in mind that it's probably wise to sock away a little more into your savings account in good months to make up for the less profitable ones.

I also recommend using www.youneedabudget.com as a planning tool if you have an irregular income. Jesse Mecham, the founder, is a friend of mine, and he's created a system that lets you spend money based on what you made *last* month—helpful if you don't know what you're going to make *next* month.

YOUR MONEY IS NOW AUTOMATIC

Congratulations! Your money management is now on autopilot. Not only are your bills paid automatically and on time, but you're actually saving and investing money each month. The beauty of this system is that it works without your involvement and it's flexible enough to add or remove accounts any time. You're accumulating money *by default*.

You might be wondering what's going to happen with the investment money. Right now, it's growing each month as you contribute to your 401(k) and Roth IRA, but it's just sitting there. You need to put it to work by investing it in something. In the next chapter, we'll talk about how you can become your own investment expert and how to go about getting the best return on your investment money.

ACTION STEPS

WEEK FIVE

1 **List all your accounts in one place (one hour).** As you start linking accounts to one another, you'll need to log in to all of them. Make your life easier by getting all the login information in one place. You'll be tweaking your accounts over the next few months, so save all the login information somewhere that you can access from home and work.

---

2 **Link your accounts together (three to five days).** To set up your Automatic Money Flow, the first step is linking accounts together. The links are free and electronic, but allow three to five days for the accounts to verify the links.

---

3 **Set up your Automatic Money Flow (five hours).** Once your accounts are linked together, set up the core of your Automatic Money Flow: automatic payments. Your system will automatically send money to your investing accounts, your savings account, and your fixed costs, and leave you money for guilt-free spending. Remember, you'll want to reset your billing cycles so you can create a well-timed Automatic Money Flow.

CHAPTER 6

THE MYTH OF FINANCIAL EXPERTISE

*Why professional wine tasters and stock pickers
are clueless—and how you can beat them*

I f I invited you to a blind taste test of a $12 wine versus a $1,200 wine, could you tell the difference? I bet you $20 you couldn't.

In 2001, Frederic Brochet, a researcher at the University of Bordeaux, ran a study that sent shock waves through the wine industry. Determined to understand how wine drinkers decided which wines they liked, he invited fifty-seven recognized experts to evaluate two wines: one red, one white.

After tasting the two wines, the experts described the red wine as *intense, deep,* and *spicy*—words commonly used to describe red wines. The white was described in equally standard terms: *lively, fresh,* and *floral.* But what none of these experts picked up on was that the two wines were *exactly the same wine.* Even more damning, the wines were actually *both* white wine—the "red wine" had been colored with food coloring.

Think about that for a second. Fifty-seven wine experts couldn't even tell they were drinking two identical wines.

There's something we need to talk about when it comes to experts.

Americans love experts. We feel comforted when we see a tall, uniformed pilot behind the controls of a plane. We trust our doctors to prescribe the right medications, we're confident that our lawyers will steer us right through legal tangles, and we devour the words of the talking heads in the media. We're taught that experts deserve to be compensated for their training and experience. After all, we wouldn't hire someone off the street to build a house or remove our wisdom teeth, would we?

ALL OUR LIVES, WE'VE BEEN TAUGHT TO DEFER TO EXPERTS... BUT ULTIMATELY, EXPERTISE IS ABOUT RESULTS.

All our lives, we've been taught to defer to experts: teachers, doctors, and investment "professionals." But ultimately, expertise is about results. You can have the fanciest degrees from the fanciest schools, but if you can't perform what you were hired to do, your expertise is meaningless. In our culture of worshipping experts, what have the results been? When it comes to finances in America, they're pretty dismal. We've earned failing grades in financial literacy—in 2008, high school seniors correctly answered a gloomy 48 percent of questions on the Jumpstart Coalition's national financial literacy survey, while college seniors answered only 65 percent right. We think "investing" is about guessing the next best stock. Instead of enriching ourselves by saving and investing, most American households are in debt. And the wizards of Wall Street can't even manage their own companes' risk. Something's not right here: Our financial experts are failing us.

When it comes to investing, it's easy to get overwhelmed by all the options: small-, mid-, and large-cap stocks; REITS; bonds; growth, value, or blend funds—not to mention factoring in expense ratios, interest rates, allocation goals, and diversification. That's why so many people say, "Can't I just hire someone to do this for me?" This is a maddening question because, in fact, financial experts—in particular, fund managers and anyone who attempts to predict the market—are often no better than amateurs. They're often *worse*. The vast majority of twentysomethings can earn more than the so-called "experts" by investing on their own.

No financial adviser. No fund manager. Just automatic investments in low-cost funds (which I'll get to in the next chapter). So, for the average investor, the value of financial expertise is a myth. There are several reasons for this that I'll detail below, but I urge you to think about how you treat the experts in your life. Do they deserve to be put on a pedestal? Do they deserve tens of thousands of your dollars in fees? If so, what kind of performance do you demand of them?

In truth, being rich is within *your* control, not some expert's. How rich you are depends on the amount you're able to save and on your investment plan. But acknowledging this fact takes guts, because it means admitting that there's no one else to blame if you're not rich—no advisers, no complicated investment strategy, no "market conditions." But it also means that you control exactly what happens to you and your money over the long term.

You know what the most fun part of this book is for me? No, it's not the personal-finance groupies that I constantly wish I had. It's the disbelieving e-mails I'm going to get after people read this chapter. Whenever I point out how people waste their money by investing in expensive mutual funds or by relying on a financial adviser who generates below-market returns, I get e-mails that say, "You're full of it." Or they say, "There's no way that's true—just look at my investment returns," not really understanding how much they've made after factoring in taxes and fees. But surely they *must* be making great returns because they wouldn't continue investing if they weren't making lots of money . . . right?

In this chapter, I'm going to show you how you can actually outperform the financial pundits by sidestepping their "expertise" (and fees) and taking the simplest approach to investing. It's not easy to learn that reliance on so-called "experts" is largely ineffective, but stick with me. I've got the data to back it up, and I'll show you a simple way to invest on your own.

Experts Can't Guess Where the Market Is Going

Before we move on to discuss how you can beat the experts, let's look a little more deeply into how they operate and why their advice so often misses the mark.

The most visible financial "experts" are the financial pundits and portfolio managers (the people who choose the specific stocks in mutual funds). They love to regale us with their predictions about where the market is going: Up! Down! They go on and on about how interest rates and oil production and a butterfly flapping its wings in China will affect the stock market. This forecasting is called timing the market. But the truth is they simply cannot predict how high, how low, or even which direction the market will go. I get e-mails from people wondering what I think about oil, currency markets, or Google every single day. Who knows about those things? I certainly don't, especially in the short term. Unfortunately, the fact is that nobody can predict where the market is going. Still, the talking heads on TV make grandiose predictions every day, and whether they're right or wrong, they're never held accountable for them.

The media feeds off every little market fluctuation. On one day, the pundits are spreading gloom and doom about a multi-hundred-point loss in the market. Then, three days later, the front page is filled with images of hope and unicorns as the market climbs 500 points. It's riveting to watch, but step back and ask yourself, "Am I learning anything from this? Or am I just being overwhelmed by information about the market going up one day and down another?" More information is not always good, especially when it's not actionable and causes you to make errors in your investing. The key takeaway here is to ignore any predictions that pundits make. They simply do not know what will happen in the future.

Even though you'd think they'd know better, fund managers also fall prey to financial hype. You can see this in the trading patterns of funds themselves: Mutual funds "turn over" stocks frequently, meaning they buy and sell funds a lot (incurring trading fees and, if held outside a tax-advantaged account, taxes for you). The managers chase the latest hot stock, confident of their abilities to spot something that millions of others have not. What's more, they also demand extraordinary compensation. Get this: In 2006, the average Goldman Sachs employee made $622,000. That's not a typo—it's the *average amount* Goldman employees made with salary and bonuses. Despite this astronomical compensation, fund managers from all companies still fail to beat the market *75 percent of the time.*

"But Ramit," you might say, "my fund is different. The manager returned 80 percent over the last two years!" That's great, but just because someone beat the market for a year or two doesn't mean they'll beat the market the next year. Think back to the year 2000. If you had

More Examples of How "Experts" Can't Time the Market

Pundits and television shows know exactly how to get our attention: with flashy graphics, loud talking heads, and bold predictions about the market that may or may not (in fact, probably not) come true. These may be entertaining, but let's look at some actual data.

Recently, Helpburn Capital studied the performance of the S&P 500 from 1983 to 2003, during which time the annualized return of the stock market was 10.01 percent. They noted something amazing: During that twenty-year period, if you missed the best twenty days of investing (the days where the stock market gained the most points), your return would have dropped from 10.01 percent to 5.03 percent. And if you missed the best *forty* days of investing, your returns would equal only 1.6 percent— a pitiful payback on your money. Unfortunately, we can't know the best investing days ahead of time. The only long-term solution is to invest regularly, putting as much money as possible into low-cost, diversified funds, even in an economic downturn.

USELESS NEWSLETTERS. A 1996 study by John Graham and Campbell Harvey investigated more than two hundred market-timing newsletters. The results were, shall we say, unimpressive. "We find that the newsletters fail to offer advice consistent with market timing," the authors deadpanned as only academics can. Hilariously, by the end of the 12.5-year period they studied, 94.5 percent of the newsletters had gone out of business. Not only did these market-timing newsletters fail to accurately predict what would happen, but they couldn't even keep their own doors open. Get a life, market timers.

I'll end with a couple of more recent examples. In December 2007, *Fortune* published an article called "The Best Stocks for 2008," which contained a special entry: Merrill Lynch. "Smart investors should buy this stock before everyone else comes to their senses," they advised. They obviously weren't counting on it being sold in a fire sale a few months later. And in April 2008, *BusinessWeek* advised us, "Don't be leery of Lehman." I'm not sure about you guys, but I'm leery of worthless risky advice couched in cute alliteration. I think I'll ignore you from now on, pundits.

looked at the fifty best-returning funds then, exactly zero would have been on the same list in 1998 or 1999. And if I asked you to name the best stocks of the past ten years, you might select Apple—but would you have guessed Oshkosh Truck? What about Gilead Sciences? Holly Corp?

> **DESPITE THEIR ASTRONOMICAL COMPENSATION, FUND MANAGERS FAIL TO BEAT THE MARKET 75 PERCENT OF THE TIME.**

The problem is that nobody can consistently guess which funds or stocks will outperform, or even match, the market over time. Anyone who claims they can is lying.

So ignore the pundits' predictions. Ignore the last year or two of a fund's performance. A fund manager may be able to perform very well over the short term. But over the long term he will almost never beat the market—because of expenses, fees, and the growing mathematical difficulty of picking outperforming stocks (more on that later in this chapter). When you're evaluating a fund, the only way to really gauge it is by looking at its track record for the last ten years or more.

How Financial Experts Hide Poor Performance

As I've shown, the "experts" are often wrong and fail to beat the market, but even more irritatingly, they know how to cover their tracks so we don't catch on to their failures. In fact, the financial industry—including both companies that administer mutual funds and so-called experts—are sneakier than you'd imagine.

One of the biggest tricks they use is to never admit they were wrong. Daniel Solin, author of *The Smartest Investment Book You'll Ever Read,* describes a study that illustrates how financial-ratings companies like Morningstar, which provides stock ratings that investors can use to get a quick take on many stocks' performance, continue to give thumbs-up ratings even as the companies they purport to be evaluating crater and lose billions of dollars of shareholder value. (Aside from their stock

Three Legendary Investors Who Prove Me Wrong—Sort of

Now, there are indeed investors who have beaten the market consistently for years. Warren Buffett, for example, has produced a 22 percent annualized return over forty years. Peter Lynch of Fidelity returned 29 percent over thirteen years. And Yale's David Swensen has returned more than 16 percent over twenty-three years. They have phenomenal investing skills and have earned their titles as some of the best investors in the world. But just because these guys can consistently beat the market doesn't mean you or I can.

Yes, theoretically, it is possible to consistently beat the market (which typically returns around 8 percent after you account for inflation) in the same way it is *possible* for me to become a heavyweight boxing champion. With millions of people around the globe trying to beat the market, statistically there are bound to be a few extreme outliers. Who knows whether their success is due to statistics or skill? But even the experts themselves agree that individual investors shouldn't expect to equal their returns. Swensen, for example, has explained that he achieves outsize returns because of top-notch professional resources, but more important, access to investments that you and I will never have, such as the very best venture capital and hedge funds, which he can use to bolster his asset allocation. Swensen recently told the *Financial Post* about his resources versus the average investor's: "I've got 20 professionals here in New Haven devoting their careers to identifying high-quality active management opportunities," he said. "An individual who devotes a couple of hours a week in the evening, at most, trying to compete with institutions that have armies of people out there? It just doesn't make sense."

ratings, they do have an excellent website with tools that I use all the time. So it's not like they're all bad.) The study found the following:

> *Forty-seven of the fifty [advisory] firms continued to advise investors to buy or hold shares in the companies up to the date the companies filed for bankruptcy.*

Twelve of the nineteen companies continued to receive "buy" or "hold" ratings on the actual date they filed for bankruptcy.

Companies like Moody's and Morningstar offer ratings of stocks and funds that are supposedly simple reflections of their value, but the idea of Morningstar's five-star ratings is actually complete nonsense. Why? For two reasons:

First, receiving five golden stars doesn't actually predict success. A 1999 study by researchers Christopher Blake and Matthew Morey showed that although the low-star ratings were on target in predicting poor-performing stocks, the high-star ratings were not accurate. They wrote: "[F]or the most part, there is little statistical evidence that Morningstar's highest-rated funds outperform the next-to-highest and median-rated fund." Just because a company assigns five shiny stars to a fund does not mean it will perform well.

A number of mutual-fund management complexes employ the practice of starting "incubator" funds. A complex may start ten small new equity funds with different in-house managers and wait to see which ones are successful. Suppose after a few years only three funds produce total returns better than the broad-market averages. The complex begins to market those successful funds aggressively, dropping the other seven and burying their records.

—BURTON G. MALKIEL, *A RANDOM WALK DOWN WALL STREET*

Second, when it comes to fund ratings, companies rely on something called *survivorship bias* to obscure the picture of how well a company is doing. Survivorship bias exists because funds that fail are not included in any future studies of fund performance for the simple reason that they don't exist anymore. For example, a company may start a hundred funds, but have only fifty left a couple of years later. The company can trumpet how effective their fifty funds are, but ignore the fifty funds that failed and have been erased from history. In other words, when you see "Best 10 Funds!" pages on mutual-fund websites and in magazines, it's just as important to think about what you *aren't* seeing as what you are: The funds on that page are the ones that didn't close down. Out of that pool of already successful funds, *of course* there will be some five-star funds.

Financial companies know very well about survivorship bias, but they care more about having a page full of funds with great performance numbers than revealing the whole truth. As a result, they've consciously created several ways to test funds quickly and market only the best-performing ones, thus ensuring their reputation as the brand with the "best" funds.

How to Engineer a Perfect Stock-Picking Record

Since we know it's almost impossible to beat the market over the long term, let's turn to probability and luck to explain why some funds seem irresistibly compelling. Although a fund manager might be lucky for one, two, or even three years, it's mathematically unlikely he'll continue beating the market. To examine probability theory, let's take a simple example of an unscrupulous scammer who wants to sell his financial services to some naive investors.

He e-mails 10,000 people, half of whom are told that Stock A will go up, the other half Stock B. "This is just a freebie e-mail to demonstrate my insider knowledge," he might say. After a couple of weeks, he notices that Stock A has indeed gone up by chance. He eliminates the Stock B group and focuses on the Stock A group, e-mailing them an "I told you so" e-mail. This time, he splits the mailing in half again. Twenty-five hundred people are told about Stock C and 2,500 are told about Stock D. If either C or D goes up, on the next cycle, at least 1,250 people will have seen him pick two stocks successfully. And each cycle will make the recipients increasingly awed by his "ability."

Because we like to create order where there is none, we will ascribe magical stock-picking abilities to the scammer—even though it was literally by chance—and buy whatever "investment success kit" he's selling. The same is true of the pages of "five-star funds" you see. Moral of the story: Don't trust purported financial expertise just because of a few impressive stats.

Pundits Worth Reading

Q: *What are your favorite personal-finance blogs?*

A: Despite all my criticism of pathetic pundits who don't know what they're talking about, there are still people who provide a fresh perspective on money issues. Here are three of my favorite bloggers.

Get Rich Slowly (www.getrichslowly.org/blog), by J. D. Roth, is a great blog covering the basics of personal finance. With a name like that, you can imagine that J. D. believes in long-term growth. He writes about managing money, investing, and even starting a side job.

The Simple Dollar (www.thesimpledollar.com) is written by Trent Hamm. He covers the saving, investing, and debt sides of personal finance. He's got great book reviews and posts about regular financial situations that people like you and I find ourselves in all the time. Plus, he posts a lot.

JLP at AllFinancialMatters (http://allfinancialmatters. com) does an excellent job of using charts and data to show how low-cost investing beats brokers. JLP is usually pretty laid back, but occasionally he loses it and can't resist calling out financial companies that take advantage of regular people (those are my favorite posts).

I also keep a public list of *all* my personal-finance bookmarks at http://delicious.com/ramitsethi/finance.

These tricks are especially insidious because you'd never know to look out for them. When you see a page full of funds with 15 percent returns, you naturally assume they'll keep giving you 15 percent returns in the future. And it's even better if they have five-star ratings from a trusted company like Morningstar. But now that we know about survivorship bias and the fact that most ratings are meaningless, it's easy to see that financial "experts" and companies are just looking to fatten their wallets, not ensure that you get the best return for your money.

I Bet You Don't Need a Financial Adviser

You've heard my rants against the media hype surrounding investment and the poor performance of most professional investors. Now there's one more category of financial professionals that I want to warn you about: financial advisers.

Some of you might say, "But Ramit, I don't have time to invest! Can't I just use a financial adviser?" Ah, yes, the old outsourcing argument. We outsource our car cleaning, laundry, and housekeeping. So why not the management of our money?

Most young people don't need a financial adviser. We have such simple needs that with a little bit of time (a few hours a week over the course of, say, six weeks) we can get an automatic personal-finance infrastructure working for us.

Plus, financial advisers don't always look out for your interests. They're supposed to help you make the right decisions about your money, but keep in mind that they're actually not obligated to do what's best for you. Some of them will give you very good advice, but many of them are pretty useless.

SOME FINANCIAL ADVISERS WILL GIVE YOU GOOD ADVICE, BUT MANY ARE PRETTY USELESS.

If they're paid on commission, they usually will direct you to expensive, bloated funds to earn their commissions. By contrast, fee-based financial advisers simply charge a flat fee and are much more reputable. (Neither is necessarily better at providing good investment returns, or your top line; they simply charge differently, affecting your bottom line.)

The key takeaway is that most people don't actually need a financial adviser—you can do it all on your own and come out ahead. But if your choice is between hiring a financial adviser or not investing at all, then sure, you should hire one. People with really complex financial situations, those who have inherited significant amounts of money, and those who truly are too busy to learn about investing for themselves also should consider seeking an adviser's help. It's better to pay a little and get started investing than to not start at all. If you're determined

So You Really Think You Need a Financial Adviser?

If you really want to look into hiring a financial adviser, here's an introductory e-mail you can adapt and send:

Hi, Mike,

I'm looking for a fee-based financial planner, and I found you on www.napfa.org. A little bit about me: I'm twenty-six and have about $10,000 in total assets—$3,000 in a Roth IRA (uninvested), $3,000 in a 401(k), and $4,000 in cash. I don't need the money any time soon, so I'm looking for investments that will maximize long-term returns while minimizing costs.

If you think you can help me, I'd like to meet for half an hour and ask you some specific questions. I'd also like to hear details on other situations in which you've worked with similar people with similar goals. Would next Friday, 2/6, at 2 P.M., work at your office? Alternatively, Monday, 2/9, is wide open for me.

Thanks, Ramit

For your thirty-minute meeting—which shouldn't cost you anything—you'll want to come prepared with questions. There are hundreds of sample questions available online (search for "financial adviser questions"), but at the very least, ask these three:

- How do you make your money? Is it through commission or strictly fee based? Are there any other fees? *(You want a fee-based adviser with no hidden fees.)*

- Have you worked with other people like me in similar situations? What general solutions did you recommend? *(Get references and call them.)*

- What's your working style? Do we talk regularly or do I work with an assistant? *(You want to know what to expect in the first thirty days, sixty days, and ninety days.)*

to get professional help, begin your search at the National Association of Personal Financial Advisors (www.napfa.org). These advisers are fee based (they usually have an hourly rate), not commission based, meaning that they want to help you, not profit off their recommendations.

But remember, many people use financial advisers as a crutch and end up paying tens of thousands of dollars over their lifetime simply because they didn't spend a few hours learning about investing. If you don't learn to manage your money in your twenties, you'll cost yourself a ton one way or another—whether you do nothing, or pay someone exorbitant fees to "manage" your money.

After seeing for four years that my financial planner wasn't providing any special return on my investment, but costing me 1.5 percent in fees each year, I made the decision to open an online brokerage account and take charge of my money.

—**SARAH PURA**, 24

Active vs. Passive Management

Please know that even with all of this doom and gloom about professional investor performance, I'm not in any way saying that investing is a waste of money. You just have to know where to invest.

Mutual funds—which are simply collections of stocks (and sometimes bonds, but usually just stocks)—are often considered the simplest and best way for most people to invest. But, as we've seen, fund managers fail to beat the market 75 percent of the time, and it can be hard to tell which funds will actually perform well over the long term. And no matter how good a mutual fund is, the returns are hampered by the large fees they charge. (Sure, there are some low-cost mutual funds, but because of the way they compensate their own portfolio managers and other employees, it's virtually impossible for them to compete with the low costs of passively managed index funds, which I'll talk more about in a minute.)

When it comes to investing, fees are a huge drag on your returns. This is a little counterintuitive since we're used to paying for service, like our gym membership or admission to Disneyland. If we're getting something out of it, we should pay a fair price, right? The key is *fair,* and many of the financial "experts" we turn to for guidance make an effort to squeeze every last cent out of us.

You see, mutual funds use something called "active management." This means a portfolio manager actively tries to pick the best stocks and give you the best return. Sounds good, right? But even with all the fancy analysts and technology they employ, portfolio managers still make fundamentally human mistakes like selling too quickly, trading too much, and making rash guesses. These fund managers trade frequently so they can show short-term results to their shareholders and prove they're doing something—anything!—to earn your money. Not only do they usually fail to beat the market, but they charge a fee to do this. Mutual funds typically charge 1.5 to 3 percent of assets managed each year. (This percentage is known as a fund's expense ratio.) In other words, with a 2 percent expense ratio and a $10,000 portfolio, you'd pay $200 per year in fees. Some funds even tack on additional sales charges, or "loads," to the purchase price (a front-end load) or sales price (back-end load) of the fund. These are just some of the tricky ways mutual fund managers make money whether they perform or not.

> ## NOT ONLY DO MOST FUND MANAGERS FAIL TO BEAT THE MARKET, THEY CHARGE A FEE TO DO THIS.

Two percent doesn't sound like much until you compare it with the alternative: "passive management." This is how index funds (a cousin of mutual funds) are run. These funds work by replacing portfolio managers with computers. The computers don't attempt to find the hottest stock. They simply and methodically pick the same stocks that an index holds—for example, the five hundred stocks in the S&P 500—in an attempt to match the market. (An index is a way to measure part of the stock market. For example, the NASDAQ index represents certain technology stocks, while the S&P 500 represents 500 large U.S. stocks. There are international indexes and even retail indexes.)

Most index funds stay close to the market (or to the segment of the market they represent). Just as the stock market may fall 10 percent one year and gain 18 percent the next year, index funds will rise and fall with the indexes they track. The big difference is in fees: Index funds have lower fees than mutual funds because there's no expensive staff to pay. Vanguard's S&P 500 index fund, for example, has an expense ratio of 0.18 percent.

Remember, there are all kinds of index funds. International index funds are relatively volatile since they follow indexes that were just recently established. General U.S.-based index funds, on the other hand, are more reliable. Since they match the U.S. stock market, if the market goes down, index funds will also go down. During the financial crisis, many index funds plummeted as they matched the market, which underwent a global drop. But over the long term, the overall stock market has consistently returned about 8 percent.

Let's look at the performance from two sides: the downside (fees) and the upside (returns). First, let's compare the fees for a passively managed fund with those for an actively managed fund.

WHAT'S A BETTER DEAL?

Assuming an 8% return on an investment of $100/month	Passively managed index fund (0.18% expense ratio)	Actively managed mutual fund (2% expense ratio)	Investors pay how much more in fees with an actively managed fund?
After 5 years, you have ...	$14,780.52	$13,488.50	$1,292.02
After 10 years, you have ...	$21,846.38	$18,193.97	$3,652.41
After 25 years, you have ...	$70,542.13	$44,649.70	$25,892.43

If your decision was determined by fees alone, index funds would be the clear choice. But let's also consider another important factor: returns.

Despite my hammering home the fact that mutual funds fail to beat the market 75 percent of the time, I will say that they do occasionally provide great returns. In some years, some mutual funds do extraordinarily well and far outperform index funds. In a good year, for example, a fund focused on Russian stocks might return 70 percent—but one or two years of great performance only gets you so far. What you really want is solid, long-term returns. So, if you're thinking about using a broker or actively managed fund, call them and ask them a simple, point-blank question: "What were your after-tax, after-fee returns for the last ten, fifteen, and twenty years?" Yes, their response must include all fees and taxes. Yes, the return must be at least ten years, because the last five years of any time period are too volatile to matter. And yes, I promise they won't give you a straight answer, because that would be admitting that they didn't beat the market consistently. It's *that* hard to do.

So, the safe assumption is that actively managed funds will too often fail to beat or match the market. In other words, if the market returns 8 percent, actively managed funds won't return at least 8 percent more than three-fourths of the time. In addition, when combined with their high expense ratios, actively managed funds have to outperform cheaper, passively managed funds by at least 2 or 3 percent just to break even with them—and that simply doesn't happen.

In his book *The Smartest Investment Book You'll Ever Read,* Daniel Solin cites a study conducted by Professor Edward S. O'Neal from the Babcock Graduate School of Management. O'Neal tracked funds whose sole purpose was to beat the market. What he discovered was that from 1993 through 1998, less than half of these actively managed funds beat the market. And from 1998 through 2003, only 8 percent beat the market. But there's more. When he looked at the number of funds that beat the market in *both* time periods, the results were "sad indeed. The number of funds that beat the market in both periods was a whopping ten—or only 2 percent of all large-cap funds . . . Investors, both individual and institutional, and particularly 401(k) plans, would be far better served by investing in passive or passively managed funds than in trying to pick more expensive active managers who purport to be able to beat the markets."

Bottom line: There's no reason to pay exorbitant fees for active management when you could do better, for cheaper, on your own.

Now that you've read about the myth of expertise, it's time to see exactly how you can invest your own money to get better returns for lower cost. In the next chapter, I'll teach you everything you need to know about investing, and we'll cover all the technical aspects of selecting and automating your investments. Let's do this.

P.S.—If you're looking for Action Steps, keep reading. This chapter is informational but in the next section you'll make some major decisons.

CHAPTER 7

INVESTING ISN'T ONLY FOR RICH PEOPLE

Spend the afternoon picking a simple portfolio that will make you rich

In the previous chapter, you read about how useless investing "experts" are—and how we can do better on our own. Now we've arrived at the Promised Land, the chapter where you'll learn how to choose your own investments, pay less in fees, and get superior performance. You're going to determine your investing style by asking yourself some key questions: Do you need your money next year or can you let it grow for a while? Are you saving up for a house? Can you withstand big day-to-day changes in the stock market, or do they make you queasy? Then you're going to research funds and pick exactly the right investments to meet your goals. This includes all your investment accounts, like your 401(k) and Roth IRA. (When someone boasts, "I have $50,000 in my portfolio," which they

(continued on page 162)

159

What's Your Investor Profile?

Do you sweat like Patrick Ewing when you look at your investment returns? Do you have a robotic, emotionless demeanor when surveying gains or losses? Take this quiz to determine your investment personality:

1. YOU TURN ON YOUR COMPUTER AND LEARN THAT THE MARKET HAS LOST 350 POINTS. YOU:

a. Laugh at the fools who track day-to-day changes and go watch *The Daily Show.*

b. Get a little nervous, log in to your investment account to check out your portfolio, and decide to sit tight and ride it out.

c. Feel your heart start to race, bite off your fingernails, log in to your account, and scream, "Sell, sell, sell!" while clicking furiously.

2. IF SOMEONE ASKED YOU WHEN YOU'D NEED THE MONEY YOU'RE INVESTING, YOU'D SAY . . .

a. "Maybe when I have wrinkles all over, a gleaming white yacht, and a twenty-five-year-old girlfriend who feeds me peeled grapes."

b. "Probably some time in the next five to fifteen years."

c. "I want it there whenever I need it, like within the next three to five years."

3. HOW DO YOU WANT TO HANDLE YOUR INVESTMENTS?

a. You want to optimize every asset of your investments and tweak your asset allocation to exactly what you want.

b. You know you should do something with your money but aren't sure yet exactly what.

c. Can't someone please handle this for me?

IF YOU CHOSE MOSTLY (A) ANSWERS, you're a type-A power investor who's focused on the long term. You're willing to give up convenience in exchange for control over every aspect of your portfolio. I recommend you pick your own asset allocation through index funds. See how on page 188.

IF YOU CHOSE MOSTLY (B)S, you're like most people reading this book: You don't need your money for the next few years, but after that, it's hard to tell what you'll need. You know you should do *something* to invest but it's not clear what—and you don't want to spend your life managing your money. This is actually a great position to be in because, while most people will give in to inertia and do nothing, you can take action. You're a perfect candidate for the 85 Percent Solution: You just want to invest and let your money grow without having to think about or monitor it all the time. I recommend a lifecycle fund (see page 180) so you can invest and get on with your life.

IF YOU CHOSE MOSTLY (C)S, you need to get your head on straight. It's one thing to be conservative—if you're afraid of losing money, you can pick investments that limit your exposure (such as a lifecycle fund that's geared toward someone a few years older than you, or a heavier emphasis on more stable, large-cap funds in your portfolio). But the more common problem is that you haven't given investing much thought at all! You want to invest and get your money out in three to five years? What the hell is wrong with you? Nobody can consistently make money in the short term.

More typically, people who answered (c) haven't invested at all. Confusion and fear of losing money gets in the way. Let's be clear: If you're not investing, in the long term you're losing money every day. It actually costs you money to park your money in a savings account as inflation eats into your earnings. Look at the chart on page 5 to see why investing makes such a difference—especially when you start early. If you're truly risk-averse, you can always balance your portfolio with more conservative investments. But don't succumb to irrational fear and not invest at all. Ironically, the people who do that are the ones who end up without enough money in the end. Check out the chart on page 75 and see why it pays to start investing today.

(continued from page 159)

would say only if they were a jackass, they're probably referring to money in their 401(k), Roth IRA, and perhaps even other investment accounts.) By the end of this chapter, you'll know exactly what to invest in—and why. And you'll do it with minimal human involvement, incurring minimal expense.

My goal for this chapter is to help you pick the simplest investment to get started—and to make your portfolio easy to maintain. By doing just those two things, you'll be on the way to getting rich. Another benefit is that you will, quite simply, become a cooler person than all of your friends. Hey, I can't deny it. You'll realize that your friend who makes $50,000 a year has no savings or investments. You'll start noticing the excuses people make to justify not investing, including "I don't have time" and "Stocks can go down, and I don't want to lose my money." Most people don't know the first thing about how to pick investments—but now you will! Ah, the Promised Land is sweet.

A Better Way to Invest: Automatic Investing

L et's be honest. Nobody really loves managing their money. I'd rather be *using* my money, like eating at Taco Bell or flying to New York to hang out with friends. Basically, I'm always on the lookout for ways to spend less time and get better results. When I was in high school and applying to colleges, for example, I created a system to write three scholarship applications per day and ended up winning more than $200,000 in six months to pay for school. These days, I manage more than seven hundred e-mails per day about PBwiki, my blog, and this book. This isn't to brag about how busy I am, but to show that when it comes to money, I'm very, very interested in paying less attention while getting better returns. I've taken pains to research investments that don't take lots of time to maintain and also pay off. That's why I urge you to combine a classic low-cost investing strategy with automation.

Automatic Investing is not some revolutionary technique that I just invented. It's a simple way of investing in low-cost funds that is recommended by Nobel laureates, billionaire investors such as Warren

Buffett, and most academics. It involves spending most of your time choosing how your money will be distributed in your portfolio, picking the investments (this actually takes the least amount of time), and then automating your regular investments so you can sit and watch TV while growing your money. Hey, we're lazy. We might as well embrace it and use it to our advantage.

Automatic Investing works for two reasons:

LOWER EXPENSES. As I discussed in Chapter 6, nothing kills your investment performance more than expensive funds that invisibly drain your returns. Investing in them is especially ridiculous when you can earn better returns with lower fees. Why would you pay for the privilege of losing your money? With Automatic Investing, you invest in low-cost funds—which replace worthless, expensive portfolio managers—and you save tens of thousands of dollars in trading fees, taxes, and overall investment expenses, outperforming most investors.

IT'S AUTOMATIC. Automatic Investing frees you from having to pay attention to the latest "hot stock" or micro-change in the market. You pick a simple investment plan that doesn't involve any sexy stocks or guessing whether the market is going up or down, and then set up automatic contributions to your investment accounts. In this way, you effectively trick yourself into investing because it requires no work from you. This means you can focus on living your life—doing your job well, spending time with friends, traveling to different countries, eating at great restaurants—instead of worrying about your money. I might well call this Zen Investing for People Who Have Real Lives. (And that is why I'll never be a naming consultant.)

TOO GOOD TO BE TRUE? The way I described Automatic Investing was basically the same as saying, "Puppies are cute." Nobody would ever disagree with it. Automatic Investing sounds perfect, but what happens when the market goes down? It's not as easy to go along for the ride then. For example, I know several people who had automatic investment plans and when the stock market incurred huge losses in late 2008, they immediately canceled their investments and took their money out of the market. Big mistake. The test of a real Automatic Investor is not when things are going up, but when they are going down. It takes strength to know that you're basically getting shares on sale—and, if you're investing for the long term, the best time to make money is when everyone else is getting out of the market.

Do You Believe Everything Your Friends Tell You?

Q: *My friends tell me that investing is too risky and that I could lose all my money. Is that true?*

A: That's an instinctive, emotional reaction, not a well-reasoned, logical response. But you have to admit: It does make sense to be scared of investing right now, especially if you don't understand how it works. With headlines screaming about sharp drops, it's easy to practice the "DNA" style of investing—the Do Nothing Approach. It's very unfortunate that the very same people who are afraid of investing in the market right now are usually the same people who buy when prices are soaring. As Warren Buffett has said, investors should "be fearful when others are greedy and greedy when others are fearful."

For you, it's different. You understand how investing works, so you can put a long-term perspective into practice. Yes, in theory it's possible for you to lose all your money, but if you've bought different investments to create a balanced (or "diversified") portfolio, you won't.

You'll notice that your friends are concerned with the downside: "You could lose everything! How will you have time to learn to invest? There are so many sharks out there to take your money."

What about the downside of the money they're losing every day by not investing?

Ask your friends what the average return of the S&P 500 has been for the past seventy years. How much money would they have if they invested $10,000 today and didn't touch it for ten years—or fifty years? They won't know because they don't even know the basic return rate to assume (try 8 percent). When people say investing is too risky, it's because they don't know what they don't know.

BOTTOM LINE: Automatic Investing may not seem as sexy as trading in hedge funds and biotech stocks, but it works a lot better. Again, would you rather be sexy or rich?

More Convenience or More Control: You Choose

I want investing to be as painless as possible for you, so here's what I'm going to do: I'll give you an easy version and a more advanced version. If you're the kind of person who wants your money to grow with the least possible effort on your part and you don't care about all the theory, turn to page 180. There you'll find a step-by-step guide for picking a single investment—a lifecycle fund—and you'll get started investing in just a few hours.

But if you're a Type A nerd like me who wants to learn how it works—and maybe even customize your own portfolio for more control—read on. I'll walk you through the building blocks of a portfolio, and I'll help you construct a portfolio that's both aggressive and balanced.

Investing Is Not About Picking Stocks

Really, it's not. Ask your friends what they think investing means and I bet they'll say, "Picking stocks." Guys, you cannot reliably pick stocks that will outperform the market over the long term. It's way too easy to make mistakes such as being overconfident about choices or panicking when your investments drop even a little. As we saw in Chapter 6, even experts can't guess what will happen to the stock market. Because they've heard it repeatedly from the many investment magazines and TV shows, people think that investing is about picking winning stocks and that anyone can be successful. They can't. I hate to say it, but not everyone is a winner. In fact, most of these so-called financial "experts" are failures.

Actually, I don't hate saying that. I'll say that to their faces again and again. Yeah, I'm a frail Indian man throwing verbal punches here on page 165 of a personal-finance book. This is how battles should be fought.

Anyway, the little-known but true fact is that the major predictor of your portfolio's volatility is not due, as most people think, to the individual stocks you pick, but instead your *mix* of stocks and bonds. In 1986, researchers Gary Brinson, Randolph Hood, and Gilbert Beebower published a study in the *Financial Analysts Journal* that rocked the financial world. They demonstrated that more than 90 percent of your portfolio's volatility is a result of your asset allocation. I know *asset allocation* sounds like a B.S. phrase—like *mission statement* and *strategic alliance*. But it's not. Asset allocation is your plan for investing, the way you organize the investments in your portfolio between stocks, bonds, and cash. In other words, by diversifying your investments across different asset classes (like stocks and bonds, or, better yet, stock funds and bond funds), you could control the risk in your portfolio—and therefore control how much money, on average, you'd lose due to volatility. It turns out that the amounts you buy—whether it's 100 percent stocks or 90 percent stocks and 10 percent bonds—make a profound difference on your returns. Later, other researchers tried to measure how closely *volatility* and *returns* were correlated, but the answer ends up being pretty complicated. Suffice it to say that asset allocation is the most significant part of your portfolio that you can control.

Think about that remarkable fact: *Your investment plan is more important than your actual investments.*

Take, for example, this book. If we apply the same principle here, it means that the way I organized this book is more important than any given word in it. That makes sense, right? Well, the same is true of investing. If you allocate your money properly—for example, not all in one stock, but spread out across different kinds of funds—you won't have to worry about a single stock possibly cutting your portfolio's value in half. Indeed, by diversifying your investments, you'll make more money as an individual investor. To know how to allocate your assets, you have to know the basic options you have for investing, which is where we're headed next.

"Since you cannot successfully time the market or select individual stocks, asset allocation should be the major focus of your investment strategy, because it is the only factor affecting your investment risk and return that you can control."

—**WILLIAM BERNSTEIN,** *THE FOUR PILLARS OF INVESTING: LESSONS FOR BUILDING A WINNING PORTFOLIO*

The Building Blocks of Investing

Again, if you're not interested in the mechanics of investing and want to skip ahead to see what the simplest investment choice is, turn to page 180. But if you want to know more about what's going on under the hood, stay with me.

THE PYRAMID OF INVESTING OPTIONS

LIFECYCLE FUNDS

More convenience

Less control

More predictable returns over the long term

INDEX FUNDS / MUTUAL FUNDS

Somewhat convenient

Can be low fees (index funds) or high fees (many mutual funds)

More control than lifecycle funds, less control than stocks/bonds

Returns are fairly predictable over the long term

STOCKS / BONDS / CASH

Individual stocks and bonds are very inconvenient to choose and maintain

High control

Stocks offer extremely unpredictable returns that typically fail to beat the market

Bonds offer extremely predictable returns, but on average return less than stocks

This Pyramid of Investing Options represents your choices for different investments. At the bottom is the most basic level, where you can invest in stocks or bonds or just hold your money in cash. I'm oversimplifying because there are tons of different kinds of stocks and bonds, but you get the idea. Above them are index and mutual funds. And finally, at the top of the pyramid, are lifecycle funds. Let's look at each category (also known as *asset class*) to see what lies beneath.

STOCKS

When you buy stock, you buy shares of a company. If the company does well, you expect your stock in it to do well. When people talk about "the market," they're talking about a collection of thirty large-cap stocks—the Dow Jones Industrial Average Index. The S&P 500 is another index of 500 stocks that I'll frequently refer to.

Overall, stocks as an entire category provide excellent returns. As we know, on average the stock market returns about 8 percent per year. In fact, you can do significantly better than the market if you pick a winning stock—or significantly worse if you pick a loser. Although stocks as a whole provide generally excellent returns, individual stocks are less clear. If you invest all your money in one stock, for example, you *might* make a huge return, but it's also possible the company could tank and you could lose it all.

Stocks have been a good way to earn significant returns over the long term, but I discourage you from picking individual stocks, because it's extremely difficult to choose winning ones on your own. The tricky thing about stocks is you never know what will happen. For example, in 2005 eBay announced that it missed Wall Street's earning expectations by *a penny* per share. The stock immediately plunged 20 percent. Was it 20 percent less useful the next day? Of course not.

In Chapter 6, I demonstrated that even professionals whose livelihoods depend on it can't predict stock returns. And remember, these are highly trained analysts who can read stock prospectuses like I can read an Indian restaurant menu—flawlessly. If these experts—who devour annual reports and understand complicated balance sheets—can't beat the market, what chance do you have of picking stocks that will go up?

You have very little chance. That's why individual investors like you and me should not invest in individual stocks. Instead, we'll choose funds, which are collections of stocks (and sometimes, for diversification, bonds). They let you reduce your risk and create a well-balanced portfolio that will let you sleep at night . . . but more on that later.

BONDS

Bonds are essentially IOUs from companies or the government. (Technically, bonds are longer-term investments of ten-plus years, whereas CDs involve lending money to a bank. Because they're very similar, let's just call them both *bonds* to simplify things.) If you buy a one-year bond, it's the same as if the bank says, "Hey, if you lend us $100, we'll give you $103 back a year from now."

The advantages of bonds are that you can choose the term, or length of time, you want the loan to last (two years, five years, ten years, and so on), and you know exactly how much you'll get when they "mature" or pay out. Also, bonds, especially government bonds, are generally stable and let you decrease the risk in your

IN GENERAL, RICH PEOPLE AND OLD PEOPLE LIKE BONDS.

portfolio. See, the only way you'd lose money on a government bond is if the government defaulted on its loans—and it doesn't do that. If it runs low on money, it just prints more of it. Now *that's* gangsta.

But because bonds are such a safe, low-risk investment, the return—even on a highly rated bond—is much lower than it would be on an excellent stock. Investing in bonds also renders your money illiquid, meaning it's locked away and inaccessible for a set period of time. Technically, you can withdraw early, but you'll face severe penalties, so it's a bad idea.

With these qualities, what kind of person would invest in bonds? Let's see: extremely stable, essentially guaranteed rate of return, but relatively small returns . . . Who would it be?

In general, rich people and old people like bonds. Old people like them because they like to know exactly how much money they're getting next month for their medication or whatever it is they need. Also, some of these grannies and grampies can't withstand the volatility of the stock market because they don't have much other income to support themselves and/or they have very little time left on this earth to recover from any downturn.

Rich people, on the other hand, tend to become more conservative because they have so much money. Put it this way: When you have $10,000, you want to invest aggressively to grow it because you want to make more money. But when you have $10 million, your goals switch from aggressive growth to preservation of capital. You'll accept lower investment returns in exchange for security and safety. So a guaranteed bond at 3 percent or 4 percent is attractive to a wealthy person—after all, 3 percent of $10 million is still a lot.

CASH

In investing terms, cash is money that's sitting on the sidelines, uninvested and earning only a little money in interest from money-market accounts, which are basically high-interest savings accounts. Traditionally, cash has been the third part of a portfolio beyond stocks and bonds. You want to have totally liquid cash on hand for emergencies, and as a hedge if the market tanks. Of course, you pay a price for this security: Cash is the safest part of your portfolio, but it offers the lowest reward. If you factor inflation, you actually *lose* money by holding cash in most accounts.

That's why I say it's *traditionally* been part of a portfolio. As long as you're contributing toward your savings goals as I described in Chapter 5, you're fine. Don't worry about having a separate cash account as part of your investments. Let's keep this simple.

Asset Allocation: The Critical Factor That Most Investors Miss

If you bought all different kinds of stocks or stock funds, you'd be diversified—but still only within stocks. That's like being the hottest person in Friendship, Wisconsin—better than not being hot, but not going to get you cast in *Gossip Girl*. (Friendship is actually a real place. My friend grew up there, and he told me what he and his buddies used to use as a gang sign: two hands clasping in friendship. I mocked him endlessly for that.)

It is important to diversify within stocks, but it's even more important to allocate *across* the different asset classes—like stocks and bonds. Investing in only one category is dangerous over the long term. This is where the all-important concept of asset allocation comes into play. Remember it like this: Diversification is *D* for going *deep* into a category (for example, buying different types of stocks: large-cap, small-cap, international, and so on), and asset allocation is *A* for going *across* all categories (for example, stocks *and* bonds).

80 YEARS OF AVERAGE ANNUAL RETURNS FOR STOCKS AND BONDS

The group at Vanguard Investment Counseling & Research recently analyzed eighty years of investment returns to help individual investors understand how to allocate their money. These numbers, which don't include inflation, give us a hint on how to maximize our investment returns.

Stocks	Bonds	Cash
Higher risk	Lower risk	Ultra-low risk. Stored in an interest-generating money-market account, not under your mattress.
10.5%	5.2%	3.8%

In determining where to allocate your assets, one of the most important considerations is the returns each category offers. Of course, based on the different types of investments you make, you can expect different returns. Higher risk generally equals higher potential for reward. Take a look at the chart above.

At first glance, it seems clear that stocks return the most. So let's all invest there!!

Not so fast. Remember, higher rewards entail higher risk, so if you're loaded up on stocks and your portfolio dips 25 percent next year, all of a sudden you're financially immobile, eating only Triscuits, waiting to see whether your money climbs back up or you die first. Hey, it had to be said.

But seriously, many of the fifty- and sixty-year-olds who have seen catastrophic drops in their portfolios should never have invested in all equities. Timing matters. If you're twenty-five years old and have dozens of years to grow your money, a portfolio made up of stock-based funds probably makes sense. But if you're older, retirement is coming up within a few decades and you'll want to tamp down your risk. I heard from tons of people in their forties, fifties, and sixties who were rocked by the stock market's decline in 2008. I can't help but feel sorry for them, but you should learn from their mistakes. Even if the market tanks, you have control over your asset allocation. If you're older—especially if you're in your sixties, for god's sake—a sizeable portion of your portfolio should be in stable bonds.

Bonds act as a counterweight to stocks, rising when stocks fall and reducing the overall risk of your portfolio. By investing part of your money in bonds, you reduce some of your overall risk. Sure, if that biotech stock went up 200 percent, you'd wish your bond money was all in the stock—but if the stock went down, you'd be glad your bonds were there as a buffer against losing everything. Although it may seem counterintuitive, your portfolio will actually have better overall performance if you add bonds to the mix. Because bonds will generally perform better when stocks fall, bonds lower your risk a lot while limiting your returns only a little.

"But Ramit," you might say, "I'm young and I want to invest aggressively. I don't need bonds." I agree. Bonds aren't really for young people in their twenties. If you're in your twenties or early thirties, and you don't necessarily need to reduce your risk, you can simply invest in all-stock funds and let time mitigate any risk. But in your thirties and older, you'll want to begin balancing your portfolio with bonds to reduce risk. And what if stocks as a whole don't perform well for a long time? That's when you need to own other asset classes—to offset the bad times.

The Importance of Being Diversified

Now that we know the basics of the asset classes (stocks, bonds, and cash) at the bottom of the pyramid, let's explore the different choices within each asset class. Basically, there are many types of stocks, and we need to own a little of all of them. Same with bonds. This is called diversifying, and it essentially means digging in to each asset class—stocks and bonds—and investing in all their subcategories.

As the table on the next page shows, the broad category of "stocks" actually includes many different kinds of stock, including large-company stocks ("large-cap"), mid-cap stocks, small-cap stocks, and international stocks. To add yet another wrinkle, none of them performs consistently. In the same year, small-cap stocks might gain huge percentages, but international stocks might tank—and this performance can vary from year to year. For example, William Bernstein notes, in 1998 U.S. large-cap stocks gained 28.6 percent, international stocks gained 20 percent, and REITs

STOCKS AND BONDS HAVE MANY FLAVORS

Stocks	Bonds
LARGE-CAP Big companies with a market capitalization ("market cap," which is defined as outstanding shares times the stock price) over $5 billion	**GOVERNMENT** An ultra-safe investment that's backed by the government. In exchange for their low risk, government bonds tend to return less than stocks as a general rule of thumb.
MID-CAP Midsized companies with a market cap between $1 billion and $5 billion	**CORPORATE** A bond issued by a corporation. These tend to be riskier than government bonds, but safer than stocks.
SMALL-CAP Smaller companies with a market cap less than $1 billion	**SHORT-TERM** Bonds with terms of usually less than three years
INTERNATIONAL INVESTMENTS Stocks from companies in other countries, including emerging markets (like China, India, and Mexico) and developed markets (like the United Kingdom, Germany, and France). Americans sometimes may buy these directly, or may have to buy them through funds.	**LONG-TERM** These bonds tend to mature in twenty or more years and, accordingly, offer higher yields than shorter-term bonds.
GROWTH Stocks whose value may grow higher than other stocks, or even the market as a whole	**MUNICIPAL** Also known as "munis," these are bonds issued by local governments.
VALUE Stocks that seem bargain priced (i.e., cheaper than they should be)	**INFLATION-PROTECTED** Treasury Inflation-Protected Securities, or TIPS, are ultra-safe investments that protect against inflation.

Note that REITs, "real-estate investment trusts"—which are types of investments that let you invest in real estate through a single ticker symbol, just like a stock—don't neatly fall into any of these categories because of their complicated structure.

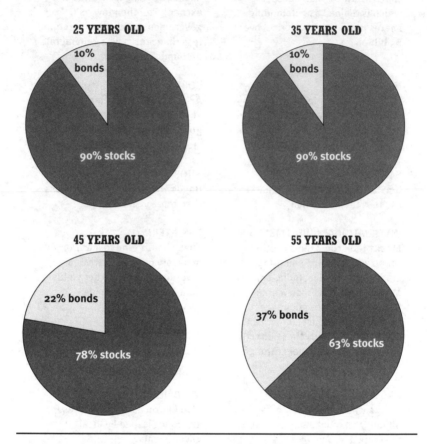

WHAT A GRANNY NEEDS: TYPICAL ASSET ALLOCATIONS BY AGE

Here's what typical investors' asset allocations—remember, that's the mix of different investments—might look like as they get older. These figures are taken from Vanguard's lifecycle funds.

25 YEARS OLD
10% bonds
90% stocks

35 YEARS OLD
10% bonds
90% stocks

45 YEARS OLD
22% bonds
78% stocks

55 YEARS OLD
37% bonds
63% stocks

(collections of real estate stocks) lost 17 percent. But in 2000, just two years later, U.S. large-cap stocks *lost* 9.10 percent, foreign stocks *lost* 14.17 percent, and REITS *gained* 31.04 percent. Similarly, different types of bonds offer different benefits, including rates of return and tax advantages.

The fact that performance varies so much in each asset class means two things: First, if you're trying to make a quick buck off investing, you'll usually lose money because you have no idea what will happen in the near future. Anyone who tells you they do is a fool or a commission-based salesman. Second, you should own different categories of stocks (and maybe bonds) to balance out your portfolio. You don't want to own only U.S. small-cap stocks, for example, or funds that own only small-cap stocks. If they didn't perform well for ten years, that would really suck. If, however, you own small-cap stocks, plus large-cap stocks, plus international stocks, and more, you're effectively insured against any one area dragging you down. So, if you were to invest in stocks, you'd want to *diversify*, buying all different types of stocks or stock funds to have a balanced portfolio.

These allocations are just general rules of thumb. Some people prefer to have 100 percent in stocks until they're in their thirties or forties. Others are more conservative and want some money in bonds. But the big takeaway here is that, if we're in our twenties and thirties, we can afford to be aggressive about investing in stocks and stock funds—even if they drop temporarily—because time is on our side.

And honestly, if you're twenty-five and just starting out, your biggest danger isn't having a portfolio that's too risky. It's being lazy and overwhelmed and not doing any investing at all. That's why it's important to understand the basics but not get too wrapped up in all the variables and choices.

Over time, you can manage your asset allocation to reduce risk and get a fairly predictable return on investments. Thirty years from now, you're going to need to invest very differently from how you do today. That's just natural: You invest much more aggressively in your twenties than in your fifties, as you get older and tell long-winded stories about yourself. So although it seems sexy to pull out a pipe and phone in your favorite stock choices to your broker, the real work in investing comes with creating an investment plan that's appropriate for your age and comfort level with risk.

All of this sounds completely reasonable: "I invest more aggressively when I'm younger, and as I get older, I get more and more conservative."

There's just one problem.

How the hell are you actually supposed to do it? What specific investments should you choose? Should you invest in individual stocks? (No.) Most people stop here, superficially thinking that investing is only about stocks, leading to frustration. Not surprisingly, when they try to think more deeply about this, they get confused and shut down, killing any impetus to invest, becoming destitute and wandering around a tumbleweed-laden desert in their twilight years. Well, almost all of that.

Don't let this happen to you! Let's go further up the Pyramid of Investing Options to cover another key to investing: funds.

Mutual Funds:
Not Bad, Pretty Convenient, but Often Expensive and Unreliable

The financial industry isn't stupid. Those people are ingenious at creating products to meet investor needs (or what the industry *wants* people to need). In 1924, mutual funds, which are just baskets filled with different types of investments (usually stocks), were invented. Instead of requiring investors to perform the Herculean task of picking individual stocks themselves, mutual funds allowed average investors to simply choose types of funds that would suit them. For example, there are large-cap, mid-cap, and small-cap mutual funds, but also mutual funds that focus on biotechnology, communication, and even Europe or Asia. Mutual funds are extremely popular because they allow you to pick one fund, which contains different stocks, and not worry about putting too many eggs in one basket (as you likely would if you bought individual stocks), monitoring prospectuses, or keeping up with industry news. The funds provide instant diversification because they hold many different stocks. Most people's first encounter with mutual funds is through their 401(k), where they choose from a bewildering array of options. You buy shares of the fund and the fund's manager picks the stocks he thinks will yield the best return.

Mutual funds are incredibly useful financial tools—over the past eighty-five years, they have proven to be very popular and extremely profitable. Compared with other investments, they've been a cash cow for Wall Street. That's because in exchange for "active management" (having an expert choose a fund's stocks), the financial companies charge big fat fees (also known as expense ratios). These fees eat a hole in your returns and make me want to poke a steel-tipped Popsicle stick into my eye. Sure, there are some low-fee funds out there, but most mutual funds have high expense ratios.

Now, I don't fault the financial companies for selling mutual funds. They got average Americans to invest, and, even after fees, mutual funds are an excellent investment choice compared with doing nothing. But things have changed. As we saw in Chapter 6, there are now better choices for investing: lower-cost, better-performing index funds. Yet, like a gold digger clasping on to her soon-to-be ex-husband, Wall Street has resisted killing its cash cow of actively managed mutual funds.

Advantages of a mutual fund: Hands-off approach means an expert money manager makes investment decisions for you. Mutual funds hold many varied stocks, so if one company tanks, your fund doesn't go down with it.

Disadvantages: Annual fees can equal tens of thousands of dollars or more over the lifetime of an investment using expense ratios, front-end loads, and back-end loads (worthless sales charges that add nothing to your returns)—all tricky ways to make mutual funds more money. Also, if you invest in two mutual funds, they may overlap in investments, meaning you may not really be diversified. Worst of all, you're paying an "expert" to manage your money, and 75 percent of them do not beat the market.

In short, mutual funds are prevalent because of their convenience, but because actively managed mutual funds are, by definition, expensive, they're not the best investment any more. Active management can't compete with passive management, which takes us to index funds, the more attractive cousin of mutual funds.

Index Funds:
The Attractive Cousin in an
Otherwise Unattractive Family

In 1975, John Bogle, the founder of Vanguard, introduced the world's first index fund. These simple funds use computers to buy stocks and match the market (such as the S&P 500 or NASDAQ). Instead of having a mutual fund's expensive staff of "experts" who try to beat the market, index funds set a lower bar: A computer matches the indexes by automatically matching the makeup of the market. For example, if a stock represents 2 percent of the S&P 500, it will represent 2 percent of the index fund. Index funds are the financial equivalent of "If you can't beat 'em, join 'em." And they do so while also being low cost and tax efficient, and requiring hardly any maintenance at all. In other words, index funds are simply collections of stocks that computers manage in an effort to match the market. There are index funds for the S&P 500, for Asia-Pacific funds, for real-estate funds, and for anything else you can imagine. Just like mutual funds, they have ticker symbols (such as VFINX).

In a radical move he originally crafted in his senior thesis at Princeton, Bogle argued that index funds would offer better performance to individual investors. Active mutual fund managers could not typically beat the market, yet they charged investors maintenance fees and incurred tremendous amounts of taxes on their frequent trading.

Just as we each think we're above average when it comes to being attractive, every mutual fund manager believes *he* can beat the market. To accomplish this, managers use fancy analysis and data, and trade frequently. Ironically, this results in lots of taxes and trading fees, which, when combined with the expense ratio, makes it virtually impossible for the average fund investor to beat—or even match—the market over time. Bogle opted to discard the old model of mutual funds and introduce index funds.

Today, index funds are an easy, efficient way to make a significant amount of money. Note, however, that index funds simply match the market. If you own all equities in your twenties (like me) and the stock

HIGH EXPENSE RATIOS COST MORE THAN YOU THINK

Amount in your portfolio	Annual expenses of a low-cost index fund (.18%)	Annual expenses of an actively managed mutual fund (2%)
$5,000	$9	$100
$25,000	$45	$500
$100,000	$180	$2,000
$500,000	$900	$10,000
$1,000,000	$1,800	$20,000

Professionals Agree— Index Funds Are Great Investments

You don't have to take my word for it. Here, a few experts on the benefits of index funds:

"I believe that 98 or 99 percent—maybe more than 99 percent—of people who invest should extensively diversify and not trade. That leads them to an index fund with very low costs."

—WARREN BUFFETT,
ONE OF AMERICA'S GREATEST INVESTORS

"When you realize how few advisers have beaten the market over the last several decades, you may acquire the discipline to do something even better: become a long-term index fund investor."

—MARK HULBERT,
EDITOR OF HULBERT FINANCIAL DIGEST

"The media focuses on the temporarily winning active funds that score the more spectacular bull's eyes, not index funds that score every year and accumulate less flashy, but ultimately winning, scores."

—W. SCOTT SIMON, *AUTHOR OF* INDEX MUTUAL FUNDS:
PROFITING FROM AN INVESTMENT REVOLUTION

market drops (like it has), your investments will drop (like mine, and everyone else's, did). Index funds reflect the market, which is going through tough times but, as history has shown, will climb back up. As a bonus for using index funds, you'll anger your friends in finance because you'll be throwing up your middle finger to their entire industry—and you'll keep their fees for yourself. Wall Street is terrified of index funds and tries to keep them under wraps with increased marketing of mutual funds and nonsense like "5-Star Funds" and TV shows that highlight action, not results.

Advantages: Extremely low cost, easy to maintain, and tax efficient.

Disadvantages: When you're investing in index funds, you typically have to invest in multiple funds to create a comprehensive asset allocation (although owning just one is better than doing nothing). If you do purchase multiple index funds, you'll have to rebalance (or adjust your investments to maintain your target asset allocation) regularly, usually every twelve to eighteen months. Each fund typically requires a minimum investment, although this is often waived with automatic monthly investments.

Okay, so index funds are clearly far superior to buying either individual stocks and bonds or mutual funds. With their low fees, they are a great choice if you want to create and control the exact makeup of your portfolio.

But what if you're one of those people who knows you'll just never get around to doing the necessary research to figure out an appropriate asset allocation and which index funds to buy? Let's be honest: Most people don't want to construct a diversified portfolio, and they certainly don't want to rebalance and monitor their funds, even if it's just once a year.

If you fall into this group, there is the option at the very top of the investment pyramid. It's an investment option that's drop-dead easy: lifecycle funds.

Lifecycle Funds: Investing the Easy Way

Whether you're just arriving here direct from page 165, or you've read through the basics of investing and decided you want to take the easy way after all, no problem—lifecycle funds are the easiest investment choice you'll ever need to make.

Lifecycle funds, also known as *target-date funds,* are my favorite investment of all because they embody the 85 Percent Solution: not exactly perfect, but easy enough for anyone to get started—and they work just fine.

Lifecycle funds are simple funds that automatically diversify your investments for you based on age. Instead of having to rebalance stocks and bonds, lifecycle funds do it for you. If more Americans owned lifecycle funds, for example, far fewer retirees would have seen precipitous drops in their retirement accounts, because the lifecycle funds would have automatically changed to a more conservative asset allocation as they approached their golden years. Lifecycle funds are actually "funds-of-funds," or collections made up of other funds, which offer automatic diversification. For example, a lifecycle fund might include large-cap, mid-cap, small-cap, and international funds. (And those funds, in turn, will hold stocks from each of those areas.) In other words, your lifecycle fund will own many funds, which all own stocks and bonds. It sounds complicated, but believe it or not, this actually makes things simple for you, because you'll have to own only *one* fund, and all the rest will be taken care of for you.

Lifecycle funds are different from index funds, which are also low cost but require you to own multiple funds if you want a comprehensive asset allocation. Multiple funds mean you have to rebalance your funds regularly, usually every year, which is a laborious process of redistributing your money to different investments so you get back to your target asset allocation. What a pain.

IF MORE AMERICANS OWNED LIFECYCLE FUNDS, FOR EXAMPLE, FAR FEWER RETIREES WOULD HAVE SEEN PRECIPITOUS DROPS IN THEIR RETIREMENT ACCOUNTS.

Luckily, lifecycle funds automatically pick a blend of investments for you based on your approximate age. They start you off with aggressive investments in your twenties and then shift investments to become more conservative as you get older. You do no work except continuing to send money into your lifecycle fund.

Lifecycle funds aren't perfect for everyone because they work on one variable alone: age. Everyone has different investment needs, and these funds aren't particularly tailored to your individual situation. As a result, you might not get the maximum possible return you could get if you picked your own portfolio. However, lifecycle funds are designed to appeal to people who are lazy. In other words, for many people the ease of use for these funds far outweighs any loss of returns that might occur from taking the one-size-fits-all approach. In my opinion, if it means it will get you investing, the benefits of having one fund that handles all of your investments make up for any shortcomings.

What About Other Kinds of Investments?

There are many different investments besides stocks, bonds, and index and lifecycle funds. You can buy precious metals, real estate, or even art; just don't expect very good returns. And despite all my dire warnings, you can also buy a couple of stocks you really like.

REAL ESTATE. For most Americans, their home is their biggest "investment," and yet, as investments go, real estate is not a very good one for individual investors. Why? Because the returns are generally poor, especially when you factor in costs like maintenance and property taxes—which renters don't pay for, but homeowners do. I'll cover real estate more in Chapter 9, but in general, most people confuse their house with an investment that they buy and sell for profit. Think about it. Who sells their house for profit and keeps the money? If your parents ever sold their house, did they move into a smaller house and enjoy the rest of that money? No! They rolled it over to the down payment for their next, more expensive house.

You want to keep each part of your portfolio balanced so no one area overshadows the rest. If you're spending $2,000 per month on your mortgage and don't have enough left over to diversify into other areas, that's not a balanced portfolio. If you do buy real estate, regardless of whether it's to live in or to invest in, be sure to keep funding the rest of your investment areas—whether that's a lifecycle fund or your own portfolio of index funds.

ART. A 1998 study at New York University produced some surprising results about art as investment. It showed that art is reliable, profitable (fine art returned 10.4 percent), and an effective hedge against portfolio volatility. However, by choosing particular art pieces as investment, you're doing essentially the same thing as trying to predict winning stocks, and after reading Chapter 6 you know how difficult that is to do. In aggregate, art investments may be quite profitable, but the trick is choosing which individual pieces will appreciate—and as you can imagine, that isn't easy.

HIGH-RISK, HIGH-POTENTIAL-FOR-REWARD INVESTMENTS. Life isn't just about lifecycle funds and index funds. Lots of people understand that, logically, they should create a well-diversified portfolio of low-cost funds. But they also want to have *fun* investing. If you feel this way, sure, use a small part of your portfolio for "high risk" investing—but treat it as fun money, not as money you need. I set aside about 10 percent of my portfolio for fun money, which includes particular stocks I like, know, and use (companies like Amazon.com that focus on customer service, which I believe drives shareholder value); sector funds that let me focus on particular industries (I own an index fund that focuses on health care); and even angel investing, which is personal venture-capital investing for private ultra-early-stage companies. (I occasionally see these angel opportunities because I work in Silicon Valley and have friends who start companies and look for early friends-and-family money.) All these are very-high-risk investments and they're funded by just-for-fun money that I can afford to lose. Still, there is the potential for great returns. If you have the rest of your portfolio set up and still have money left over, be smart about it, but invest a little in whatever you want.

Lifecycle funds aren't all created equal—some of them are more expensive than others—but as a general rule, they're low cost and tax efficient. Best of all, they take no work beyond automatically contributing money once a month, quarter, or year. You won't have to actively invest and monitor and rebalance on your own, because lifecycle funds handle the messy work for you. Cool, right?

One thing to note is that you'll need between $1,000 and $3,000 as a minimum to buy in to a fund. If you don't have it, go to page 106 and add a savings goal for "lifecycle fund." Once you save the minimum needed to invest, you can open your fund and set up an automatic transfer each month.

All right, let's check out an example of two low-cost lifecycle funds. In the table on the next page, you can see how the allocations in both funds change based on your age. When you're in your twenties, more of your assets are in stocks because you can afford to take more risks. When you're in your fifties, the balance shifts so you are more heavily invested

LIFECYCLE FUNDS AUTOMATICALLY ADJUST AS YOU GET OLDER

Here's a comparison of two popular lifecycle funds. These funds target roughly the same age—someone in his or her twenties—and assume retirement at age sixty-five. You should pay special attention to the minimum initial investment (it matters if you don't have a lot of money lying around) and the asset allocation, which will help you determine which fund most suits your risk tolerance. Remember, these are only two example funds; you can choose among many lifecycle funds offered by companies like the ones I list on page 187.

	Vanguard Target Retirement 2050 (VFIFX)	T. Rowe Retire 2045 (TRRKX)
Minimum initial investment	$3,000	$1,000 if within an IRA, $2,500 otherwise
Minimum monthly investment	None (but you should send some money every month)	None (but you should send some money every month)
Asset allocation at 25 years old	90% stocks, 10% bonds	88% stocks, 9% bonds, 3% cash
35 years old	90% stocks, 10% bonds	86% stocks, 11% bonds, 3% cash
45 years old	78% stocks, 22% bonds	74% stocks, 23% bonds, 3% cash
55 years old	63% stocks, 37% bonds	58% stocks, 38% bonds, 4% cash

The major benefit to a lifecycle fund is that you set it and forget it. You just keep sending money and your fund will handle the allocation, trading, and maintenance, automatically diversifying for you. If you invest in a lifecycle fund, you could literally spend minutes *per year* on your investments. You may not agree with the exact allocation of the fund, but frankly it's close enough. As you know, 85 percent correct is way better than nothing at all.

in stable, lower-risk bonds. We saw this same approach when we talked about allocating your assets across stocks, bonds, and index funds. But the difference with lifecycle funds is that they automatically do this rebalancing for you.

Getting Your Hands Dirty: Choosing and Buying Your Investments

By now, you should know what you want to invest in: a lifecycle fund or index funds. If you're even considering buying individual stocks because you think you can beat the market or it's sexier, I want you to take all your money, put it in a big Ziploc bag along with this book, and light it on fire. Just save the middleman.

If you don't want to spend a billion years managing your money and you're satisfied with the 85 Percent Solution of investing in a convenient fund that's good enough and will free you up to live your life and do what you love, then go for a lifecycle fund. If you're more of a personal-finance geek, are willing to spend some time on your finances, and want more control, then choose index funds. Whichever category you fall into, you'll want to figure out exactly *what* to invest in. Let's get started.

The Investment Most Americans Have: Your 401(k)

As we discussed in Chapter 3, if you get a 401(k) match from your employer, you need to pay into your 401(k) before you do any other investing. If your employer doesn't offer a 401(k) match, skip to the Roth IRA section on the next page. You should have already set up your 401(k), but now it's time to focus on how you allocate the money you're investing in it. (If you had to pick funds when you opened your account, you can always go back in and change your allocation. Just ask your human resources person for the proper form or, better yet, change it on your 401(k) website.)

You know how I love reducing choice to get people to take action? Well, the companies that offer 401(k)s take this to an extreme: They offer a few investment funds for you to choose from—usually the options are called something like *aggressive investments* (which will be a fund of mostly stocks), *balanced investments* (this fund will contain stocks and bonds), and *conservative investments* (a more conservative mix of mostly bonds).

If you're not sure what the different choices mean, ask your HR representative for a sheet describing the differences in funds. Note: Stay away from "money market funds," which is just another way of saying your money is sitting, uninvested, in cash. You want to get your money working for you.

As a young person, I encourage you to pick the most aggressive fund they offer that you're comfortable with. As you know, the more aggressive you are when younger, the more money you'll likely have later. This is especially important for a 401(k), which is an ultra-long-term investment account.

Depending on what company your employer uses to administer your 401(k), your fund options may be a little pricey in terms of expense ratios (I consider anything over 0.75 percent expensive), but on balance, you're getting huge tax advantages and employer-match benefits. So, it's worth it to invest in these funds, even if they aren't perfect.

Investing Using Your Roth IRA

After your 401(k) match, the next best place to invest is your Roth IRA. (I'm sure I don't need to remind you that in addition to accruing earnings tax-free, one of the primary benefits of Roth IRAs is the flexibility of choosing any funds you want.)

When you send money to your Roth IRA account, it just sits there. You'll need to invest the money to start making good returns. The easiest investment is a lifecycle fund. You can just buy it, set up automatic monthly contributions, and forget about it. (If you really want more control, you can pick individual index funds instead of lifecycle funds, which I'll discuss on page 188.)

The Rule of 72

The Rule of 72 is a fast trick you can do to figure out how long it will take to double your money. Here's how it works: Divide the number 72 by the return rate you're getting, and you'll have the number of years you must invest in order to double your money. (For the math geeks among us, here's the equation: 72 ÷ return rate = number of years.) For example, if you're getting a 10 percent return rate from an index fund, it would take you approximately seven years (72 ÷ 10) to double your money. In other words, if you invested $5,000 today, let it sit there, and earned a 10 percent return, you'd have $10,000 in about seven years. And it doubles from there, too. Of course, you could have even more by adding a small amount every month using the power of compounding.

CHOOSING A LIFECYCLE FUND FOR YOUR ROTH IRA

Two companies with popular lifecycle funds are Vanguard and T. Rowe Price, both of which are great. Vanguard's Target Date 2045 fund (that is, assuming you'll retire around sixty-five, your "target date" of retirement will be somewhere around 2045) has a very low 0.19 percent expense ratio. The minimum investment to get started is $3,000, and you can set up monthly recurring contributions of at least $100 each. (Note: Vanguard also charges a $30 annual account maintenance fee which you can get waived by signing up at Vanguard.com and getting your account notifications by e-mail instead of snail mail.)

The T. Rowe Price Retirement 2045 Fund has an expense ratio of 0.74 percent, which is costlier than Vanguard but still a fair price. One advantage is that the fund requires only a $1,000 minimum to invest if you're doing it within a Roth IRA.

Other popular companies with lifecycle funds include Schwab, Fidelity, and TIAA-CREF. Check their websites or call them up (see page 87 for some contact information). You want to look for lifecycle funds, which may also be called *target-date retirement funds*. Note: Those target dates are just a suggestion. You can choose any lifecycle fund, depending on your age and risk tolerance. So if you're twenty-five and pretty risk averse, you can pick a fund designed for someone older, which will give you a more conservative asset allocation.

BUYING INTO YOUR LIFECYCLE FUND

Now that you've identified a lifecycle fund to invest in, actually buying it is an easy process.

Log in to your Roth IRA (which you opened in Chapter 3). Your login information should be handy if you followed my tip on page 88.

You'll need to have at least enough cash in it to cover the minimum investment of the fund, which is often between $1,000 and $3,000. Some companies waive the minimums if you agree to set up an automatic $50 or $100 investment every month (which you should). But some, like Vanguard, won't waive the fees no matter what. If you really want a fund that requires a minimum investment, but you don't have the money, you'll need to save up the necessary amount before you can buy into the fund. So, once you have enough money in your account, type in the ticker symbol for your lifecycle fund (it will look something like VFINX). If you don't know it, you can search for it right from your account.

Then, click "buy." Voilà!

With each fund you buy, you'll be able to set up automatic contributions so you don't have to contribute manually each month.

So You Want to Do It on Your Own

So you aren't satisfied with one lifecycle fund, and you want to pick your own index funds to construct your portfolio in your Roth IRA. Are you sure?

If you're looking for one investment that gets you 85 percent of the way there—which you won't have to monitor, rebalance, or even pay attention to—then just use a lifecycle fund from the above section. (Can you tell that I'm a big lifecycle fan?)

Remember, most people who try to manage their own portfolios fail at even matching the market. They fail because they sell at the first sign of trouble, or because they buy and sell too often, thereby diminishing their returns with taxes and trading fees. (Think of all the people who sold off their 401(k)s in late 2008, not really understanding that there were bargains to be had by simply continuing their consistent investing. It was fear—not strategy.) The result is tens of thousands of dollars lost over a lifetime. Plus, if you buy individual index funds, you'll have to rebalance every year to make sure your asset allocation is still what you want it to be (more on this in a minute). Lifecycle funds do this for you, so if you just want an easy way to invest, use one.

THE KEY TO CONSTRUCTING A PORTFOLIO IS NOT PICKING KILLER STOCKS! IT'S FIGURING OUT A BALANCED ASSET ALLOCATION THAT WILL LET YOU RIDE OUT STORMS AND SLOWLY GROW OVER TIME.

But if you want more control over your investments and you just *know* you're disciplined enough to withstand market dips and to take the time to rebalance your asset allocation at least once a year, then choosing your own portfolio of index funds is the right choice for you.

All right, let's do this. If you've read this far, I guess my warnings and harassment didn't dissuade you from building your own portfolio. If I can't scare you, I might as well help you.

As we discussed earlier, the key to constructing a portfolio is not picking killer stocks! It's figuring out a balanced asset allocation that will let you ride out storms and slowly grow, over time, to gargantuan proportions. To illustrate how to allocate and diversify your portfolio, we're going to use David Swensen's recommendation as a model. Swensen is pretty much the Warren G of money management. He runs Yale's fabled endowment, and for more than twenty years he has generated an astonishing 16.3 percent annualized return, whereas most managers can't even beat 8 percent. That means he has doubled Yale's money every 4.5 years from 1985 to today. Best of all, Swensen is a genuinely good guy. He could be making hundreds of millions each year running his own fund on Wall Street, but he chooses to stay at Yale, making just over $1 million per year, because he loves academia. "When I see colleagues of mine leave universities to do essentially the same thing they were doing but to get paid more, I am disappointed because there is a sense of mission," he's said. I love this guy.

Anyway, Swensen suggests allocating your money in the following way:

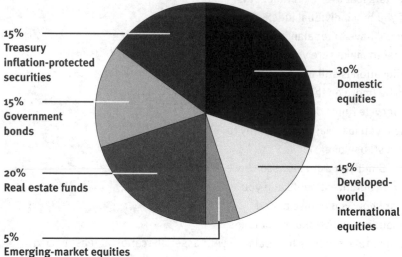

THE SWENSEN MODEL OF ASSET ALLOCATION

15% Treasury inflation-protected securities

15% Government bonds

20% Real estate funds

5% Emerging-market equities

30% Domestic equities

15% Developed-world international equities

30 percent—Domestic equities: U.S. stock funds, including small-, mid-, and large-cap stocks

15 percent—Developed-world international equities: funds from developed foreign countries, including the United Kingdom, Germany, and France

5 percent—Emerging-market equities: funds from developing foreign countries such as China, India, and Brazil. These are riskier than developed-world equities, so don't go off buying these to fill 95 percent of your portfolio.

20 percent—Real estate funds: also known as REITs, short for real estate investment trust. REITs are funds that invest in mortgages and residential and commercial real estate, both domestically and internationally.

15 percent—Government bonds: fixed-interest U.S. securities, which provide predictable income and balance risk in your portfolio. As an asset class, bonds generally return less than stocks.

15 percent—Treasury inflation-protected securities: also known as TIPS, these treasury notes protect against inflation. Eventually you'll want to own these, but they'd be the last ones I'd get after investing in all the better-returning options first.

A significant amount of math went into Swensen's allocation, but the most important takeaway is that no single choice represents an overwhelming part of the portfolio. As illustrated by the tech bubble of 2001 and the real estate crash of 2007, any sector can drop at any time. When it does, you don't want it to drag your entire portfolio down with it. As we know, lower risk generally equals lower reward. But the coolest thing about asset allocation is that you can actually reduce your risk while maintaining an equivalent return.

Swensen's theories are great, but how do we make them real and pick funds that match his suggestions? By picking a portfolio of low-cost funds, that's how.

Choosing your own index funds means you'll need to dig around and identify the best index funds for you. I always start researching at the

Keep It Manageable

Q: *How many funds should I invest in?*

A: If you're wondering how many funds you should own, I'd encourage you to keep it simple. Ideally you should have just one (a lifecycle fund). But if you're picking your own index funds, as a general guideline, you can create a great asset allocation using anywhere from three to seven funds. That would cover domestic equities, international equities, real estate investment trusts, and perhaps a small allocation to treasury bonds. Remember, the goal isn't to be exhaustive and to own every single aspect of the market. It's to create an effective asset allocation and move on with your life. And if you're looking for those funds, check page 180.

YOU CANNOT JUST PICK RANDOM FUNDS AND EXPECT TO HAVE A BALANCED ASSET ALLOCATION.

most popular companies: Vanguard, Schwab, and T. Rowe Price. (You'll find their phone numbers and websites on page 87.) I especially like etrade.com's research tools, which let you easily see how much the funds cost, what their fees are, and what types of stocks they contain.

When you visit these websites, you'll be able to research funds (you may have to click "Products and Services" on many of the sites) to make sure they're low-cost and meet your asset allocation goals.

The first thing you want to do when picking index funds is to minimize fees. Look for the management fees ("expense ratios") to be low, around 0.2 percent, and you'll be fine. Really, anything lower than 0.75 percent is okay. Most of the index funds at Vanguard, T. Rowe Price, and Fidelity offer excellent value. Remember: Expense ratios are one of the few things you can control, and higher fees cost you dearly—and they just put money in Wall Street's pocket. See the chart on page 157 for a comparison of how these fees can affect you.

Second, you want to make sure the fund fits into your asset allocation. After all, the reason you're choosing your own index funds is to have more control over your investments. Use David Swensen's model as a baseline and tweak as necessary if you want to exclude certain funds or prioritize which are important to you. For example, if you have limited money and you're in your twenties, you'd probably want to buy the stock funds first so you could get their compounding power, whereas you could wait until you're older and have more money to buy the bond funds to mitigate your risk. In other words, when you look for various funds, make sure you're being strategic about your domestic equities, international equities, bonds, and all the rest. You cannot just pick random funds and expect to have a balanced asset allocation. I use the Instant X-Ray tool (www.morningstar.com/cover/tools.html), which lets me compare various funds' asset allocations to see how well they cover domestic investments, foreign investments, bonds, and more. It's a great tool to help drill into your asset allocation and make sure your funds are well diversified.

Third, note that you should absolutely look at how well the fund has returned over the last ten or fifteen years, but remember that, as they say, past performance is no guarantee of future results.

Dollar-Cost Averaging: Investing Slowly Over Time

When I want to sound smart and intimidate people, I calmly look at them, chew on a muffin for a few seconds, and then abruptly throw it against a wall and scream, "DO YOU DOLLAR-COST AVERAGE???" People are often so impressed that they slowly inch away, then turn around and whisper to people around them. I can only surmise that they are discussing how clever and knowledgeable I am.

Anyway, *dollar-cost averaging* is a fancy phrase that refers to investing regular amounts over time, rather than investing all your money into a fund at once. This is the essence of Automatic Investing, which lets you consistently invest in a fund so you don't have to guess when the market is up or down. For example, if you have $12,000 available to invest, you could invest $1,000 per month for a year. (Remember: If you set up Automatic Investing at regular intervals, most funds waive transaction fees.)

But if you have the cash, why would you invest at regular intervals instead of all at once? Imagine if you invest $10,000 tomorrow and the stock drops 20 percent. At $8,000, it will need to increase 25 percent (not 20 percent) to get back to $10,000. By investing over time, you hedge against any drops in the price—and if your fund does drop, you'll pick up shares at a discount price. In other words, by investing over a regular period of time, you don't try to time the market. Instead, you use time to your advantage.

This can all be automated, of course. In Chapter 5, we covered your automatic infrastructure. To set up Automatic Investing, configure your investment accounts to automatically transfer money in from your checking account each month. See page 131 for details.

To make this a little easier, when you click "Products and Services" on most sites, you'll be able to find a fund screener that will let you add search filters like "international index funds with an expense ratio of less than 0.75%" to find funds that fit your criteria. Remember, this isn't simple. Creating your own portfolio takes significant research.

As an example of what you might end up with, here's a sample portfolio made of all Vanguard funds:

Stocks ("Equities")

30 percent—Total Market Index/equities (VTSMX)

20 percent—Total International Stock Index/equities (VGTSX)

20 percent—REIT index/equities (VGSIX)

Bonds

5 percent—U.S. treasury bond index/bonds (VFISX)

5 percent—Vanguard Intermediate-Term Treasury Fund (VFITX)

5 percent—Vanguard Long-Term Treasury Fund (VUSTX)

15 percent—TIPS bond index/bonds (VIPSX)

These are just a few of the literally thousands of index funds that exist. You can be flexible with the funds. If you want to be more or less aggressive, you can change the allocation to match your risk tolerance. For example, if you look at those funds and say, "Man, I'll never get around to owning seven funds," then be realistic with yourself. Maybe you want to buy the stock funds but just one bond fund for now. Maybe you don't need to think about TIPS yet. Pick the number of funds that will let you get started, realizing that you can adjust it later on to get a balanced asset allocation.

Spend time identifying the funds that will help you build a full, balanced asset allocation over time. You don't need to get all seven funds listed above—even one is better than nothing. But you should have a list of funds that you'll eventually buy to round out your allocation.

BUYING INTO INDIVIDUAL INDEX FUNDS

Once you've got a list of index funds you want to own in your portfolio—usually three to seven funds—start buying them one by one. If you can afford to buy into all the funds at once, go for it—but most people can't do this, since the minimum for each fund is between $1,000 and $3,000.

Just like with a lifecycle fund, you want to set a savings goal to accumulate enough to pay for the minimum of the first fund. Then you'll buy that fund, continue investing a small amount in it, and set a new savings goal to get the next fund. Investing isn't a race—you don't need a perfect asset allocation tomorrow. Here's how to handle buying multiple index funds over time.

Let's say you check your Conscious Spending Plan from Chapter 4, and it allows you to invest $500 per month after contributing to your 401(k). Assuming all of your funds have a $1,000 minimum, you'd set a savings goal of $1,000 for Index Fund 1 and save for two months. Once you accumulated enough to cover the minimum, transfer that $1,000 from savings to your investment account and buy the fund. *Now,* set up a contribution of $100 per month to the fund you just bought ($50 or $100 is usually the minimum amount you can automatically contribute). Then take the remaining $400 per month set aside for investing ($500 total minus the $100 you're investing in Index Fund 1) and start another savings goal toward Index Fund 2. Once you've saved enough, buy Index Fund 2. Repeat this process as

> **INVESTING ISN'T A RACE—YOU DON'T NEED A PERFECT ASSET ALLOCATION TOMORROW.**

necessary. Sure, it may take a few years to get to the point where you own all the index funds you need, but remember you're taking a forty- or fifty-year outlook on investing—it's not about the short term. This is the cost of constructing your own perfect portfolio.

Note: Once you own all the funds you need, you can split the money across funds according to your asset allocation—but *don't* just split it evenly. Remember, your asset allocation determines how much money you invest in different areas. For example, if you have $250 per month and you buy seven index funds, the average person who knows nothing (i.e., most people) would split the money seven ways and send $35 to each. That's wrong. Depending on your asset allocation, you'd send more or less money to various funds, using this calculation: (Your monthly total amount of investing money) $\times$ (Percentage of asset allocation for a particular investment) = Amount you'll invest there. For example, if you're investing $1,000 per month and your Swensen allocation recommends 30 percent for domestic equities, you'd calculate ($1,000) $\times$ (0.3) = $300 toward your domestic-equity fund. Repeat for all other funds in your portfolio.

Finally, if you opt for investing in your own index funds, you'll have to rebalance about once a year, which will keep your funds in line with your target asset allocation. I'll cover that in the next chapter.

HOW TO WRESTLE WITH A BEAR—AND WIN

Why I'm Not Worried About the Economy

by J.D. Roth of www.getrichslowly.org

As I write this, the U.S. is in the midst of a financial crisis. The stock market has dropped more than 22 percent in the past two weeks. It's down 36 percent for the year. People are panicked. They're pulling money out of mutual funds at record rates—$46 billion last week alone.

I'm not one of them.

In fact, I just made the largest investment of my life, moving $46,000 in my 401(k) from cash into a Fidelity index fund. Am I scared? You bet. $46,000 is a hell of a lot of money. But I'm taking my cues from Warren Buffett, the world's richest man, who in 2004 gave this advice: "Be fearful when others are greedy and greedy when others are fearful."

Or, to put it in more familiar terms, "Buy low, sell high."

I think the market is low right now, so I've made a lump-sum investment. But buying low can be intimidating. Suppose the markets never go back up? Nobody wants to wrestle with a bear. I'm taking a risk by attacking the beast head on.

Moves like this don't bother me as much as they might bother other people (my wife, for example) because my risk tolerance is high. I have twenty or thirty years to go before retirement. That's two or three decades to recover from any further market drops.

Risk and reward go hand in hand. The historically high returns of the stock market are impossible without risk; anyone who tells you otherwise is lying. But not everyone can stomach having all of their investments in stocks and mutual funds.

If your risk tolerance is low (if you're scared of bears), or you're approaching retirement, it's best to keep your money someplace safe, such as bond funds or high-yield savings accounts. I keep cash equal to a few months of expenses in savings. I have a friend who is far less risk-tolerant than I am who keeps an entire year of expenses in savings. (Please, if you're going to set this much money aside, put it into a high-yield savings account or certificates of deposit!)

Even if your risk tolerance isn't all that high, you can still invest in the stock market, even during downturns. Dollar-cost averaging is an excellent way to do this. Dollar-cost averaging simply means making regular, scheduled investments instead of buying into the stock market all at once. It's a way to mitigate risk. An indexed mutual fund decreases risk because your money is diversified across many stocks. Dollar-cost averaging decreases risk even further because your money is diversified across time.

Buying low can be intimidating. Suppose the markets never go back up?

When I was dollar-cost averaging, I set up a system through ShareBuilder (sharebuilder.com), an online brokerage that's a subsidiary of ING Direct, though there are many other ways to do it. On the first of every month, ShareBuilder pulled $250 from my credit union and used the money to buy shares of index funds inside my Roth IRA. The process was painless. I invested every month, whether the market was up or down. It let me ignore the news and enjoy life knowing my long-term plan was in motion.

Dollar-cost averaging makes investing easy: you set it and forget it.

But don't just take my word for it. Here are a handful of sites that offer tools and tricks to help you tangle with bear markets:

■ http://tinyurl.com/dollarcostaveraging—Michael Fischer's video presentation about the virtues of dollar-cost averaging
■ http://tinyurl.com/fearofinvesting—Erin Burt offers five tricks to conquer your fear of investing
■ http://tinyurl.com/riskquiz—Rutgers University helps you assess your risk tolerance
■ http://tinyurl.com/stupidinvestors—Ben Stein on why "smart" investors are sometimes stupid
■ http://tinyurl.com/DCAbenefits—A great introduction to the benefits of dollar-cost averaging

In Why Smart People Make Big Money Mistakes and How to Correct Them, Gary Belsky and Thomas Gilovich point to research that shows "the pain people feel from losing $100 is much greater than the pleasure they experience from gaining the same amount." Don't let the bear scare you. You can wrestle with him and come out ahead.

J.D. Roth writes about smart personal finance at getrichslowly.org.

WEEK SIX

1 Figure out your investing style (30 minutes). Decide whether you want the simple investment options of a lifecycle fund, or more control (and the complexity) of index funds. I recommend a lifecycle fund as the 85 Percent Solution.

2 Research your investments (3 hours to 1 week). If you've decided on a lifecycle fund, research the funds from Vanguard, T. Rowe Price, and Schwab (see page 87 for contact info). This should take a few hours. If you're constructing your own portfolio, it will take more time (and more money to meet the minimums of each fund). Use the Swensen model as a basic template and prioritize which funds you'll buy today and which you'll get later. Once you decide on an asset allocation, research funds using a fund screener like the one in your investing account, Morningstar X-Ray, or the great one on www.etrade.com.

3 Buy your fund(s) (1 hour to 1 week). Buying a lifecycle fund is easy: First, transfer money to your investment account. (For 401(k)s, you should already be directing money from each paycheck into your 401(k) account. For Roth IRAs, this money should be waiting in your savings account from Chapter 5. If you don't have cash lying around to invest, set a savings goal and wait until you have enough to invest in your first fund.) Once the money is ready and has been transferred to your investment account, log in to your account, enter the ticker symbol, and you're finished. If you're buying individual index funds, you'll usually need to buy one at a time and set up savings accounts for the others.

Yes! You're now an investor! And not only that, but you've reached the end of the six-week program. You've optimized your credit cards and bank accounts and started investing—and, even better, you've tied your system together so it works automatically with hardly any effort on your part. There's just a little more: In the next chapter we'll focus on how to maintain your investments. Then, in the last chapter, I'll address all those random questions you have about money and life in general. But the truth is, by making it all the way through this chapter, you've already done all the hard work.

CHAPTER 8

EASY MAINTENANCE

You've done the hard work: Here's how to maintain (and optimize) your financial infrastructure

You may have noticed that this chapter is one of the shortest in the book. That's because you've already put the 85 Percent Solution into place and dealt with the most important parts of your finances: your credit cards, bank accounts, spending, and investments. Most people are still struggling with paying their monthly bills. So congratulations. But—of course there's a *but*—if you're seriously nerdy and want to know more about enhancing your finances, this is the chapter for you. We'll cover a few topics that will help you optimize your investments even further. Remember, though: This is extra credit, so don't feel the need to follow the advice in this chapter unless you really want to.

Feed Your System

In the previous chapter, you chose your investments and set things up so they run automatically. The automatic system is great, but it's fueled by only one thing: the money you feed it. That means that your system is only as strong as the amount you put in it. The earlier chapters in this book were about implementing the 85 Percent Solution—getting started was the hardest and most important step. It didn't matter if you were contributing only $100 per month. But now it's about the raw volume you put into your system—more in, more out. Do you really want to wait twenty-five years to have $100,000? If not, feed your system as much money as possible now. Every dollar you invest today will be worth many more tomorrow.

HOW RICH WILL I BE IN . . .

How much will your monthly investment be worth, assuming an 8 percent return?

IF YOU INVEST . . .	$100/ month	$500/ month	$1,000/ month
After 5 years . . .	$7,347	$36,738	$73,476
After 10 years . . .	$18,294	$91,473	$182,946
After 25 years . . .	$95,102	$475,513	$951,026

Don't just take it from me, though. Go to www.dinkytown.net and open up one of their investment calculators. Enter in your monthly investment contribution, assuming an 8 percent return—don't forget to factor in taxes if you're not using a Roth IRA. You'll likely see that your current contributions will grow more slowly than you thought. But by adding a small amount per month—even $100 or $200 more—the numbers will change dramatically.

In Chapter 4, I outlined a Conscious Spending Plan that suggested general percentages of income to allocate for savings and investing. Your first goal was to aim for those percentages. Now it's time to move beyond those amounts so you can save and invest as much as possible. I can hear you screaming, "Are you kidding? I can't squeeze out another cent. I hate you, Ramit!" This is not about me wanting to deprive you. Actually, quite the opposite: Because compounding works so effectively, the more you save now, the more you'll have later (by a huge amount). You saw this in the dinkytown.net calculator. Now, go in and play around with your Conscious Spending Plan to see how you can eke out a little more to put toward your investments every month. Optimizing your plan might involve doing some serious bargaining when you make major purchases like a car or house (see Chapter 9). Or you might need to cut your expenses as ruthlessly as possible. (Don't forget to check out my "Save $1000 in 30 Days Challenge" at www.iwillteachyoutoberich.com/30daychallenge.) You may even think about negotiating a higher salary or getting a higher-paying job (see page 234). No matter how you go about it, be sure that you're shoveling the maximum amount possible into your system every month. Remember, it's never easier to do this than when you're in your twenties and thirties—and the more you feed into your system now, the sooner you'll be rich.

Ignore the Noise

N ow that you've mastered the basics of personal finance and set up your automated system, you're going to start noticing how badly most other people are managing their money. Here, for example, are three real recent quotes from my highly educated friends:

Q: *"I don't know what to do with my 401(k). I was advised to put it all in money market for now since mutual funds are not doing well. Is this right? How do you know when the downturn has hit bottom? Somebody said that it may take five years to get this mortgage mess turned around!"*

MY RESPONSE: The day-to-day movements of the market shouldn't concern you. If you have a long time horizon, you're automatically investing each month. When the market is going up, your system will automatically buy fewer shares. When the market is going down, it will buy more shares. Over time, you'll do far better than speculators who try to predict where the market will go.

Q: *"Forget index funds. I made a 67 percent return with my Russian mutual fund last year, and that's after fees."*

MY RESPONSE: It doesn't matter what happened last year, it matters what happens in the next ten to twenty years. Plus, if a fund goes up, it can also go down. That's why asset allocation is more important—and less risky—than a superstar fund.

Q: *"Dude, you're wasting your money on renting in San Francisco. Why don't you buy a house?"*

MY RESPONSE: Renting is actually an excellent decision in certain markets—and real estate is generally a poor financial investment, which I cover on page 250.

Look, you've decided on Automatic Investing because it's a simple, low-cost way of investing. You've seen the research indicating that it beats traditional fund managers. And yet, every time your friends ask

> ## UNLIKE OTHER PEOPLE, WHO WORRY ABOUT MONEY (BECAUSE THEY NEVER LEARNED HOW IT WORKS), YOU GET TO FOCUS ON THE THINGS YOU LOVE.

you one of those questions or you see a report about the "plunging" stock market, you'll be tempted to change your investing style. Buy that tech company's stock! Sell oil, it's no good! The sky is falling!!! This is especially true in tumultuous times, like during the global financial crisis of 2008. One day the market dropped 700 points, the next week it soared 900 points. As a result, the pundits were out in full force, making all sorts of absurd claims. The volatility spooked people, and ordinary Americans started withdrawing from the market. For most people, fear guides their investment decisions.

Ignore it all. As I discussed in Chapter 6, the benefit of Automatic Investing is that you don't have to focus on these heart-pounding stock reports from pundits and magazines every day! Unlike other people, who will clasp their hands and worry about money (because they never took a couple of hours to learn how it works), you get to focus on the things you love: hanging out with friends, visiting your family, traveling, or whatever you want to do. Ignore the noise. Force yourself to resist logging in to your investment account more than once a month—that's it. If you've set up your asset allocation and are consistently funding it, stick to your guns. You're investing for the long term, and when you look back, day-to-day changes (even the cataclysmic plunges of 2008) will seem like minor blips—which they are.

Rebalancing Your Investments

I f you have a diversified portfolio, some of your investments, such as international stocks, may outperform others. To keep your asset allocation on track, you'll want to rebalance once a year so your international stocks don't become a larger part of your portfolio than you intended. Think of your investment portfolio like your backyard: If you want your zucchini to be only 15 percent of your backyard, and they grow like crazy and end up taking over 30 percent, you'll want to rebalance by either cutting the zucchini back, or by getting a bigger yard so that the zucchini is back to covering only 15 percent. I know, I know—I should become an organic gardener. Ladies, it's hard to deny that I am a Renaissance man.

The good news: If you've chosen a lifecycle fund as described on page 180, you can skip this section—those funds handle rebalancing for you.

But if you've chosen to manage your own asset allocation, you'll need to rebalance every twelve to eighteen months. Otherwise, within a couple of years, your allocation will be completely skewed. For example, let's say you create an asset allocation based on the Swensen model:

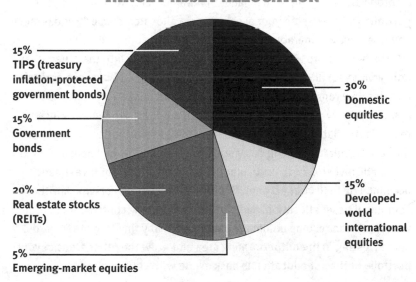

TARGET ASSET ALLOCATION

15%
TIPS (treasury inflation-protected government bonds)

15%
Government bonds

20%
Real estate stocks (REITs)

5%
Emerging-market equities

30%
Domestic equities

15%
Developed-world international equities

Now let's assume that domestic equities gain 50 percent one year. (For easy calculations, let's hold all other investments constant.) All of a sudden, domestic equities represent a larger part of your portfolio, and all the other numbers are out of whack.

ALLOCATION AFTER DOMESTIC EQUITIES JUMP 50%

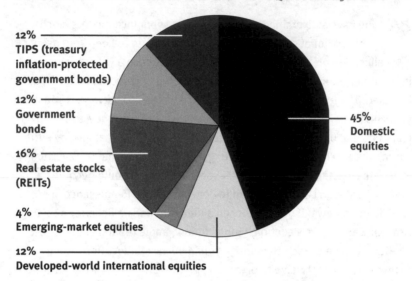

12%
TIPS (treasury
inflation-protected
government bonds)

12%
Government
bonds

16%
Real estate stocks
(REITs)

4%
Emerging-market equities

12%
Developed-world international equities

45%
Domestic
equities

Although it's great that one of your investment areas is performing well, you want to keep your allocation in check so one sector isn't disproportionately larger or smaller than the others. Rebalancing your portfolio will make sure your assets remain allocated properly and protect you from being vulnerable to one specific sector's ups and downs.

The best way to rebalance is to plow more money into the other areas until your asset allocation is back on track. How? Assuming your domestic equities now represent 45 percent of your asset allocation—but should actually be only 30 percent— stop sending money there temporarily and redistribute that 30 percent of your investment contribution evenly over the rest of your investment categories. You can do this by "pausing" your automatic investment to particular funds from within your investment account. Log in to your account, find the fund that's out of whack with your initial asset allocation, and stop your automatic contributions. (Don't worry, you can resume automatic payments at any time.) In other words, stop investing in the outperforming area and grow the other areas of your portfolio until your allocation is back in line with your goals.

Check out the chart on the next page to see how it works. As you can see, in this case, after eight months you're back on target, more or less, and can go back to your original allocations.

Note: There's another way to rebalance, but I don't like doing it. You can rebalance by selling the outperforming equities and plowing the money into other areas to bring the allocation back under control. I hate selling because it involves trading fees, paperwork, and "thinking," so I don't recommend this.

Don't forget to set a calendar reminder to resume your automatic payments. With two minutes of math, which you may consider torture (unless you're Asian), you can know exactly when to resume your payments.

If, on the other hand, one of your funds has *lost* money, that will also knock your asset allocation out of whack. In this case, you can pause the other funds and add money to the loser until it returns to where it should be in your portfolio. To keep the math simple, I recommend the Portfolio Allocator at www.morningstar.com to help guide your rebalancing.

And remember, if you've invested in a lifecycle fund (see page 180), this will be automatically taken care of for you—yet another reason I like them.

Stop Worrying About Taxes (and the 85 Percent Solution for Handling Them)

People worry about taxes too much, and they make all kinds of bad decisions to avoid them. Listen to me: You pay taxes only if you make money. If you're paying 30 percent in taxes on something, it means you made 70 percent elsewhere, so do not freak out about taxes. Plus, it's your damned civic duty. Want to complain about taxes? Go take a ride on a road anywhere in Africa or Southeast Asia. After two hours of bouncing in the back of a rickshaw, the top of your skull will be permanently dented and you'll look like a coal worker from the *Titanic*. So give me a break, pay your taxes, do your civic duty.

(continued on page 210)

Rebalancing Your Portfolio

$10,000 PORTFOLIO AFTER GAIN OF 50% IN DOMESTIC EQUITIES

Value		$12,727	← New portfolio value
	Allocation	**Value**	
Domestic	45%	$5,727	←
International	12%	$1,500	←
Emerging Markets	4%	$500	←
REITs	16%	$2,000	←
Bonds	12%	$1,500	←
TIPS	12%	$1,500	←

	Month 2		Month 3		Month 4	
Value	$13,727		$14,727		$15,727	
	Allocation	Value	Allocation	Value	Allocation	Value
Domestic	42%	$5,727	39%	$5,727	36%	$5,727
International	12%	$1,710	13%	$1,920	14%	$2,130
Emerging Markets	4%	$610	5%	$720	5%	$830
REITs	16%	$2,260	17%	$2,520	18%	$2,780
Bonds	12%	$1,710	13%	$1,920	14%	$2,130
TIPS	12%	$1,710	13%	$1,920	14%	$2,130

Note: In some cases, the numbers in the above columns don't add up to 100%

Because your domestic equities now represent 45 percent of your portfolio, rather than the targeted 30 percent, you have to take action. Pause your automatic contribution to domestic equities and reallocate that 30 percent by distributing it evenly to the other five asset classes (e.g., each would get an additional 6 percent). $1,000 monthly contributions will now be allocated as follows:

0%: Put this investment on pause and evenly distribute the 30% across the other asset classes (i.e., 6% for each).

21%: The target is 15%, so add 6% and you'll get 21%. Monthly contribution: $210

11%: The target here is 5%, so you again add 6%. Monthly contribution: $110

26%: Target is 20%. Monthly contribution: $260

21%: Target is 15%. Monthly contribution: $210

21%: Target is 15%. Monthly contribution: $210

Month 5		Month 6		Month 7		Month 8	
$16,727		$17,727		$18,727		$19,727	
Allocation	Value	Allocation	Value	Allocation	Value	Allocation	Value
34%	$5,727	32%	$5,727	31%	$5,727	29%	$5,727
14%	$2,340	14%	$2,550	15%	$2,760	15%	$2,970
6%	$940	6%	$1,050	6%	$1,160	6%	$1,270
18%	$3,040	19%	$3,300	19%	$3,560	19%	$3,820
14%	$2,340	14%	$2,550	15%	$2,760	15%	$2,970
14%	$2,340	14%	$2,550	15%	$2,760	15%	$2,970

because of the variables of rounding.

MANAGING ASSET ALLOCATION WITH MULTIPLE ACCOUNTS AND MINIMAL EFFORT

by nickel of www.fivecentnickel.com

*I*nvestment experts have argued for years that asset allocation is one of the most important factors in determining your success as an investor. In other words, picking the proper mix of investment types in the proper proportions is the key to maximizing your returns while minimizing your risk. While entire books have been written about how to determine a proper allocation, much less attention has been paid to the ins and outs of maintaining this balance, especially when you (and perhaps a spouse) are managing multiple investment accounts.

Consider the case of a married couple with a taxable investment account, two Roth IRAs, and two 401(k) accounts. Even with a relatively simple allocation of X percent in domestic stocks, Y percent in international stocks, and Z percent in bonds, maintaining the proper allocation can get complicated. If you've chosen a lifecycle fund, none of this is really relevant, since you can just choose the same fund in all of your accounts. But if you're handling your own asset allocation, how do you keep managing multiple investments simple?

THE ONE POT SOLUTION. *The solution is simple: Treat all of your accounts as one big pot of money. Instead of trying to hit the proper X/Y/Z allocation in each account, shoot for maintaining that allocation overall. In order to make this work with the least effort possible, keep one account as your "variable" account and make the others static. The variable account will contain a mix of different funds, which you can rebalance based on your target asset allocation. The static accounts will each contain a single type of investment, whether it's domestic equities, international equities, or bonds. For example, your Roth IRA could contain a few different funds (and would be the variable account), while your wife's 401(k) could be a static account, which you'd only use to buy domestic equities.*

If you need to rebalance your overall portfolio, log in to your variable account and make changes. For example, if your international equities have grown faster than your other investments, and are now disproportionately higher than you want, log into your variable account and exchange some of your international holdings into domestic stocks and/or bonds. Alternatively, you can change your ongoing contributions to put the international funds on "pause" until things even out.

So how should you decide which assets go where? I have several guiding principles: First and foremost, tax-inefficient (i.e., income-generating) assets such as bonds should go into a tax-advantaged account like an IRA or 401(k). Conversely, taxable accounts should only hold tax-efficient investments like equity index funds, and you should try to make these accounts static to minimize the tax consequences associated with selling your investments when rebalancing. Finally, since withdrawals from Roth accounts such as a Roth IRA or Roth 401(k) will be completely tax free, you should seek to maximize growth in those accounts by picking aggressive investments.

> **Keeping one asset type per account eliminates the need to rebalance within each individual account.**

The real benefit here is that keeping one asset type per account eliminates the need to rebalance within each individual account. Instead, rebalancing becomes a matter of tweaking the holdings within your variable account to bring your overall allocation back into line.

You'll handle ongoing contributions in much the same way. All contributions made into a static account go directly into its chosen asset class. For instance, all contributions into a 100 percent bond account would go to purchase bonds—and so on. You can then balance out your contributions across your variable account(s) so that your total contributions are in proportion with the desired X/Y/Z mix.

THE DOWNSIDE. The only real drawback to this strategy is that, in an extremely turbulent market, your allocation might get so far out of line that you can't correct it by rebalancing your overall holdings across accounts. For example, in the latter half of 2008, stocks dropped dramatically. So if you wanted to rebalance by selling bonds and buying more stocks, you might not have had enough bonds available to exchange into stocks in your variable account(s). In such cases, you'd have to "unlock" one of your static accounts and use that to help rebalance your portfolio. For the most part, however, you won't have to do this, and this strategy will save you a ton of headaches.

---

nickel writes about personal finance at http://www.fivecentnickel.com.

(continued from page 205)

Okay, that was a weird tangent. I hate to say this, but aside from the very basics of saving on taxes (like taking advantage of tax-deferred accounts and not selling investments before holding them for a year), chances are you don't make enough to worry about them. You certainly don't need to make investment decisions—like buying tax-efficient municipal bonds—to save on taxes. People in their twenties who do this have usually read something in some magazine and then they start scheming ways to avoid the tax man. Let's be honest. Once you start making too much to invest in your Roth IRA, you'll need more help in this department. But for now, follow that old adage: "Don't let Uncle Sam make your investment decisions."

THE ONE THING YOU NEED TO KNOW ABOUT TAXES AND INVESTMENTS

Invest as much as possible into tax-deferred accounts like your 401(k) and Roth IRA. Because retirement accounts are tax advantaged, you'll enjoy significant rewards. Your 401(k) money won't be taxed until you withdraw it many years down the line, and your Roth IRA earnings won't be taxed at all. More important, you won't have to worry about the minutiae, including picking tax-efficient funds or knowing when to sell to beat end-of-year distributions. By taking this one step of investing in tax-advantaged retirement accounts, you'll sidestep the vast majority of tax concerns.

Investing in tax-advantaged retirement accounts is the 85 Percent Solution for taxes. Sure, you could create complicated tax structures, start putting money away in 529s for your kids, and use the annual gift allowance to give thousands away to others in gifts—but who the hell needs to do that right now? Investing as much as possible in tax-deferred accounts is the answer to 85 percent of your tax questions.

WHY YOU SHOULD THINK TWICE ABOUT SELLING

In general, any time you sell your investments, you'll be eligible to pay taxes when April 15th rolls around. The government has created incentives for long-term investing: If you sell an investment that you've held for less than a year, you'll be subject to ordinary income tax, which is usually 25 to 35 percent. Most people who buy a stock and make $10,000 in nine months and stupidly decide to sell it really pocket only $7,500.

If, however, you hold your investment for more than a year, you'll pay only a capital-gains tax, which in most cases is currently 15 percent (depending on your income, it could even be less). This is a strong incentive to buy and hold for the long term. In the above example of a $10,000 gain, if you sold it after one year and were taxed at 15 percent, you'd pocket $8,500.

Here's the trick: If you've invested within a tax-advantaged retirement account, you don't have to pay taxes in the year that you sell your investment. In a 401(k), which is tax deferred, you'll pay taxes much later when you withdraw your money. In a Roth IRA, by contrast, you've already paid taxes on the money you contribute, so when you withdraw, you won't pay taxes at all.

Since you presumably made a good investment, why not hold it for the long term? In Chapter 6, we covered how people can't time the market. In Chapter 3, I showed you how buy-and-hold investing produces dramatically higher returns than frequent trading. And once you've factored in taxes, the odds are stacked against you if you sell. This is yet another argument for not buying individual stocks, and instead using lifecycle funds or index funds to create a tax-efficient, simple portfolio. Remember, all of this assumes that you made a *good investment*.

Bottom line: Invest in retirement accounts and hold your investments for the long term. Until your portfolio swells to roughly $100,000, that's about all you need to know.

Knowing When to Sell Your Investments

In your twenties and thirties, there are only three reasons to sell your investments: You need the money for an emergency, you made a terrible investment and it's consistently underperforming the market, or you've achieved your specific goal for investing.

YOU NEED THE MONEY FOR AN EMERGENCY

If you suddenly need money for an emergency, here's your hierarchy of where to get it.

1. Use your savings account.

2. Sell any valuables that aren't critical to you. Seriously—use eBay. I'll be honest: You probably won't get a lot of money from selling valuables (people have a tendency to overvalue their own property compared with what others will pay for it). But selling some of your own goods is an important psychological step—it will let you prove how serious you are both to yourself and to your family (which will help if you're asking them for help).

3. Ask your family if you can borrow the money from them. *Note:* This doesn't work if your family is crazy.

4. Use the money in your retirement accounts. You can always withdraw the principal you contributed to your Roth IRA penalty-free, although you'll be severely retarding your money's ability to compound over time. With a 401(k), you can take money out for "hardship withdrawals," which typically include medical expenses, buying a home, tuition, preventing foreclosure, and funeral expenses, but you'll probably still pay early-withdrawal fees. If it comes to this, consult your HR representative. But I urge you to avoid cashing out your retirement accounts because of the penalties and taxes involved.

5. Use your credit card only as a last resort. I can't emphasize this enough: The chances are very good that your credit card will gouge you when you repay it, so don't do this unless you're truly desperate.

YOU MADE A TERRIBLE INVESTMENT THAT'S CONSISTENTLY UNDERPERFORMING

This point is largely moot if you invested in an index fund or series of index funds, because they reflect the entire market's performance. If it's going down, that means the entire market is down. If you believe the market will recover, that means investments are on sale for cheaper prices than before, meaning not only should you *not* sell, but you should keep investing and pick up shares at a cheaper price.

But let's talk about this conceptually to understand when to sell an investment for poor performance. If you pulled up a list of your investments and saw the chart at the top of the next page, what would you do?

"Ramit," you might say frantically. "This stock sucks! I need to sell it before I lose all my money!"

Not so fast. You have to look at the context before you decide what to do. For instance, if the example is a consumer-goods stock, how is the rest of the consumer-goods industry doing? (*Note:* You can research

CONSUMER-GOODS STOCK

Date	Price	Date	Price
6/3/2002	33.43	1/3/2006	23.78
1/2/2003	31.53	6/1/2006	23.90
6/2/2003	31.01	1/3/2007	26.29
1/2/2004	35.55	6/1/2007	27.68
6/1/2004	35.45	1/2/2008	22.91
1/3/2005	26.45	5/2/2008	20.61
6/1/2005	28.17		

industries by going to Yahoo Finance, clicking on "Investing," and then on "Industries.")

By looking at the stock *and* the surrounding industry (see chart below), you see that the entire industry is in decline. It's not your particular investment. They're *all* doing poorly. Now, this raises questions about the industry, but it also gives you a context to explain your stock's plunging returns. And just because they're plunging, by the way, doesn't mean that you should sell immediately. All industries experience declines at one time or another. In fact, looking at the chart below, I'd dig in more to see what was happening with the industry. Is it still viable? Are there competitors

CONSUMER-GOODS INDUSTRY INDEX

Date	Price	Date	Price
6/3/2002	50	1/3/2006	38
1/2/2003	49	6/1/2006	36
6/2/2003	45	1/3/2007	32
1/2/2004	42	6/1/2007	30
6/1/2004	44	1/2/2008	31
1/3/2005	40	5/2/2008	29
6/1/2005	38		

replacing it? (For example, if you own shares in a company that's producing cassette-playing Walkmans, chances are that business is not coming back.) From looking at the above chart, it appears that the stock is performing in line with the rest of the industry. If you think the industry or investment is simply going through a cyclical downturn, then hang on to the investment and continue regular purchases of shares. If, however, you think the industry won't recover, you may want to sell the investment.

Now if your stock looked like *this*, I might consider selling:

STOCK FROM INDUSTRY A

Date	Price	Date	Price
6/3/2002	43	1/3/2006	23.78
1/2/2003	31.53	6/1/2006	23.9
6/2/2003	31.01	1/3/2007	26.29
1/2/2004	35.55	6/1/2007	27.68
6/1/2004	35.45	1/2/2008	22.91
1/3/2005	26.45	5/2/2008	20.61
6/1/2005	28.17		

INDUSTRY A INDEX

Date	Price	Date	Price
6/17/2002	335.97	1/3/2006	372.26
1/2/2003	317.39	6/1/2006	355.64
6/2/2003	324.38	1/3/2007	388.98
1/2/2004	351.22	6/1/2007	425.47
6/1/2004	358.26	1/2/2008	406.19
1/3/2005	346.81	5/2/2008	372.74
6/1/2005	363.26		

As you can see, this stock really had been underperforming against its industry index.

Once you decide it's time to sell an investment, the process is easy. You simply log in to your investment account, browse to the investment you want to sell, and then click "Sell." If you're selling outside of a retirement account, there are many tax implications, such as tax-loss harvesting (which lets you offset capital gains with losses), but since most of us will invest all of our money in tax-efficient retirement accounts, I'm not going to get into these issues here. I want to emphasize that I almost never have to sell investments because I rarely make specific stock investments. If you pick a lifecycle fund or build a portfolio of index funds instead, you rarely have to think about selling. My advice: Save your sanity and focus on more important things.

YOU ACHIEVED YOUR SPECIFIC GOAL

Buy and hold is a great strategy for ultra-long-term investments, but lots of people invest in the medium to short term to make money for specific goals. For example, "I'm going to invest for a dream vacation to Thailand. . . . I don't need to take the trip any time soon, so I'll just put $100/month into my investing account." Remember, if your goal is less than five years away, you should set up a savings goal in your savings account. But if you've invested money for a longer-term goal and you've achieved it, sell and don't think twice. That's a great investing success, and you should use the money for whatever your original goal was.

Giving Back: Elevating Your Goals Beyond the Day-to-Day

Most people spend their entire lives handling the day-to-day issues of money and never get ahead. How am I going to pay off that loan? Oh man, why did I buy that $300 jacket? Damn, I thought I canceled that subscription.

If you've followed the steps in this book, you've moved past these basic questions. Your accounts work together automatically. You know how much you can afford to spend going out and how much you want to save each month. If something goes wrong, your system lets you easily see if you need to cut costs, make more money, or adjust your lifestyle. It's all there.

Financial Options for Super-Achievers: Make the Ten-Year Plan That Few Others Do

I'm always surprised by the e-mails I get from people who have optimized every part of their investing strategy and are nonetheless *still* looking for more ways they can optimize their finances. It's easy: Just ask people five to ten years older than you what they *wish* they had started earlier, then do that. You'll get three answers right off the bat:

1. CREATE AN EMERGENCY FUND. An emergency fund is simply another savings goal that is a way to protect against job loss, disability, or simple bad luck. Most people in their twenties don't need emergency funds because we can just borrow money from our other savings goals or, worst case, go home to Mom and Dad. But if you have a mortgage or you need to provide for your family, an emergency fund is a critical piece of being financially secure. To create one, just set up an extra savings goal and then funnel money to it in the same way you would your other goals. Eventually, your emergency fund should contain six months of spending money (which includes *everything:* your mortgage, other loans, food, transportation, taxes, gifts, and anything else you would conceivably spend on).

2. INSURANCE. As you get older and more crotchety, you'll want more and more types of insurance to protect yourself from loss. This includes home-owner insurance (fire, flood, and earthquake) and life insurance. If you own a home, you need insurance, but young, single people don't need life insurance. First of all, statistically, we hardly ever die, and the insurance payout is useful only for people who depend on your livelihood, like your spouse and kids. Beyond that, insurance is really out of the scope of this book, but if you're truly interested, I encourage you talk to your parents and their friends, and search for "life insurance" online to research the various options. You probably don't need to buy a bunch of insurance options right now, but you can certainly set up a savings goal so when you *do* need them, you'll have money to use. One last thing: Insurance is almost never a good investment, despite what financial salespeople (or clueless parents) will tell you. So use it as protection from downside risk—like for fires or accidental death when you have a family—but don't think of it as a growth investment.

3. CHILDREN'S EDUCATION. Whether or not you have children yet, your first goal should be to excel financially for yourself. I always get confused when I see people on TV who are in debt yet want to save for their children's education. What the hell? Listen up, Momma: First, get out of debt and save for your own retirement. *Then* you can worry about your kids. That said, just as Roth IRAs are great retirement accounts, 529s—educational savings plans with significant tax advantages—are great for children's education. If you've got kids (or know that one day you will) and some spare cash, pour it into a 529.

These are just a few of the things you'll be forced to think about in the next ten years. The best way to prepare yourself is to talk to successful people who are somewhat older than you and have their act together. Their advice can be invaluable—and can give you an edge on planning for the next decade.

That means it's time to think about elevating your goals beyond the day to day. Whereas most people might be so consumed with the minutiae of money that they've never thought about getting rich ("I just want to pay off this debt."), you can set larger goals of doing the things you love using money to support you.

I'm afraid this will sound sanctimonious to some of you, but I really don't mean it to be. I believe that part of getting rich is giving back to the community that helped you flourish. There are lots of traditional ways to do this, like volunteering at a soup kitchen or becoming a Big Brother or Big Sister. I wanted to try to contribute on a bigger scale (plus I find that my jokes are not so welcome at soup kitchens). So, in 2006, I created The Sethi Scholarship (scholarships.ramitsethi.com), which awards money and mentoring to one entrepreneurial young person per year. (Fun fact: The first year I launched it, not one person applied.) When I told friends I had launched a scholarship, they looked at me in disbelief. "That's ridiculous," they said. "I could never have enough money to launch a scholarship." They said this while wearing $150 jeans and eating a $40 dinner. How easy would it be for them to set a savings goal and sock away money to give to others? Look, my scholarship is for $1,000. You don't need to be rich to give back. Even $100 helps. And it doesn't have to be a scholarship, either. Sites like Kiva.org let you give directly to poor third-world communities. Or you can donate to your high school, local library, environmental action groups, the Red Cross—whatever means the most to you. And if you're short on cash, donate your time, which is often more valuable than money.

If you think about it, philanthropy mirrors the very same *I Will Teach You to Be Rich* principles you read in this book: The simplest step can get you started. But, as with managing their money, people over-complicate things and create artificial barriers to prevent themselves from giving back. You don't have to be rich to be a philanthropist, just as you don't have to be rich to invest. The point is that now you've got a personal-finance system that few others have. This allows you to elevate your goals beyond making it through the daily grind. When you think back to last year, what was the one big thing you accomplished for others? What will it be this year?

If I could hope for one thing from this book, it would be that you become a master of conscious spending—and then apply those skills to help those around you. Maybe it will be by establishing a scholarship, or mentoring a needy kid, or even just helping your friends manage their money for free. Whatever it is, you're now in the very top tier of investing knowledge. You've moved beyond managing your money for short-term goals and you're thinking strategically about your money and how it can help you to be rich—and how to share that with others.

If this were a movie, it would be raining, violin music would be swelling in the background, and a young soldier would slowly raise his hand to salute an elderly general. With all this talk about giving back, it would be very emotional, and a single tear would be rolling down someone's cheek.

But we've got one last chapter to read. From the thousands of e-mails and blog comments I've received over the years, I know there are a few common issues that come up regularly. Apparently, life isn't all about dissecting the nuts and bolts of asset allocation and creating compound-growth charts. Who knew? In the next chapter, I'll cover the specifics of money and relationships, buying a car and your first house, and managing the daily questions that come up in your financial life. Last chapter! Let's do it.

CHAPTER 9

A RICH LIFE

The finances of relationships,
weddings, buying a car, and your first house

What does *rich* mean to you? I brought this up in the introduction, but throughout this book we've spent a lot of time talking about *money*. As I've said before, that's great, but I believe being rich is about much more than that. For me, it's about freedom— it's about not having to think about money all the time and being able to travel and work on the things that interest me. It's about being able to use money to do whatever I want—and not having to worry about my budget, asset allocation, or how I'll ever be able to afford a house.

But that's just me. Being rich probably means something different to you. In this chapter, I'm going to address some of the most common questions I've received about life and money. I hope my answers will help you live a richer life.

Student Loans— Pay Them Down or Invest?

Student loans are a big kick in the face that the real world has arrived. CNN reports that the average college graduate has around $20,000 of student loans—plus, as the U.S. Public Interest Research Group recently indicated, more than $2,500 of credit card debt. It can seem hard to get ahead when you have the baggage of student loans weighing you down. The good news is that student loans were probably an excellent financial decision (unless you ended up being an artist or actor . . . In those cases, get a real job). College graduates far outearn those with only a high school degree. Still, if you have $20,000 of debt hanging over your shoulders, you're going to want to know how to handle it. Although we already talked about getting out of student debt in Chapter 1, there's one additional question I constantly get asked: "Should I invest or pay off my student loans?"

INVESTING VS. PAYING OFF STUDENT LOANS

It can be difficult to hear the drumbeat of "invest early!" when you're scrambling to pay $500 or $1,000 in student loans each month. But when it comes to putting money toward investing or your student loans, you really have three choices:

- *Pay the minimum monthly payment on your student loans and invest the rest.*

- *Pay as much as possible toward your student loans and then, once they are paid off, start investing.*

- *Do a hybrid 50/50 approach, where you pay half toward your student loans (always paying at least the minimum) and send the other half into your investment accounts.*

Technically, your decision comes down to interest rates. If your student loan had a super-low interest rate of, say, 2 percent, you'd want to pursue option one: Pay your student loans off as slowly as possible because you can make an average of 8 percent by investing in low-cost funds. However, notice I said *technically*. That's because money management isn't always rational. Some people aren't comfortable having any debt at all and want to get rid of it as quickly as possible. If having debt keeps you awake at night, follow option two and pay it off as soon as possible—but understand that you could be losing lots of growth potential just so you can be more comfortable.

I recommend you take a close look at option three, and here's why: The interest rate on most student loans these days is similar to what you'd get in the stock market, so frankly your decision will be a toss-up. All things being equal, the money you would stand to make by investing would be about the same amount that you'll pay out in interest on your student loan, so basically it's a wash. It won't really matter whether you pay off your student loans or invest, because you'll get roughly the same return. *Except for two things:* compound interest and tax-advantaged retirement accounts. When you invest in your twenties and early thirties, you get huge benefits from compound interest. If you wait until you're older to invest, you'll never be able to catch up on those earnings. Plus, if you're investing in tax-advantaged accounts like 401(k)s and Roth IRAs (see Chapter 3), you're getting gains from tax benefits. That's why I would consider a hybrid split, paying off your debt with part of your money and investing with the rest. The exact split depends on your risk tolerance. Most people will simply choose a 50/50 split to keep things simple, but if you're more aggressive, you'll probably want to invest more.

LOVE AND MONEY

MONEY HAS A HUGE EFFECT ON RELATIONSHIPS. JUST TAKE A LOOK AT your day-to-day life: I bet you have a friend who never leaves enough of a tip at restaurants or never pays you back when you lend him money. Nothing is more annoying than someone who mistreats you with money— and those are just your *friends*! Imagine when you have a husband or wife, and you have to share bank accounts and responsibilities for rent and car payments and everything else. You better believe money will be an issue.

That's why I want to spend some time talking about how to handle money in your different relationships—your relationship with your parents, your boyfriend or girlfriend, your future spouse. I thought about dealing with money and your children, too, but considering I am planning to buy my kids paper towels instead of shoes, I may not be the best person to talk about that.

Letting Your Parents Manage Your Money Is Dumb

You wouldn't believe how many questions I get from smart, educated people who think it's fine to let their parents manage their money. When you think about it, it is not that surprising. Parents who offer to let their kids send cash to the family money manager have probably coddled their kids for their entire lives. Do you want to let your folks feed you with a bottle and change your diaper, too? Don't be one of these jackasses.

It's time to grow up. Even though parents have good intentions, offering to handle money management is one of the worst things they can do for their kids. At our age, we should be learning how to manage our money ourselves. No financial advisers, no B.S. And if we make mistakes, that's okay—maybe we lose $100 or even $1,000 now and again, but we learn from those mistakes. By doing this we get confident enough to be increasingly aggressive with our investments. Plus, chances are good that after reading this book you know more than your parents do about managing money anyway.

> **IT'S TIME TO GROW UP. AT OUR AGE, WE SHOULD BE LEARNING HOW TO MANAGE OUR MONEY OURSELVES. NO FINANCIAL ADVISERS, NO B.S.**

If you take the lazy route and send your money to your parents, a few things happen. First, you develop a hands-off mentality: "Well, I don't have to worry about it." GOD, IF I HEAR THIS ONE MORE TIME, I AM GOING TO JUMP UP AND BEAT SOMEONE WITH AN ONION. (That way it's unclear why they're crying.) But as I've said over and over, investing is largely hands off once you do the initial research. Buy and hold means buy something and . . .

hold it! Not too hard once you've done your homework. Plus, if it's your own money and you made the investment yourself, you'll actually *want* to track its progress. Trust me, it's kind of fun.

Second, if your parents invest your money, you don't get the kind of transparent information you would if it were your own investment. Sure, you could probably get your parents' password and log in every once in a while and check . . . but would you? Also, if their entire portfolio went up 30 percent, what does that mean for your money (which was probably invested at a different time than their money)? How much did you actually make? I hate math, so I would avoid having to calculate this at all costs.

Third, you want to give yourself bottom-line accountability for any gains or losses. No blaming your parents, their financial adviser (who is paying *his* bills using the fees he charges you), or your parents' fancy full-service account for charging you fees. Your investments should be yours, and so should the wins or losses. It's fine to rely on your parents for advice, and your friends and the Internet are always there to help with evaluating investments, too. But in the end, the decisions should be yours.

Finally, now that you've read this book, you can probably beat your parents' return. (Go to Chapter 6 and revisit the myth of financial expertise to see why.) So please, if your parents suggest you just invest with them, tell them why you'd rather do it on your own.

How to Help Parents Who Are in Severe Debt

As you could probably tell from my rant on parents and money, I'm a big fan of being self-sufficient with your money—whether or not your parents offer to help you out.

But sometimes your parents are in financial trouble of their own. If your parents are in a lot of debt, it can be very tough on your relationship with them—especially if they reach out to you and ask for help. In this case, your biggest challenge is not going to be coming up with a technical personal-finance solution for their problem. Instead, it's going to be persuading them to change decades of bad money-management habits. Work through this delicately but firmly. They'll probably be coping with the crushing guilt of having to rely on their son or daughter to help them with their finances, but don't let them get caught up in feeling bad. Instead, identify where their money is going, set up a plan using the hierarchy of investing (see page 76), and then help your parents make the tough decisions that will be necessary. My readers have used what I've taught them to persuade their parents to do anything from finally setting up a retirement account (when they were in their fifties) to selling their house and downsizing their entire lives.

Every situation is different, but here are some questions you can ask. (Remember: Tread gently. Nobody likes talking about money—especially if it means having to admit to their kids that they need help.)

- *How do they feel about their money? Why?*
- *How much do they make per month? How much do they spend?*
- *What percentage of their income are they saving?*
- *Do they pay fees for their bank accounts and credit cards?*
- *What's their average monthly credit card balance? Why isn't it zero? How could they get it there?*
- *Do they have any investments? If so, how did they choose them?*
- *Do they own mutual fund(s)? How much are they paying in fees?*
- *Are they maximizing their 401(k), at least as much as their company matches?*
- *What about other retirement vehicles like a Roth IRA? Do they have one?*
- *Do they read www.iwillteachyoutoberich.com? NO? WHY NOT, POPS?!?! (Note: I highly recommend that you scream this really loudly at them.)*

Your parents might not have answers to all these questions, but listen closely to what they *do* tell you. I'd encourage you to take the 85 Percent Solution approach and figure out one or two major actions they could take to improve their financial situation. Maybe it means setting up an automatic savings account, or focusing on paying off one credit card so they can feel a small sense of accomplishment. Think back to when you didn't know anything about money and it was incredibly overwhelming. Now you can use what you've learned to help your parents make small changes that will have big results.

The Dreaded "DTR" Conversation with Your Boyfriend or Girlfriend—About Money

Remember how painful those "Define the Relationship" conversations were back in college? Now imagine you have to sit down and talk about money while wishing you could use the sweat from your forehead to drown yourself. Sure, you and your boyfriend or girlfriend might have had an occasional chat about money. But when you're getting serious—whether you're recently engaged or moving in together or just at a point where your decisions start to really affect each other—it's important to spend some time talking about your money and your financial goals. Talking about money with your partner might sound painful, but I promise you it doesn't have to be awkward. As corny as it sounds, it can actually bring you closer together—*if* you know what to ask and stay calm. And if your girlfriend/boyfriend isn't a nut job with $300,000 in credit card debt.

The specific tactics aren't as important as your attitude going in. The key is to start by *asking their advice*. Yes, even if you don't need

> **THE KEY IS TO START BY ASKING THEIR ADVICE. YES, EVEN IF YOU DON'T NEED IT!**

it! Bring the topic up lightly. "Hey, I've been trying to learn about money lately . . . What do you think about investing versus saving?" If you don't get an answer, try this: "Okay, hey, I have another question . . . What do you think about my spending? Is there anything you think I should change?" I guarantee you they'll have an opinion on *that*—and although you're sacrificing yourself, at least it'll get the conversation started.

After a few days, ask for their financial advice again: "What do you think—should I pay off my credit card or my student debt?" (Of course, you already know the answer from page 220.) Then, a few days later, tell them you've been doing some more research. "I picked up a book on personal finance and it had some really interesting stuff in it," you can say. "What do you think about talking about our money together?"

(It is optional to add something like, "The book is by an amazing, weird, gracious author named Ramit Sethi, and I visit his website every day.")

When you sit down to talk, once again start by asking your partner's opinions: "I know you use cash to pay for everything, but this guy says we should use credit cards to build our credit and track spending. What do you think?" The goal of this meeting should be to agree that money is important to both of you, and that you want to work together to help each other with finances. That's it!

If things go well during your first conversation, ask if your boyfriend or girlfriend would be willing to sit down again to go over both of your finances together. Remember, it's not about criticizing or noting things that are being done wrong—it's about figuring out ways to help each other so you can grow together. Some phrases you can use:

- *"You're really good at [X] and I want you to help me with my finances."*
- *"We're going to join our lives together, and I want money to be a part of that."*
- *"One plus one equals three,"* which explains why you two can combine money smarts to create synergies. *Note:* Only MBAs or consultants can use this line with a straight face.

THE BIG MEETING

This is the big day when you both lay bare all your finances and work through them together. But remember, it's not really such a dramatic step, since you've been slowly working toward this for weeks.

It should take about four or five hours to prepare for this meeting. You'll each want to bring the following:

- *A list of your accounts and the amount in each*
- *A list of debts and what the interest rates are*
- *Monthly expenses (see page 104 for details)*
- *Your total income*
- *Any money that is owed to you*
- *A list of short-term and long-term financial goals*

When you sit down, put the paper aside and start by talking about goals. From a financial perspective, what do you want? What kind of lifestyle do you expect? What about vacations in the next year? Does either of you need to support your parents?

Then look at your monthly spending. This will be a sensitive conversation because nobody wants to be judged. But remember, keep an open mind. Show yours first. Ask, "What do you think I could be doing better?" And then it's your partner's turn.

Spend some time talking about your attitudes toward money. How do you treat money? Do you spend more than you make? Why? How did your parents talk about money? (One of my friends has horrible money-management skills, which is confusing because she's so disciplined and smart. After years of knowing her, one day she told me that her dad had declared bankruptcy *twice,* which helped me understand the irrational way she approached money.)

> **SPEND SOME TIME TALKING ABOUT YOUR ATTITUDES TOWARD MONEY. HOW DO YOU TREAT MONEY? DO YOU SPEND MORE THAN YOU MAKE? WHY?**

The most important goal of this conversation is to set up a plan to manage your money, including your credit cards, bank accounts, budget, and investment accounts. Essentially, you want to work through this book with your partner.

Your immediate goal should be to set up a few short- and long-term savings goals, such as a year-end trip and/or something a little more major like buying a car or putting a down payment on a house. At this point, it's probably better not to run through all the numbers for a really large purchase because it can get overwhelming. Just set up a savings goal or two and set up an automatic monthly transfer for each of you. Longer term, you and your girlfriend/boyfriend should work together to get on the same page with your money attitudes. When you set a goal together ("We're going to save enough to put a $30,000 down payment on a house"), you'll both be able to commit to working toward it.

LIVING TOGETHER: WHAT TO DO IF ONE OF YOU MAKES MORE MONEY THAN THE OTHER

The first question to ask is "Do you realize you're living in sin?" Just kidding, I don't give a damn.

Once you and your girlfriend or boyfriend start sharing expenses, questions will invariably come up about how to handle money on a daily basis—especially if one of you has a higher income than the other. When it comes to splitting bills, there are a couple of options.

The first, and most intuitive, choice is to split all the bills 50/50. But that doesn't work for everyone.

As an alternative, how about this fresh idea from Suze Orman? She encourages dividing expenses based proportionately on income. For example, if your monthly rent is $1,000, here's how you might split it up:

DIVIDING EXPENSES BASED ON INCOME

	You	Your partner
Monthly income	$3,000	$2,000
Rental payment	$600 (3,000 / 5,000 = 60%)	$400 (2,000/5,000 = 40%)

WHAT TO DO IF YOUR PARTNER SPENDS MONEY IRRESPONSIBLY

This is the most common complaint I hear from newlywed readers. "Ramit," they write, "my husband spends way too much money on video games. How are we supposed to save money? When I tell him this, he tunes me out and the next day, he's buying something else."

The solution to this is to *elevate the conversation beyond you and your partner.* If you keep trying to tell your partner not to spend money on something, he or she will resent it and ignore you. More than anything, people hate to be judged for their spending, so if you continue making it personal ("You can't spend that much on shoes each month!"), you'll get nowhere.

Instead, keep it simple. Turn to page 106 in Chapter 4 and look at how much it costs to save for common purchases like vacations, Christmas gifts, or a new car. Then have a conversation about what your savings goals are and how much you need to save to reach them—and come to a savings plan that you both agree on.

If you do this, the next time you have an argument about spending, you can steer it away from you and your partner and instead make it about *the plan*. Nobody can get defensive when you're pointing to a piece of paper (rather than pointing at the other person). Say, "Hey, cool iPhone. Are we still on track to hit our savings goal?" This is hard to argue with if you say it in an innocent voice. In fact, they definitely can't get defensive, because they agreed to the plan! By focusing on the plan, not the person, you sidestep the perception of being judgmental and work on bringing spending in line with your goals. This is the way handling money is supposed to work.

The $28,000 Question: Why We're All Hypocrites About Our Wedding (and How to Save for Yours)

A while back, I was out with some friends, including one who was planning her wedding. Because both my sisters had recently gotten married, I suggested she check out a nearby stationery store for her invitations. "It's really expensive, like fourteen dollars per invitation," I told her. "But at least you can get some ideas for design." She looked at me and without a hint of arrogance said, "Oh, I'll check it out. I actually talked to my family and we have an unlimited budget for the wedding."

That one sentence rendered me speechless. She wasn't bragging. She was just saying it matter-of-factly: Her wedding could cost *anything* and that was totally fine. She comes from a very wealthy family, so this isn't so unusual. What *is* unusual, however, is that so many people will scoff at the above story—and then proceed to spend ungodly amounts on their own wedding while steadfastly insisting how absurd "most" people are. I want to help plan for these large life events. But be prepared—you're going to have to confront the hypocrisy that we all have when it comes to these purchases.

OF COURSE *YOUR* WEDDING WILL BE SIMPLE

When my sister called me to tell me that she'd gotten engaged, I was out with my friends. I ordered champagne for everyone. When my other sister told me she was getting married a few months later, I told all my friends again. Then I found out they were each having both an East Coast wedding and a West Coast wedding—for a total of four Indian weddings in a few months! I ordered a round of cyanide and made mine a double.

That's what got me started thinking about weddings. The average American wedding costs almost $28,000, which, *The Wall Street Journal* notes, is "well over half the median annual income in U.S. households." Hold on: Just wait a second before you start rolling your eyes. It's easy to say, "These people should just realize that a wedding is about having a special day, not about putting yourself in crippling debt."

But guess what? When it's your wedding, you're going to want everything to be perfect. Yes, you. So will I. It'll be your special day, so why *not* spend the money to get the extra-long-stemmed roses or the filet mignon? My point isn't to judge people for having expensive weddings. Quite the opposite: The very same people who spend $28,000 on their weddings are the ones who, a few years earlier, said the same thing you're saying right now: "I just want a simple wedding. It's ridiculous to go into debt for just one day." And yet, little by little, they spend more than they planned—more than they can afford—on their special day. Look, there's nothing wrong with wanting your day to be perfect. Let's just acknowledge it and figure out how to achieve our goals.

SO WHAT SHOULD YOU DO?

Knowing the astonishingly high costs of weddings, what can you do? I see three choices:

Cut costs and have a simpler wedding. Great idea, but frankly, most people are not disciplined enough to do this. I don't say this pejoratively, but statistically: Most people will have a wedding that costs tens of thousands of dollars.

Do nothing and figure it out later. This is the most common tactic. I spoke to a recently married person who spent the previous eight months planning her wedding, which ended up becoming a very expensive day. Now, months later, she and her husband don't know how to deal with the resulting debt. If you do this, you are a moron. But you are in good company, because almost everybody else does it, too.

Budget and plan for the wedding. Ask ten people which of these choices they'll make, and every single one of them will pick this one. Then ask them how much money they're saving every month for their wedding (whether they're engaged or not). I guarantee the sputtering and silence will be worth it. This is a great idea in theory but is almost never followed in practice.

If you think about it, we actually have all the information we need. The average age at marriage is about twenty-seven for men and twenty-six for women. We know that the average amount of a wedding is about $28,000. So, if you really are committed to not going into debt for your wedding, here's the astonishing amount you should be saving (whether you're engaged or not):

SCARY FIGURES

Your Age	Months until wedding	Monthly amount needed to save
20	84	$333
21	72	$389
22	60	$467
23	48	$583
24	36	$778
25	24	$1,167
26	12	$2,333
27	1	$28,000

Most of us haven't even conceived of saving this amount for our weddings. Instead, we say things like

- *"Wow, that's a lot. There's no way I can save that. Maybe my parents will help. . . ."*
- *"My wedding won't be like that. It'll be simple and elegant."*

- *"I'll think about it when I get engaged."*
- *"Luckily, I won't have to pay for it."* (Who will? Is your future spouse also thinking like this?)
- *"I have to marry someone rich."* (I've heard people say this, and they were only half joking.)

More commonly, though, we don't think about this at all: one of the most major expenditures of our lifetimes, which will almost certainly arrive in the next few years, and we don't even sit down for ten minutes to think about it. Something's broken here.

SURPRISING WEDDING MATH

This is pretty cool in a sickening, gut-wrenching kind of way. I set up a simulation to see which levers were the most powerful in reducing wedding costs. To be honest, I thought reducing the number of guests would produce the biggest result.

I was wrong.

Interestingly, changing the number of guests doesn't change the cost as much as you'd imagine. In the example on the next page, reducing the headcount by 50 percent reduces the cost only 25 percent.

Beyond the obvious—negotiating for better prices on the venue and food—the best suggestion I've heard about cutting wedding costs is to tackle the *fixed* costs. One of my friends, for example, actually flew in a photographer from the Philippines for his wedding. It sounds extravagant, but even with the flight, he saved $4,000. In another example, my sister had her invitations designed and printed in India for a fraction of what it would have cost in the United States.

In Chapter 4, I encouraged you to pick the one or two biggest problem areas in your spending and address them. Your wedding is no different: You want to look at the biggest expenses with a fine-toothed comb. Pick the biggest two or three expenditures and relentlessly cut their costs. Your honeymoon is going to cost $5,000? See if you can get someone to give you frequent flier miles as a wedding gift, check for travel deals online, enlist your second cousin who's a travel agent, or see if your credit card offers any perks you can use. Bridesmaids' dresses cost $4,000? Cut it in half by going with a local dress store. Chances are, it's better to optimize the three biggest cost areas by 30 percent than to get a 10 percent reduction in everything (and it'll keep you sane).

SAMPLE WEDDING COSTS

Variable costs		
Guests	150	75
Open bar/person	$20	$20
Lunch/person	$30	$30
Reception/person	$120	$120
Subtotal	$25,500	$12,750
Fixed costs		
DJ	$1,000	$1,000
Photographer	$4,000	$4,000
Rentals: tables, chairs, linens	$1,500	$1,250
Flowers	$750	$600
Hotel for guests	$750	$750
Invitations	$1,000	$750
Rehearsal dinner	$1,500	$1,500
Honeymoon	$5,000	$5,000
Dress	$800	$800
Limo	$750	$750
Rings	$5,000	$5,000
Bridesmaids' dresses	$4,000	$4,000
Misc.	$2,000	$2,000
Subtotal	$28,050	$27,400
Grand total	$53,550	$40,150

You can run the simulation yourself to check out how your own planning stacks up. Visit the live wedding-cost spreadsheet at www.iwillteachyoutoberich.com/wedding.

WORK AND MONEY

I'VE SAID IT BEFORE AND I'LL SAY IT AGAIN: FUNDAMENTALLY, THERE ARE two ways to get more money. You can earn more or you can spend less. Cutting costs is great, but I personally find increasing earnings to be a lot more fun. Because most of our income comes from work, it's an excellent place to optimize and earn more. In fact, negotiating your salary at a new job is the fastest legal way to make money. Your starting salary is even more important than you think because it sets the bar for future raises and, in all likelihood, your starting salary at future jobs. A $1,000 or $2,000 salary increase, in other words, can equal many times that over your career. Now let me show you how to get thousands by negotiating for a better salary.

Negotiating Your Salary, I Will Teach You to Be Rich Style

In Chapter 4, I wrote about asking for a raise at your current job. But the single best time to negotiate salary is when you're starting a *new* job. You have the most leverage then and—with some basic preparation—you can earn $5,000 or $10,000 in a simple ten-minute conversation, then retire to a nearby café for a light lunch. Delightful.

When I coach people on negotiation, I pretend to be the hiring manager and ask the toughest questions they might get. My friends don't like this, possibly because I also repeatedly crack jokes about taking the "role play" further than I should, but I force them to do it and they later thank me. When we're finished—four to five hours later—they're exhausted and cranky. But the people I've coached end up negotiating, on average, $6,000 more in salary.

Negotiating is 90 percent about mind-set and 10 percent about tactics. Most people don't believe they should negotiate. They're afraid of being "rude" or of having the employer rescind their offer. That almost never happens, especially because the company may have already spent up to $5,000 recruiting you. If you negotiate, you explicitly communicate that you value yourself more highly than the average employee. Are you average? If not, why would you settle for an average salary?

HIGHLIGHT THE WAYS YOU'LL HELP YOUR COMPANY HIT ITS GOALS.

The basics of negotiating are very simple:

1. Remember that nobody cares about you.

Most new employees come to the table talking about how much *they* want to make. To be totally honest, as a hiring manager, I don't really care what you want to make. I would like to sit in the back of a Bentley with two hot twins and be fed a Taco Bell Grill Stuft Burrito with extra jalapeños. So when you're negotiating, remember this: When it comes to you, your manager cares about two things—how you're going to make him look better, and how you're going to help the company do well.

NEGOTIATING TACTIC: Always frame your negotiation requests in a way that shows how the *company* will benefit. Don't focus on the amount you'll cost the company. Instead, illustrate how much *value* you can provide to the company. If your work will help them drive an initiative that will make $1 million for the company, point that out. Tie your work to the company's strategic goals—and show the boss how you'll make him look good. Highlight how you'll make your boss's life easier by being the go-to person he can hand anything to. And remember that your company will make much more off your work than they pay you, so highlight the ways you'll help your company hit its goals. Your key phrase here is "Let's find a way to arrive at a fair number that works for both of us."

2. Have another job offer—and use it.

This is the single most effective thing you can do to increase your salary. When you have another job offer, your potential employers will have a newfound respect for your skills. It's like seeing the hot girl in the bar who's surrounded by guys. You want her more because everyone else does, too.

(continued on page 238)

How My Friend Got a 28 Percent Raise by Doing Her Homework

I recently helped my friend Rachel, twenty-five, negotiate a job offer, and at my request, she wrote up the process:

First the big picture: I got a 28 percent raise in base salary, which comes out to more than $1,000/hour based on how much time I spent getting the job. Plus stock options, which at least allow me the luxury of dreaming about being a gazillionaire.

I've applied to, and been ignored for, many, many job openings—more than I care to share. Despite this, I decided to jump back into the job market a few months ago after doing marketing for a large hotel in San Francisco. I found a marketing manager position on a site called VentureLoop (Craigslist for startups) and through it I sent in a resume, which snagged a phone interview, which was followed by an in-person interview, which was followed by an offer letter.

Sounds like a cakewalk, right? Actually, the VP of Marketing told me that I had the least experience of anyone she was interviewing—then she hired me anyway. I can't pinpoint exactly why I was successful in getting this job in contrast to all of my past attempts, but I can think of a few things that probably made the difference. My strategies weren't rocket science but they involved time and effort, two things that definitely make a difference separating you from the pack.

1. I BROKE DOWN THEIR JOB POSTING line by line and wrote down my skills and projects I'd worked on that directly related to their description.

2. I RESEARCHED THEIR WEBSITE EXTENSIVELY, read articles about the company, and looked up the management teams' backgrounds so that I could speak knowledgeably about the company and why I was a good fit.

3. I PREPARED A SPIEL ABOUT MY SOMEWHAT ECLECTIC RESUME, which can look unfocused if not set in the proper context.

4. I CALLED AN EXPERT ON START-UPS, finance, bargaining, and a half dozen other things to get some outside counsel. Ramit gave me some key advice, including, "Tell them you want to get your hands dirty," and "Suggest three things you would do to improve/enhance their marketing efforts." Yes, he does talk just like he writes on his blog.

5. I ACTUALLY TOOK RAMIT'S ADVICE, which is where a lot of my work came in. I dreamed up three proposals for generating greater interest at trade shows, better responses to direct marketing efforts, and increased name recognition in the general population.

Wow! So the interview must have gone really well, right? Not quite . . . and Rachel's description of what she did is a classic case of turning a missed opportunity into a chance to win.

I never actually found a good opportunity to mention my ideas (this despite a four-hour interview). I e-mailed the proposals to my potential boss instead. I then individually e-mailed every person I spoke to that day to thank them for their time. Might have been overkill, but then again, my e-mail flurry may have been the tipping point for my hiring.

My references later told me that the VP had been impressed with my energy and intelligence, and had decided she would rather train someone with potential than hire a more experienced, and perhaps less flexible, individual. Three weeks of research and planning paid off with an entirely new career—a pretty stellar return on the investment of my time.

Just notice how this is the exact embodiment of everything this book stands for. Rachel carefully researched her options, took action, reached out to more experienced people for advice, and came in with a presentation that was better than everyone else's (so much so that she actually didn't have to negotiate much). And when she didn't get a chance to show off all of her presentation, she sent it by e-mail—even though some people would think that was "weird."

Getting rich isn't about one silver bullet or secret strategy. It happens through regular, boring, disciplined action. Most people see only the results of all this action—a winnable moment or an article in the press. But it's the behind-the-scenes work that really makes you rich.

(continued from page 235)

NEGOTIATING TACTIC: Interview with multiple companies at once. Be sure to let each company know when you get another job offer, but *don't* reveal the amount of the exact offer—you're under no obligation to. In the best case, the companies will get into a bidding war and you'll profit while watching two multinational firms rumble over you. I can think of no better way to spend a casual weekday.

3. Come prepared (99 percent of people don't).

Don't just pick a salary out of thin air. First, visit www.salary.com and www.payscale.com to get a median amount for the position. Then, if you can, talk to people currently at the company (if you know someone who has recently left, even better—they'll be more willing to give you the real information) and ask what the salary range really is for the job. Finally—

> **BRING A STRATEGIC PLAN OF WHAT YOU WANT TO DO IN THE POSITION AND HAND IT TO YOUR HIRING MANAGER.**

and this is important—bring a plan of how you'll hit your goals to the negotiating session.

NEGOTIATING TACTIC: Most of the negotiation happens outside the room. Call your contacts. Figure out the salary amount you'd love, what you can realistically get, and what you'll settle for. And don't just ask for money. Literally bring a strategic plan of what you want to do in the position and hand it to your hiring manager. Do you realize how few people come to a negotiation with a plan for their role? This alone could win you $2,000 to $5,000. And, of course, it allows you to negotiate on the value you're going to bring to the company, not just the amount they'll pay you.

4. Have a toolbox of negotiating tricks up your sleeve.

Just as in a job interview, you'll want to have a list of things in your head that you can use to strengthen your negotiation. Think about your strong points and figure out ways you might be able to bring them to the hiring manager's attention. For example, I often ask, "What qualities make someone do an extraordinary job in this position?" If they say, "The

(continued on page 242)

Five Things You Should *Never* Do in a Negotiation

1. DON'T TELL THEM YOUR CURRENT SALARY. Why do they need to know? I'll tell you: So they can offer you just a little bit more than what you're currently making. If you're asked, say, "I'm sure we can find a number that's fair for both of us." If they press you, push back: "I'm not comfortable revealing my salary, so let's move on. What else can I answer for you?" (*Note:* Typically first-line recruiters will ask for these. If they won't budge, ask to speak to the hiring manager. No recruiter wants to be responsible for losing a great candidate, so this will usually get you through the gatekeeper. Also, some government jobs require you to reveal your salary. But if a place insists that you reveal your prior salary, it's a pretty good sign that it's not a great job.)

2. DON'T MAKE THE FIRST OFFER. That's their job. If they ask you to suggest a number, smile and say, "Now come on, that's your job. What's a fair number that we can both work from?"

3. IF YOU'VE GOT ANOTHER OFFER FROM A COMPANY THAT'S GENERALLY REGARDED TO BE MEDIOCRE, DON'T REVEAL THE COMPANY'S NAME. When asked for the name, just say something general but true, like, "It's another tech company that focuses on online consumer applications." If you say the name of the mediocre company, the negotiator is going to know that he's got you. He'll tear down the other company (which I would do, too), and it will all be true. He won't focus on negotiating, he'll just tell you how much better it will be at his company. So withhold this information.

4. DON'T ASK "YES" OR "NO" QUESTIONS. Instead of "You offered me fifty thousand dollars. Can you do fifty-five thousand?" say, "Fifty thousand dollars is a great number to work from. We're in the same ballpark, but how can we get to fifty-five thousand?"

5. NEVER LIE. Don't say you have another offer when you don't. Don't inflate your current salary. Don't promise things you can't deliver. You should always be truthful in negotiations.

ADVICE
FROM THE
BLOGOSPHERE

MAKE SURE A RAISE GOES TO YOUR BOTTOM LINE, NOT TO YOUR HEAD

How to Turn Small Raises into Long-Term Financial Success

by Trent Hamm of www.thesimpledollar.com

Every year, many Americans receive a welcome addition to their paycheck: a cost-of-living raise. This raise is a small percentage (between 3 and 4 percent) of salary that is added to keep pace with the increase in inflation. Some of us get even luckier, and receive a performance-based raise or a promotion.

I know the joys of receiving a raise—and I also know how tempting it can be to spend the extra money. When I received my first significant raise as a working adult, which amounted to roughly a 10 percent increase in my salary, I celebrated. I bought an iPod and a pile of video games, and then later I "invested" the rest of that raise in some vintage baseball cards.

To a small degree, that kind of behavior is fine. It's great to celebrate our successes in life—when our hard work pays off, it's natural and healthy to do something fun to mark that occasion, whether it's to buy something new or to go out on the town.

CELEBRATE A LITTLE—AND THEN GET SMART. As with many things in life, however, true success is achieved by finding a healthy balance. So when you receive a raise, don't feel bad about celebrating—but do it modestly. Go out for a dinner date with your partner, or buy a DVD you've been thinking about picking up. And that's where the celebration should stop. A mere increase in your income is not a call to change your standard of living.

Instead, use your raise to put yourself in a better financial position. Start by calculating how much your take-home pay will increase each month after your raise and then plan on setting aside most of that extra money. The next step is to automatically transfer that amount from your checking account to your savings account each time you're paid, so that you're never tempted to check your account balance and spend more than you should.

What do you do with that saved amount? You have a lot of options. If you're still carrying student loans or credit card debt, you can use it to accelerate your repayment plan, which will allow you to systematically eliminate your personal debt more quickly. Another smart move is to simply let it build up in your savings account as an emergency fund. This cash will come in handy if you need a major car repair or if you lose your job, for example. Another tactic is to invest it toward a long-term goal, like a home for yourself and your (potential) family or for retirement.

BE LIKE WARREN BUFFETT. *Storing away your extra income also has a second benefit: it keeps you from growing your standard of living in step with the growth in your paycheck. While it can be very tempting to do this, I encourage you to look at the story of Warren Buffett. His abilities as a businessman and investor have made him the richest man in America, yet he still lives in the same modest house in Omaha, Nebraska, that he's lived in for much of his adult life. Buffett realized long ago that having money doesn't require you to spend it and that the money you don't spend can be invested, growing from a small amount today into a large amount tomorrow. His $50 billion net worth certainly attests to it.*

Trent Hamm, author of *365 Ways to Live Cheap,* blogs about applying frugal living tactics to everyday life at www.thesimpledollar.com

> When you receive a raise, don't feel bad about celebrating—but do it modestly. ...A mere increase in your income is *not* a call to change your standard of living.

(continued from page 238)

person should be very focused on metrics," I say, "That's great that you said that—we're really on the same page. In fact, when I was at my last company, I launched a product that used an analytical package to . . ."

NEGOTIATING TACTIC: Have a repertoire of your accomplishments and aptitudes at your fingertips that you can include in your responses to commonly asked questions. These should include the following:

- Stories about successes you've had at previous jobs that illustrate your key strengths

- Questions to ask the negotiator if the conversation gets off track ("What do you like most about this job?" "Oh, really? That's interesting, because when I was at my last job, I found . . .")

5. Negotiate for more than money.

Don't forget to discuss whether or not the company offers a bonus, stock options, flexible commuting, or further education. You can also negotiate vacation and even job title. *Note:* Startups don't look very fondly on people negotiating vacations, because it sets a bad tone. But they *love* negotiating stock options, because top performers always want more, as it aligns them with the company's goals.

NEGOTIATING TACTIC: Your line is "Let's talk about total comp," which refers to your total compensation—not just salary, but everything. Treat them each as levers: If you pull one up, you can afford to let another fall. Use the levers strategically—for example, by conceding something you don't really care about—so you can both come to a happy agreement.

6. Be cooperative, not adversarial.

If you've gotten to the point of negotiating a salary, the company wants you and you want them. Now you just need to figure out how to make it work. It's not about you demanding more or them screwing you for less. Negotiation is about finding a cooperative solution to creating a fair package that will work for both of you. So check your attitude: You should be confident, not cocky, and eager to find a deal that benefits you both.

NEGOTIATING TACTIC: The phrase to use here is "We're pretty close . . . Now let's see how we can make this work."

7. Smile.

I'm not joking. This is one of the most effective techniques in negotiation. It's a disarming technique to break up the tension and demonstrates that you're a real person. When I was interviewing for college scholarships, I kept getting passed over until I started smiling—and then I started winning a bunch of them.

NEGOTIATING TACTIC: Smile. Really, do it.

8. Practice negotiating with multiple friends.

This sounds hokey, but it works better than you can imagine. If you practice *out loud*, you'll be amazed at how fast you improve. Yet nobody ever does it because it feels "weird." I guess it also feels "weird" to have an extra $10,000 in your pocket, jackass. For example, one of my friends thought it was too strange to practice negotiating, so when he faced a professional hiring manager, he didn't have a prayer. Later, he came to me like a clinically depressed Eeyore, whining about how he didn't negotiate. What could I say? This lack of practice can cost, on average, $5,000 to $10,000.

CHECK YOUR ATTITUDE: YOU SHOULD BE CONFIDENT, NOT COCKY, AND EAGER TO FIND A DEAL THAT BENEFITS YOU BOTH.

NEGOTIATING TACTIC: Call over your toughest, most grizzled friend and have him grill you. Don't laugh during the role play—treat it like it's a real negotiation. Better yet, videotape it—you'll be surprised how much you learn from this. If it sounds ridiculous, think about the benefits of not only the additional money, but the respect you'll get from your boss for a polished, professional negotiation.

9. If it doesn't work, save face.

Sometimes, the hiring manager simply won't budge. In that case, you need to be prepared to either walk away or take the job with a salary that's lower than you wanted. If you do take the job, always give yourself an option to renegotiate down the line—and get it in writing.

NEGOTIATING TACTIC: Your line here is "I understand you can't offer me what I'm looking for right now. But let's assume I do an excellent job over the next six months. Assuming my performance is just extraordinary, I'd like to talk about renegotiating then. I think that's fair, right?" (Get him to agree.) "Great. Let's put that in writing and we'll be good to go."

If you want to learn more about negotiation, I've put together a package of in-depth negotiation videos and tips. Check out www.iwillteachyoutobe rich.com/negotiate-like-an-Indian for details.

HOW TO SAVE THOUSANDS ON BIG-TICKET ITEMS

WHEN IT COMES TO SAVING MONEY, BIG PURCHASES ARE YOUR CHANCE to shine—and to dominate your clueless friends who are so proud of not ordering Cokes when they eat out, yet waste thousands when they buy large items like furniture, a car, or a house. When you buy something major, you can save massive amounts of money—$2,000 on a car or $40,000 on a house—that will make your other attempts to save money pale in comparison. Big-ticket items like these, however, are where people most commonly make mistakes. They don't comparison shop, they overpay because a salesperson cons them into spending too much, and worst of all they then think they got a good deal. Don't be one of these people!

A Fresh Look at Buying a Car

It's strange how many people make an effort to save on things like clothes and eating out, but when it comes to large purchases like cars, make poor decisions and erase any savings they've accumulated along the way.

Let me first tell you that the single most important decision associated with buying a car is not the brand or the mileage or the rims (please jump off a bridge if you buy specialty rims). Surprisingly, from a financial perspective, the most important factor is *how long you keep the car before selling it*. You could get the best deal in the world, but if you sell the car after four years, you've lost money. Instead, understand how much you can afford, pick a reliable car, maintain it well, and drive it for as long as humanly possible. Yes, that means you need to drive it for more than ten years, because it's only once you finish the payments that the real savings start. And by taking good care of your car, you can save even more enormous piles of money over the long term—and you'll have a great car.

There are four steps to buying a car: Budgeting, Picking a Car, Negotiating Like an Indian, and Maintaining Your Car.

First, ask yourself how buying a car fits into your spending and saving priorities (see Chapter 4). If you're satisfied with a used Toyota Corolla and would rather put your extra money toward investing for growth, great. On the other hand, if you really love BMWs and can afford to buy one, then you should do it. This is conscious spending, applied.

Once you've thought about where your car fits into your priorities, you need to look at your Conscious Spending Plan and decide what you're willing to allocate toward your car each month. This is the number you keep in your back pocket as the number you can afford *to spend up to*. Ideally you'll spend less. (*Note:* Ignore the advertisements for "$199/month." Those are scammy introductory rates that are simply not real.)

So, knowing that there will be other expenses involved in the total expense of having a car, you want to decide how much you want to spend on the car itself. For example, if you can afford a total monthly payment of $500 toward your car, you can probably afford a car that costs $200 to $250 per month. (For example, my monthly car payment of $350.75 actually adds up to around $1,000 when I factor in insurance, gas, maintenance, and $200/month San Francisco parking.) With a budget of around $200 per month for your car itself, that means you can afford a car that costs around $12,000 over five years. Pretty sobering compared with what most people think they can afford, right? This shows you how easy it is to overspend on a car.

IF YOU PICK A CRAPPY CAR, YOU ARE A MORON

Please, pick a good car. There are some cars that are just objectively bad decisions that nobody should ever buy. For example, has anyone with an IQ over 42 ever consciously chosen to buy a Chevy Lumina? Sadly, many

Dos and Don'ts for Your First Car

Do

- **INVESTIGATE RECENT GRADUATE INCENTIVE PLANS** for first-time car buyers. Many car companies offer programs that give rebates or special financing if you're a new grad and have reasonably good credit. Google it to find companies that are offering deals.

- **CALCULATE TOTAL COST OF OWNERSHIP** (TCO). This means you figure out how much you'll be spending over the life of the car— these expenses can have a big effect on your finances. Besides the cost of the car and the interest on your loan, the TCO should include maintenance, gas, insurance, and resale value. By understanding even a rough ballpark of how much these "invisible" costs will run you, you'll be able to save more accurately—and avoid surprises when you get a $600 car-repair fee.

- **BUY A CAR THAT WILL LAST YOU AT LEAST TEN YEARS,** not one that looks cool. Looks fade and you're still going to be stuck with the payments. Optimize for the long term.

Don't

- **LEASE.** Leasing nearly always benefits the dealer, not you. It appeals to people who want the newest car and are willing to pay exorbitant amounts and get nothing to show for it—so, wealthy people who want new cars every two years, and in some cases, businesses for tax reasons. Not you! Buy a car and hold it for the long term. *Consumer Reports* research recently "determined that buying a car—in this case, the best-selling 2008 Honda Accord EX, at $24,495—would cost $4,597 less over five years than closed-end leasing for exactly the same model." If that doesn't persuade you not to lease, I don't know what will.

- **SELL YOUR CAR IN FEWER THAN SEVEN YEARS.** The real savings come once you've paid off your car loan and driven it for as long as possible. Most people sell their cars far too early. It's much cheaper to maintain your car well and drive it into the ground.

- **ASSUME YOU HAVE TO BUY A USED CAR.** Run the numbers. Over the long term, a new car may end up saving you money, if you pick the right new car, pay the right price, and drive it for a long time. See below for my story on buying a new car.

- **STRETCH YOUR BUDGET FOR A CAR.** Set a realistic budget for your car and don't go over it. Be honest with yourself. Other expenses will come up—maybe car related, maybe not—and you don't want to end up struggling because you can't afford your monthly car payment.

people I know are seduced by the shiny new cars at the dealership. But it's important to remember that you're not just buying the car for today—you're buying it for the next ten-plus years. Buying a flashy car can be like dating a hot yet vapid girl: The hotness will wear off after a little while, and all you'll be left with is the unsatisfying person beneath. That is why when I'm checking girls out, I always exclaim loudly to my friend, "HEY, MAN, REMEMBER, WE HAVE TO OPTIMIZE FOR THE LONG TERM." Trust me, when girls overhear that, they can't resist me.

First, any car you evaluate must fit within your budget. This will eliminate most cars automatically. Do not even look at cars you can't afford.

Second, the car must be a *good car*. "But Ramit," you might say, "who can say what a good car is? One man's trash is another man's treasure." Listen, there is one person who will say what a good car is: me. Here's what makes a good car:

- **RELIABILITY.** When I bought my car, above all, I wanted one that would not break down. I have enough stuff going on in my life, and I want to avoid car-repair issues that cost time and money as much as possible. Because this was a high priority, I was willing to pay slightly more for it.

- **A CAR YOU LOVE.** I've written time and time again about consciously spending on the things you love. For me, since I'd be driving the car for a long time, I wanted to pick one that I really enjoyed driving. And like a dutiful Indian son, I love not having to worry about it breaking down.

- **RESALE VALUE.** One of my friends bought a $20,000 Acura Integra, drove it for about seven years, and then sold it for 50 percent of the price. That means she got a fantastic deal on driving a new car for seven years. To check out how your potential cars will fare, visit www.kbb.com and calculate resale prices in five, seven, and ten years. You'll be surprised how quickly most cars depreciate and how others (Toyotas and Hondas especially) retain their value.

- **INSURANCE.** The insurance rates for a new and used car can be pretty different. Even if they're only slightly different (say, $50/month), that can add up over many years.

- **FUEL EFFICIENCY.** With gas prices on a roller-coaster ride, you may want to hedge your bets and consider a very fuel-efficient, or even a hybrid, car. This could be an important factor in determining the value of a car over the long term.

- **THE DOWN PAYMENT.** This is important. If you don't have much cash to put down, a used car is more attractive because the down payment (i.e., money you have to pay when you buy the car) is typically lower. And if you put $0 down, the interest charges on a new car will be much more. In my case, I had cash available to put down.

- **INTEREST RATE.** The interest rate on your car loan will depend on your credit, which is why having a good credit score matters (see page 16). If you have multiple sources of good credit, your interest rate will be lower. This becomes more important over a longer-term loan. Each car dealership will negotiate differently. Don't be afraid to walk out if the dealer tries to change the finance terms on you at the last minute. This is a common trick.

CONQUERING CAR SALESPEOPLE BY OUTNEGOTIATING THEM

I've seen more than my share of negotiations—including watching my dad negotiate with car dealers for multiple days. I think we actually ate breakfast at a dealership once.

You must negotiate mercilessly with dealers. I have never seen as many people make bad purchasing decisions as when they're in a car dealer's office. If you're not a hardball negotiator, take someone with you who is. If possible, buy a car at the end of the year, when dealers are salivating to beat their quotas and are far more willing to negotiate. Their saliva is your salvation!

I also highly recommend using Fighting Chance (www.fightingchance .com), an information service for car buyers, to arm yourself before you negotiate. The service costs $39.95 and it's completely worth it. You can order a customized report of the exact car you're looking for, which will tell you *exactly* how much car dealers are paying for your car—including details about little-known "dealer withholding." For instance, I spent a month on the site researching and planning and then bought my car for $2,000

> **I HAVE NEVER SEEN AS MANY PEOPLE MAKE BAD PURCHASING DECISIONS AS WHEN THEY'RE IN A CAR DEALER'S OFFICE.**

under invoice. The service also provided specific tips for how to negotiate from the comfort of your sofa. You don't even have to set foot in a dealership until the very end.

Here's how I did it:

When I decided to buy—at the end of December, when salespeople are desperate to meet their quotas—I faxed seventeen car dealers and told them exactly which car I wanted. I said I was prepared to buy the car within two weeks and, because I knew exactly how much profit they would make off the car, I would go with the lowest price offered to me. The same day, as I sat back with a cup of Earl Grey tea and a Taco Bell burrito, faxes started rolling in from the dealers. After I had all the offers, I called the dealers, told them the lowest price I'd received, and gave each of them a chance to beat it. This resulted in a bidding war that led to a downward spiral of near-orgasmic deals.

In the end, I chose a dealer in Palo Alto who sold me the car for $2,000 under invoice—a nearly unheard-of price. I didn't have to waste my time going to multiple dealerships, and I didn't have to bother with slimy car salesmen. I went into only one dealer's office: the winning one.

BORING BUT PROFITABLE: MAINTAINING YOUR CAR

I know that keeping your car well maintained doesn't sound sexy, but it will make you rich when you eventually sell your car. So take your car's maintenance as seriously as your retirement savings: As soon as you buy your car, enter the major maintenance checkpoints into your calendar so you remember them. Here's a hint: The average car is driven about fifteen thousand miles per year. You can use that number as a starting point to calculate a maintenance schedule based on the car manufacturer's instructions.

Of course, you also need to have regular oil changes, watch your tire pressure, and keep your car clean. I keep a record of each service I have, along with any notes. When I sell my car, I'll show the documentation to the buyer to prove how meticulous I've been (and charge the buyer accordingly). People often forget this and slap their foreheads when they go to sell their car, only to be negotiated down (by someone like me) for not keeping detailed maintenance records. Don't let yourself get outmaneuvered by a lack of paperwork.

The Biggest Big-Ticket Item of All: Buying a House

If I asked people, "Hey, would you like to make a hundred thousand dollars in one year?" who wouldn't say yes? And if I sweetened the offer by saying you'd have to spend only ten hours per week that year to do it, I guarantee every single person I asked would go for it. So why don't people spend that amount of time researching the biggest purchase of their lives? By doing the research that 99 percent of other people don't, you can save tens of thousands of dollars on your house over the life of your loan. That's why, when I hear about people who "fell in love" with a house and then "had to have it on the spot," I am reminded why I wish I could pull a red wagon full of tomatoes everywhere I go.

Buying a house is the most complicated and significant purchase you'll make, so it pays to understand everything about it beforehand. I mean *everything*. This isn't a pair of pants at Banana Republic. When you buy a house worth hundreds of thousands of dollars, you should be an expert on the tricks and common mistakes most home buyers make. You should know all the common real estate terms, and how to push and pull to get the best deal. And you should understand that houses are primarily for living in, not for making huge cash gains.

Look, if you buy a house without opening up a spreadsheet and entering some numbers, you are a fool. Remember, if you can save $75,000 or $125,000 over the entire course of a thirty-year loan just by educating yourself a little, it's certainly worth your time. I'm going to help you figure out if buying a house is right for you, and then I'm going to give you an overview of the things you'll need to do over the next few months—at least three months, probably twelve—to prepare to buy. I can't cover all the tips here, but I'll get you started with the basics.

WHO SHOULD BUY A HOUSE?

From our earliest days, we're taught that the American dream is to own a house, have 2.5 kids, and retire into the sunset. In fact, I have friends who graduated from college and the first major purchase they wanted to make was a house. What the hell? No budget, no 401(k), but they wanted to buy a house? When I ask my younger friends why they want to buy a house, they stare at me blankly. "They're a good investment," they reply like brainless automatons who are at risk of being smacked by me.

Actually, houses really aren't very good investments in general. But I'll cover that in a minute. Back to who should buy:

First and foremost, you should buy a house only if it makes financial sense. In the olden days, this meant that your house would cost no more than 2.5 times your annual income, you'd be able to put at least 20 percent of the purchase price down, and the total monthly payments (including the mortgage, maintenance, insurance, and taxes) would be about 30 percent of your gross income. If you make $50,000 per year before taxes, that means your house would cost $125,000, you'd put $25,000 down, and the total monthly payments would be $1,250 per month. Yeah, right. Maybe if you live in the Ozarks.

Things are a little different now, but that doesn't explain the stupidity of people who purchase houses for ten times their salaries with zero money down. Sure, you can stretch those traditional guidelines a little, but if you buy something you simply can't afford, it *will* come around and bite you in the ass.

Let me be crystal clear: Can you afford at least a 10 percent down payment for the house? If not, set a savings goal and don't even think about buying until you reach it. Even if you've got a down payment, you still need to be sure you make enough money to cover the monthly payments. You might be tempted to think, "Oh, I'm paying $1,000/month for my apartment, so I can definitely afford $1,000 for a house!" Wrong. First off, chances are you'll want to buy a nicer house than you're currently renting, which means the monthly payment will likely be higher. Second,

THE BOTTOM LINE: BUY ONLY IF YOU'RE PLANNING TO LIVE IN THE SAME PLACE FOR TEN YEARS OR MORE.

when you buy a house, you'll owe property taxes, insurance, and maintenance fees that will add hundreds per month. If the garage door breaks or the toilet needs repairing, that's coming out of your pocket, not a landlord's—and home repairs are ridiculously expensive. So even if your mortgage payment is the same $1,000/month as your rental, your real cost will be about 40 to 50 percent higher—in this case, more like $1,500/month when you factor everything in.

Bottom line: If you don't have enough money to make a down payment and cover your total monthly costs, you need to set up a savings goal and defer buying until you've proven that you can hit your goal consistently, month after month.

Next thing to think about: Are the houses you're looking at within your price range? It's funny how so many people I know want to live only in the grandest possible house. Sure, your parents may live in one of those now, but it probably took them thirty or forty years to be able to afford it. Unless you're already loaded, you need to readjust your expectations and begin with a starter house. They're called that for a reason—they're simple houses that require you to make trade-offs but allow you to get started. Your first house probably won't have as many bedrooms as you want. It won't be in the most amazing location. But it will let you get started making consistent monthly payments and building equity.

Finally, will you be able to stay in the house for at least ten years? Buying a house means you're staying put for a long time. Some people say five years, but the longer you stay in your house, the more you save. There are a few reasons for this: If you sell through a traditional realtor, you pay that person a huge fee—usually 6 percent of the selling price. Divide that by just a few years, and it hits you a lot harder than if you had held the house for ten or twenty years. There are also the costs associated with moving. And depending on how you structure your sale, you may pay a significant amount in taxes. The bottom line here: Buy only if you're planning to live in the same place for ten years or more.

I have to emphasize that buying a house is not just a natural step in getting older. Too many people assume this and then get in over their heads. Buying a house changes your lifestyle forever. No matter what, you have to make your monthly payment every month—or you'll lose your house and watch your credit tank. This affects the kind of job you can take and your level of risk tolerance. It means you'll need to save for a six-month emergency plan in case you lose your job and can't pay your mortgage. In short, you really need to be sure you're ready for the responsibility of being a home owner.

Of course, there are certainly benefits to buying a house and, like I said, most Americans will purchase one in their lifetime. If you can afford it and you're sure you'll be staying in the same area for a long time, buying a house can be a great way to make a significant purchase, build equity, and create a stable place to raise a family.

THE TRUTH: REAL ESTATE IS A POOR INVESTMENT FOR INDIVIDUAL INVESTORS

Americans' biggest "investments" are their houses, but real estate is also the place where Americans lose the most money. Realtors (and most home owners) are not going to like me after this section, but in truth, real estate is the most overrated investment in America. It's a purchase first— a very expensive one—and an investment second.

As an investment, real estate provides mediocre returns at best. First, there's the problem of risk. If your house is your biggest investment, how diversified is your portfolio? If you pay $2,000 per month to a mortgage, are you investing $6,000 elsewhere to balance your risk? Of course not. Second, the facts show that real estate offers a very poor return for individual investors. Yale economist Robert Shiller found that "from 1890 through 1990, the return on residential real estate was just about zero after inflation."

I know this sounds crazy, but it's true. We fool ourselves into thinking we're making money when we're simply not. For example, if someone buys a house for $250,000 and sells it for $400,000 twenty years later, they think, "Great! I made $150,000!" But actually, they've forgotten to factor in important costs like property taxes, maintenance, and the opportunity cost of not having that money in the stock market. The truth is that, over time, investing in the stock market has trumped real estate quite handily—even now—which is why renting isn't always a bad idea.

I'm not saying buying a house is always a bad decision. It's just that you should think of it as a purchase, rather than as an investment. And, just as with any other purchase, you should buy a house and keep it for as long as possible. Do your homework and then negotiate. And know your alternatives (like renting).

BUYING VS. RENTING: THE SURPRISING NUMBERS

I want to show you why renting is actually a smart decision for many people, especially if you live in an expensive area like New York or San Francisco. But first, let's get rid of the idea that renters are "throwing away money" because they're not building equity. Any time you hear clichés like that—from *any* area of personal finance—beware. It's just not true, and I'll show you the numbers to prove it.

The total price of buying and owning a house is far greater than the house's sticker price. Take a look at this research from the Office of Federal Housing Enterprise Oversight.

When you rent, you're not paying all those other assorted fees, which effectively frees up tons of cash that you would have been spending on a mortgage. *The key is investing that extra money.* If you do nothing with it (or, worse, spend it all), you might as well buy a house and use it as a forced savings account. But if you've read this far, chance are good that you'll take whatever extra money you have each month and invest it.

Of course, like buying, renting isn't best for everyone. It all depends on your individual situation. The easiest way to see if you should rent or buy is to use *The New York Times*'s excellent online calculator "Is It Better to Rent or Buy?" It will factor in maintenance, renovations, capital gains, the costs of buying and selling, inflation, and more. You can find it at www.nytimes.com/2007/04/10/business/2007_BUYRENT_GRAPHIC.html.

THE COST OF BUYING A HOME OVER 30 YEARS

	2007
Purchase Price (typical single-family home)	$290,000
Interest @ 6.41%; total = $291,000 (after tax: 33% bracket)	$195,000
Taxes & Insurance ($6,000 / year)	$180,000
Maintenance ($300 / month)	$108,000
Major Repairs & Improvements	$300,000
Total Costs	**$1,073,000**

Note: 6.41% was the average mortgage-interest rate in 2006; the national median home price was $222,000. Source: Office of Federal Housing Enterprise Oversight.

BECOMING A HOME OWNER: TIPS FOR BUYING YOUR NEW HOUSE

Like any area of personal finance, there are no secrets to buying a house. But it does involve thinking differently from most other people, who make the biggest purchase of their lives without fully understanding the true costs. Although I may be aggressive with my asset allocation, I'm conservative when it comes to real estate. That means I urge you to stick by tried-and-true rules, like 20 percent down, a 30-year fixed-rate mortgage, and a total monthly payment that represents no more than 30 percent of your gross pay. If you can't do that, wait until you've saved more. It's okay to stretch a little, but *don't* stretch beyond what you can actually pay. If you make a poor financial decision up front, you'll end up struggling—and it can compound and become a bigger problem through the life of your loan. Don't let this happen, because it will undo all the hard work you put into the other areas of your financial life.

If you make a good financial decision when buying, you'll be in an excellent position. You'll know exactly how much you're spending each month on your house, you'll be in control of your expenses, and you'll have money to pay your mortgage, invest, and take vacations, buy a TV, or whatever else you want to do.

Here are some of the things you'll need to do to make a sound decision.

Myths About Owning a Home

"PRICES ALWAYS GO UP IN REAL ESTATE" (OR, "THE VALUE OF A HOUSE DOUBLES EVERY TEN YEARS"). Not true. We can see this now in a very obvious way with the recent real estate crash. But most insidiously, net house prices haven't increased when you factor in inflation, taxes, and other homeowner fees. They appear to be higher because the sticker price is higher, but you have to dig beneath the surface.

"YOU CAN USE LEVERAGE TO INCREASE YOUR MONEY." Home owners will often point to leverage as the key benefit of real estate. In other words, you can put $20,000 down for a $100,000 house, and if the house climbs to $120,000, you've effectively doubled your money. Unfortunately, leverage can also work against you if the price goes down. If your house declines by 10 percent, you don't just lose 10 percent of your equity—it's more like 20 percent once you factor in the 6 percent realtor's fees, the closing costs, new furniture, and other expenses.

"I CAN DEDUCT MY MORTGAGE INTEREST FROM MY TAXES AND SAVE A BUNCH OF MONEY." Be very careful here. Tax savings are great, but people forget that they're saving money they ordinarily would never have spent. That's because the amount you pay out owning a house is much higher than you would for any rental when you include maintenance, renovations, and higher insurance costs, to name a few. So although you will certainly save money on your mortgage interest specifically, the net-net is usually a loss. As Patrick Killelea from the real-estate site www.patrick.net says, "You don't get rich spending a dollar to save 30 cents!"

1. Check your credit score. The higher your score, the better the interest rate on your mortgage will be. If your credit score is low, it might be a better decision to delay buying until you can improve your score. (See page 17 for details on bettering your score.) Good credit translates into not only a lower total cost, but lower monthly payments. The table on the next page from www.myfico.com shows how interest rates affect your mortgage payments on a thirty-year fixed $300,000 loan.

THE EFFECT OF CREDIT SCORES
ON A MORTGAGE PAYMENT

FICO score	APR*	Monthly payment
760–850	4.384%	$1,499
700–759	4.606%	$1,539
680–699	4.783%	$1,571
660–679	4.997%	$1,610
640–659	5.427%	$1,690
620–639	5.973%	$1,793

* APR figures calculated in January 2009.

2. Save as much money as possible for a down payment. Traditionally, you had to put 20 percent down. In recent years, people were allowed to put as little as zero down—but it's become all too clear that that was a very bad idea. If you can't save enough to put 20 percent down, you'll have to get something called Private Mortgage Insurance (PMI), which serves as insurance against your defaulting on your monthly payments. PMI costs between 1 and 1.25 percent of the mortgage, plus an annual charge. The more you put down, the less PMI you'll have to pay. If you haven't been able to save at least 10 percent to put down, stop thinking about buying a house. If you can't even save 10 percent, how will you afford an expensive mortgage payment, plus maintenance and taxes and insurance and furniture and renovations and . . . you get the idea. Set a savings goal (page 106) for a down payment, and don't start looking to buy until you reach it.

3. Calculate the total *amount of buying a new house.* Have you ever gone to buy a car or cell phone, only to learn that it's way more expensive than advertised? I know I have, and most of the time I just bought it anyway because I was already psychologically set on it. But because the numbers are so big when purchasing a house, even small surprises will end up costing you a ton of money. For example, if you stumble across an unexpected cost for $100 per month, would you really cancel the paperwork for a new home? Of course not. But that minor charge would add up to $36,000 over the lifetime of a thirty-year loan—plus the opportunity cost of investing it. Remember that the closing costs—including all administrative fees and expenses—are usually between 2 and 5 percent of the house price. So on a $200,000 house, that's $10,000. Keep in mind that ideally the total price shouldn't be much more than three times your gross annual income. (It's okay to stretch here a little if you don't have any debt.) And don't forget to factor in insurance, taxes, maintenance, and renovations. If all this sounds a little overwhelming, it's telling you that you need to research all this stuff before buying a house. In this particular case, you should ask your parents and other home owners for their surprise costs or check out www.fool.com/homecenter/deal/deal04.htm.

4. Get the most conservative, boring loan possible. I like a thirty-year fixed-rate loan. Yes, you'll pay more in interest compared with a fifteen-year loan. But thirty-year loans are more flexible because you can *always* pay extra toward your loan and pay it off faster if you want. But you probably shouldn't. *Consumer Reports* simulated what to do with an extra $100 per month, comparing the benefits of prepaying your mortgage versus investing in an index fund that returned 8 percent. Over a twenty-year period, the fund won 100 percent of the time. As they said, ". . . the longer you own your home, the less likely it is that mortgage prepayment will be the better choice."

5. Don't forget to check for perks. The government wants to make it easy for first-time homebuyers to purchase a house. Many state and local governments offer benefits for first-time home buyers. Check out www.hud.gov/buying/localbuying.cfm to see the programs in your state. Also, check with your employer, who may offer special first-time home-buying rates. Ask—it's worth it. Finally, don't forget to check with any associations you belong to, including local credit unions and teacher's associations. You may get access to special lower rates. Hell, check even your Costco membership (they offer special rates for members, too).

6. Use online services to comparison shop. You may have heard about www.zillow.com, which is a rich source of data about home prices all over the United States. Also check out www.redfin.com, which is disrupting the real-estate market by letting home buyers get access to more information—like local tax records—online. You can do your research online and Redfin will send an agent to negotiate for you. They claim an average savings of $14,000. For your homeowner's insurance, check www.insure.com to comparison shop. And don't forget to call your auto insurance company and ask them for a discounted rate if you give them your homeowner's insurance business.

How to Tackle Future Large Purchases

We've covered weddings, cars, and houses, but there are plenty of other major expenses that people don't plan ahead for—just think about having kids! The problem is that, as we've seen, if you don't plan ahead, it ends up costing you much more in the end. The good news is that there is a way to anticipate and handle almost any major expense you'll encounter in life.

1. Acknowledge that you're probably not being realistic about how much things will cost—then force yourself to be. If you've read this whole book (and taken even half of my advice), you're probably better at your finances than 95 percent of other people, but you're still human. Sorry, but your wedding will be more expensive than you planned. Your house will have costs you didn't account for. Having a head-in-the-sand approach, however, is the worst thing you can do. Bite the bullet, sit down, and make a realistic plan of how much your big purchases will cost you in the next ten years. Do it on a napkin—it doesn't have to be perfect! Just spend twenty minutes and see what you come up with.

2. Set up an automatic savings plan. Because almost nobody will take my recommendation to make a budget to forecast major purchases, I suggest just taking a shortcut and setting up an automatic savings plan (see page 133). Assume you'll spend $28,000 on your wedding, $20,000 on a car, $20,000 for the first two years of your first-born kid, and however much you'll need for a typical down payment for a house in your city. Then figure out how much you need to save. If you're twenty-five, and you're going to buy a car and get married in three years, that's $45,000 ÷ 36 months = $1,250 per month. "But Ramit," you might say in an annoying whine, "that's more than a thousand dollars per month. I can't afford that!"

Okay, can you afford $300? If so, that's $300 more than you were doing yesterday.

3. You can't have the best of everything, so use the P word. Priorities are essential. Like I said, it's human nature to want the best for our wedding day or first house, and we need to be realistic about acknowledging that. But we also need to acknowledge that we simply can't have the best of everything. Do you want the filet mignon or an open bar at your wedding? Do you want a house with a backyard or a neighborhood with better local schools? If you have the costs down on paper, you'll know exactly which trade-offs you can make to keep within your budget. If you haven't written anything down, there will appear to be no trade-offs necessary. And that's how people get into staggering amounts of debt.

For the things you decide aren't that important, beg, borrow, and steal to save money: If you're getting married, use a public park instead of a ballroom, ask your baker friend to make the cake. If you're buying a car, cut out the sunroof so you can get the model you want. And whatever you do, negotiate the hell out of big-ticket purchases. This is where, if you plan ahead, time can take the place of money.

A Rich Life for You—and Others

If I've been successful, the end of this book is the beginning of a rich future for you. We know that being rich isn't just about money. We know that most people around us have strong opinions about money, yet are clueless with their own. And we know that conscious spending can be fun (especially when it's automated). But now that you know how money really works, there's one other thing: Not enough people know about being rich. It's not some mythical thing that happens only to Ivy League grads and lottery winners. *Anyone* can be rich—it's just a question of what rich means to you. In my definition, I've always believed in getting really good at something, then passing it on to others. You're great at managing your finances and goals now. Would you do me a favor and pass the word along to your friends to help them focus on their goals, too? A rich life is about more than money. It starts by managing your own. And it continues by helping others become rich.

INDEX

a

Accounts, linking together, 131–33
Age, asset allocation and, 171–72, 174,
    175, 180–81, 183–85
Airline rewards, 21, 28, 29
Á la Carte Method, 100–101
Angel investing, 183
Annual percentage rates (APRs), 19, 22,
    25–26, 39
  credit scores and, 16–17, 256–57
  highest, paying credit card with, 41, 42
  negotiating down, 42–43, 46, 110
Art, investing in, 182
Asset allocation, 166, 170–72, 175, 202
  age and, 171–72, 174, 175, 180–81,
    183–85
  lifecycle funds and, 180–81, 183–85
  with multiple accounts, 208–9
  rebalancing and, 180, 181, 189, 203–5,
    206–7, 209
  Swensen model of, 189–91, 192, 195
ATMs, 53
Automatic Investing, 162–64, 202–3
  401(k) contributions and, 79–80, 82,
    129, 132, 136
  Roth IRA contributions and, 87, 88, 89,
    90, 129, 132, 137, 187, 188, 195
Automatic Money Flow, 125–42
  bill paying through checking accounts
    and, 52, 130, 132–33, 138
  bill paying through credit cards and,
    52, 130, 132, 137–38
  direct deposit of paychecks and, 58, 65,
    129, 133, 136
  irregular income and, 139–41
  linking accounts for, 131–33, 142
  payment of credit card accounts and,
    22–23, 39–40, 46, 47, 48, 132, 138
  savings accounts and, 129, 132, 136–37
  setting up transfers and payments for,
    133–38, 142
  student loan payments and, 36
  synchronizing bills for, 133–36
  time-saving benefits of, 126–27, 128–31
  two paychecks a month and, 138–39

b

Balance transfers, 32–33, 43–46
Bank of America, 50, 53

Banks and bank accounts, 6, 49–68
  author's personal setup for, 55
  basics for, 52–54
  best options for, 61–63
  choosing, 58–61
  credit unions vs., 57
  fees and, 50–51, 52, 56, 58, 59, 60, 61,
    63–67, 110, 116
  finding perfect setup for, 56–57
  marketing tactics of, 59
  minimum balances and, 58, 59, 60, 61,
    63, 65
  money-making tactics of, 50–51
  need for both savings and checking,
    54–55
  optimizing, 63–67
  separate, for discretionary spending,
    115–16
  see also Checking accounts; Online
    banks; Savings accounts
Bernstein, William, 166, 172–74
Big-ticket purchases, 244–60
  automatic savings plan for, 259–60
  cars, 244–50
  homes, 250–59
  weddings, 229–34
Bill paying, automated:
  through checking accounts, 52, 130,
    132–33, 138
  through credit cards, 52, 130, 132,
    137–38
Bogle, John, 177–78
Bonds, 167, 168–69, 171, 180
  asset allocation and, 166, 170–72, 174,
    175, 180–81, 183–85, 190–91
  categories of, 173
Boyfriends or girlfriends, 225–29
  laying bare your finances with, 226–27
  sharing expenses with, when income is
    unequal, 227–28
  talking about money with, 225–27,
    228–29
Brokerages:
  discount vs. full-service, 86
  see also Investment brokerage accounts
Budgeting, 92–93, 103, 109
  see also Conscious Spending Plan
Buffett, Warren, 149, 162–63, 164, 179,
    196, 241

c

Cable TV, 100, 101, 132
Capital-gains tax, 211
Career, investing in, 77
Car insurance, 18, 31, 248
Cars, 244–50
    choosing, 245–48
    dos and don'ts for, 246–47
    leasing, 246
    maintaining, 250
    negotiating with dealers for, 248–49
    total cost of, 245, 246
Cash advances, 32–33
Cash-back credit cards, 20–21
Cash investments, 166, 167, 169, 171, 197
CDs, 168–69
Cell phone service contracts, 30
Change, sustainable, 111–15
Cheapness, frugality vs., 94–96
Checking accounts, 52, 53–54, 68
    automated bill paying through, 52, 130,
        132–33, 138
    best options for, 61–62
    direct deposit of paychecks to, 58, 65,
        129, 133, 136
    finding perfect setup for, 56–57
    interest on, 52, 61
    online, 62, 68
    overdraft fees and, 50–51, 65–67,
        110, 116
    sifting through options for, 57–61
Children's education, saving for, 217
Compounding, 70, 78, 80, 187, 192, 201, 221
Concierge services, 31
Conscious Spending Plan, 9, 93–94, 103–24
    Automatic Money Flow and, 128–31
    big purchases and, 245
    envelope system and, 115–17
    focusing on big wins and, 109–11, 124
    freelancers and, 141
    guilt-free spending money and, 108
    increasing your earnings and, 117–20
    long-term investments and, 106, 195
    maintaining, 121–23, 124
    monthly fixed costs and, 104–6
    optimizing, 108–17, 124
    savings goals and, 106–8, 200–201
    setting realistic goals and, 111–15
    unexpected and irregular expenses and,
        121–22
    unexpected income and, 122–23
Credit, 14–17
    unraveling of (2008), 15, 19

Credit card debt, 19, 35, 37–47, 48, 135,
    220, 241
    aggressively paying off, 38–40
    calculating amount of, 41
    cash flow and, 44
    emotional damage of, 39
    five steps to ridding yourself of, 40–47
    Ladder of Personal Finance and, 76,
        82–83
    prioritizing, 41–42, 44–45
    sources of money for paying down, 43–47
Credit cards, 6, 17–35, 59, 133
    APRs of. See Annual percentage rates
    author's personal setup for, 28
    automated bill paying through, 52, 130,
        132, 137–38
    automatic payment of accounts, 22–23,
        39–40, 46, 47, 48, 132, 138
    balance transfers and cash advances
        from, 32–33, 43–46
    benefits of, 18, 29–31, 137, 139
    cash-back, 20–21
    closing accounts and, 32
    disputing charges and, 30
    e-mail notifications and, 138
    emergencies and, 212
    fees of, 19, 22, 23–25, 28, 40
    increasing available credit on, 26–29, 37
    keeping for long time, 26
    missing payments on, 22, 23, 24
    mistakes to avoid with, 32–35
    new, getting, 19–21
    number of, 21
    paying only minimum payments on, 18,
        38, 39
    paying on time, 22–23
    from retail stores, 33–34
    reviewing bills for, 139
    reward programs of, 21, 28, 29
    secured, for people with no income, 20
    tracking calls related to, 27
    unsolicited offers for, 19–20, 109
Credit reports, 15, 16, 21, 48
Credit scores (FICO scores), 15, 16–17, 21, 48
    managing credit cards and, 21, 22, 23, 24,
        25, 28, 32, 33, 38
    mortgages and, 16–17, 256–57
Credit unions, 57, 61
Credit utilization rate, 28–29, 32
Curve of Doing More Before Doing Less,
    126–27

d

Debit cards, 52, 53

discretionary spending and, 115–16
overdraft fees and, 50, 51, 110, 116
Debt:
    help for parents in, 223–24
    paying off, 76, 82–83, 90, 220–21, 241
    student loans and, 35–36, 220–21, 241
    see also Credit card debt
Direct deposit of paychecks, 58, 65, 129,
    133, 136
Diversification, 166, 170, 172–75, 181
Dollar-cost averaging, 197
Dow Jones Industrial Average, 168

e

Earnings:
    increasing, 117–20
    irregular, 139–41
    unequal, living together and, 227–28
    unexpected income and, 122–23
    see also Raises; Salary
80/20 analysis, 109
85 Percent Solution, 8
Emergencies, raising money for, 211–12
Emergency fund, 216, 241, 253
Emigrant Direct, 51, 63
Envelope system, 115–17
Expense ratios, 156, 157, 176, 177, 178,
    186, 187, 192
Experts. See Financial expertise

f

Federal Deposit Insurance Corporation
    (FDIC), 52
FICO scores. See Credit scores
Fidelity, 187, 192
Financial advisers, 153–55
Financial expertise, 143–58
    active vs. passive management and,
        155–58
    engineering a perfect stock-picking
        record and, 151
    legendary investors and, 149
    market-timing newsletters and, 145
    personal-finance blogs and, 152
    pundits' and fund managers' inability to
        predict market and, 2–3, 145–50, 165, 168
    ratings of stocks and funds and, 148–52
529s, 217
Fixed costs, 104–6, 107, 130
Flexo, 44–45
401(k)s, 77–82, 176
    amount to contribute to, 76, 77, 89
    automatic contributions to, 79–80, 82,
        129, 132, 136

common concerns about, 80–81
early withdrawal of money from, 80, 81,
    85, 212
employer match and, 71, 76, 78, 79, 81,
    82, 89
investing money in, 4, 81, 83, 185–86,
    189, 198, 201, 209
paying credit card debt with, 46
setting up, 77, 82, 90
statistics on, 71, 72
switching jobs and, 80–81
tax-deferred growth of, 78, 80, 81, 210, 211,
    221
Freelancing, 120, 139–41
    Conscious Spending Plan and, 141
    quarterly estimated tax payments and,
        135
Friends, money issues with, 221
Frugality:
    cheapness vs., 94–96
    prioritizing spending and, 97
Fund managers, poor performance of,
    144–51, 155
Fun money, 107, 108, 130

g

Get Rich Slowly, 152
Gifts, saving money for, 106–7
Girlfriends. See Boyfriends or girlfriends
Global financial crisis of 2008, 3, 6
    stock market declines and, 7, 70, 71–72,
        178–79, 180–81, 189, 196, 202, 209
    unraveling of credit and, 15, 19
Goldman Sachs, 146
Google Calendar, 134–35
Government bonds, 169, 191
Gym memberships, 100–101

h

Hamm, Trent, 152, 240–41
Home, purchasing of, 250–59
    determining if appropriate, 251–53, 255
    as investment, 251, 253–54, 256
    renting vs., 254
    saving for down payment on, 108, 252,
        257
    tips for, 255–59
    total cost of, 254, 255, 257–58
    see also Mortgages
Home equity line of credit (HELOC), 46
Homeowner's insurance, 216, 259
HSBC Direct, 63
Hulbert, Mark, 179

i

Impulse buying, 135

Income. See Earnings; Raises; Salary

Index funds, 155, 156–57, 167, 177–80, 185,
186, 197, 201–2, 209, 211, 212, 258
buying into, 194–95, 198
choosing, 191–94, 198
constructing portfolio of, 188–95
expense ratios of, 157, 178, 192
rebalancing portfolio and, 180, 181, 189,
203–5, 206–7, 209
Swensen allocation model and, 189–91,
192, 195

Inflation, 7, 53, 70, 170, 240, 253, 256

Information glut, 4–5

ING Direct, 51, 62–63

Insurance:
car, 18, 31, 248
homeowner's, 216, 259
life, 216–17

Interest:
on bank accounts, 51, 52, 53, 54, 59, 60,
61
on car loans, 248
on mortgages, tax deduction for, 256
on student loans, 220, 221
see also Annual percentage rates

International equities, 157, 190, 203

Investing, 9, 11, 12, 69–90, 109, 143–215
active vs. passive management and,
155–58
in art, 182
asset allocation and, 166, 170–72, 175,
180–81, 183–85, 189–91, 202, 208–9
automatic, 162–64, 202–3
concerns about risks of, 164
Conscious Spending Plan and, 106
determining your style of, 160–61, 198
diversification and, 166, 170, 172–75, 181
dollar-cost averaging and, 197
five systematic steps for, 76–77
401(k)s and, 4, 81, 83, 185–86, 189, 198,
201, 209
high-interest savings accounts vs., 69–70
high-risk, high-potential-for-reward, 183
increasing monthly contribution and,
200–201
knowing when to sell and, 211–15
letting your parents manage your
accounts and, 222–23
maintaining system of, 200–218
market downturns and, 163
myth of financial expertise and, 143–58

nonretirement accounts and, 77, 78, 79
paying off student loans vs., 220–21
Pyramid of Investing Options and, 167
in real estate, 182, 202, 251, 253–54, 256
rebalancing portfolio and, 180, 181, 189,
203–5, 206–7, 209
Roth IRAs and, 83, 186–95, 198, 209
for specific goal, 215
starting early and, 4–5
summary of advantages of, 81
tax concerns and, 205, 209, 210–11, 215
time to double money and, 187
underperformance and, 212–15
young people's poor attitudes and
behaviors and, 71–75
in your own career, 77
see also Bonds; Index funds; Lifecycle
funds; Mutual funds; Stocks

Investment brokerage accounts:
automatic transfers to, 87, 88, 89, 90,
129, 132, 137, 187, 188, 195
choosing, 86–88
keeping track of, 88

IRAs, 81, 141, 209
see also Roth IRAs

j

Jenkins, Richard, 107

JLP at AllFinancialMatters, 152

Job offers:
multiple, salary negotiations and, 235,
238, 239
negotiating, 236–37

l

Ladder of Personal Finance, 76–77

Late fees, of credit cards, 22, 23, 24

Leasing cars, 246

Leverage, 256

Lifecycle funds (target-date funds), 167,
180–85, 186, 189, 203, 205, 211
buying into, 188, 198
choosing, 187–88, 198

Life insurance, 216–17

Loads, of mutual funds, 156, 177

Lynch, Peter, 149

m

Malkiel, Burton G., 150

Materialism, 74

Media, personal advice and, 5–6

Millionaires, behaviors of, 73–74

Money-market funds, 4, 170, 186

Moody's, 150

Morningstar, 148–50, 152
Mortgages, 50, 216, 253, 255, 258
   credit scores and, 16–17, 256–57
   paying extra on, 77, 258
   tax deductions and, 256
Mutual funds, 167, 176–77, 180
   active vs. passive management and,
      155–58, 177, 178
   fees of, 155–56, 157, 163, 176, 177, 178, 179
   managers' inability to predict or beat
      market and, 144–51, 155, 177, 178
   ratings of, 148–50
   see also Index funds

Negotiating:
   with car dealers, 248–49
   for job offers, 236–37
   for salary in new job, 120, 234–44
Newsletters, market-timing, 147
"Next $100" concept, 128
Nickel (of www.fivecentnickel.com), 208–9

O'Neal, Edward S., 158
Online banks, 51
   checking accounts of, 62, 68
   high-interest savings accounts of, 51–52,
      53, 54, 59, 62–63, 65, 68, 69–70
Online shopping, 135
Overdrafts, 50–51, 65–67, 110, 116

Parents, 222–24
   managing their kids' money, 222–23
   in severe debt, helping, 223–24

Partners. See Boyfriends or girlfriends
Paychecks:
   automatic 401(k) contributions and,
      79–80, 82, 129, 132, 136
   direct deposit of, 58, 65, 129, 133, 136
PBwiki, 88, 131
Philanthropy, 140, 217–18
Pyramid of Investing Options, 167

q

Quicken, 134

r

Raises:
   negotiating, 117–20
   uses for, 122–23, 240–41
Rate-chasing, 34, 60

Real estate:
   as investment, 182, 202, 251, 253–54, 256
   see also Home, purchasing of
Real estate funds (REITs), 190
Rebalancing portfolio, 180, 181, 189, 203–5,
      206–7, 209
Rent, paying, 132–33
Renting vs. buying home, 202, 252, 254
Retail stores, credit cards from, 33–34
Retirement savings, 73, 107
   see also 401(k)s; Roth IRAs
Reward programs, of credit cards, 21, 28, 29
"Rich," meaning of, 10, 219, 260
Risk tolerance, 196–97
Roth, J. D., 152, 196–97
Roth IRAs, 76, 81, 83–89
   automatic contributions to, 87, 88, 89,
      90, 129, 132, 137, 187, 188, 195
   choosing discount-brokerage investment
      account for, 86–88
   early withdrawal of money from, 84, 85,
      212
   investing money in, 83, 186–95, 198, 209
   restrictions on, 84–85
   setting up, 85–86, 88, 90
   tax benefits of, 83–84, 210, 211, 221
Rule of 72, 187

s

Salary:
   annual, computing from hourly rate, 119
   negotiating, 120, 234–44
   see also Earnings; Raises
S&P 500, 168
Savings accounts, 53–54, 68, 85
   automatic transfers to, 129, 132, 136–37
   best options for, 62–63
   FDIC insurance for, 52
   finding perfect setup for, 56–57
   interest on, 51, 53, 54, 59, 60, 61
   online, 51–52, 53, 54, 59, 62–63, 65, 68,
      69–70
   raises and, 241
   set up for specific goals, 113, 129
   sifting through options for, 57–61
Savings goals, 112–13, 134
   automatic transfers and, 129
   Conscious Spending Plan and, 106–8,
      200–201
   down payment on home and, 108, 252,
      257
   freelancing and, 141
   increasing amount of, 200–201
   Jenkins's 60 Percent Solution and, 107

large purchases and, 259–60
lifecycle and index fund minimums and, 183, 194–95
with partner, 227, 228–29
Schwab, 87, 187, 192
checking accounts of, 62, 68, 115–16
Schwartz, Barry, 4
Sector funds, 183
Selling investments, 211–15
Selling valuables, 212
SEP-IRAs, 141
Simon, W. Scott, 179
Simple Dollar, The, 152
60 Percent Solution, 107
Snowball method, 41–42
Solin, Daniel, 148, 158
Solo 401(k)s, 141
Spending, 2, 46–47, 91–124, 140
cheapness vs. frugality and, 94–96
of friends, judging, 99
planning and, 93–94, 103–24. See also Conscious Spending Plan
raises and, 240–41
subscriptions vs. Á la Carte Method and, 100–101
talking to your partner about, 227, 228–29
tracking, 130, 137
on what you love, 9, 97–103
Stock market, 75, 253
annualized returns of, 70, 171
declines in (2008), 7, 70, 71–72, 178–79, 180–81, 189, 196, 202, 209
Stock options, 242
Stocks, 167, 168, 171, 180
asset allocation and, 166, 170–72, 174, 175, 180–81, 183–85, 190–91
categories of, 173
diversification and, 166, 170, 172–75, 181
picking, 165–66, 185, 189
ratings of, 148–50

underperforming, 212–15
see also Index funds; Mutual funds
Student loans, 35–36, 241
investing vs. paying off, 220–21
Subscriptions, 100–101, 111, 130
Survivorship bias, 150
Swensen, David, 149, 189–91, 192, 195

Target-date funds. See Lifecycle funds
Taxes:
401(k)s and, 78, 186, 210, 211, 221
freelancing and, 135
investment decisions and, 205, 209, 210–11, 215
mortgage deduction and, 256
Roth IRAs and, 83–84, 210, 211, 221
stock trading and, 146, 178, 189
TIAA-CREF, 187
Trapani, Gina, 134–35
Treasury inflation-protected securities (TIPS), 191
Trip-cancellation insurance, 31
T. Rowe Price, 87, 184, 187, 192

Unexpected expenses, 121, 122

Vanguard, 87, 157, 171, 177–78, 184, 187, 188, 192, 194
Volatility, 165–66

Wang, Jim, 112–13
Warranty extensions, 18, 31
Weddings, 37, 229–34
dealing with high cost of, 230–32
reducing costs of, 232–34
saving for, 107, 231
Wells Fargo, 53, 59, 65–67, 116
